OPEN WATER

Mikael Rosén

CHRONICLE BOOKS

SAN FRANCISCO

CONTENTS

Foreword — 7

Introduction — 9

Chapter 1
BACK TO THE FUTURE 13

Before Johnny Weissmuller played Tarzan in the movies 90 years ago, he was the world's fastest swimmer. He claimed that his times would never be beaten. Nowadays, both senior citizens and children swim faster than Weissmuller. To understand how this is possible, we need to look at innovative Japanese swimmers, the breakthrough of the safety razor, and two top-notch swimmers who never got to swim in the Olympic Games.

Chapter 2
SWIMMING IS FOR EVERYONE 53

In many ways swimming is an equal sport: men and women train together and people from all over the world are represented among the world's top swimmers. But it hasn't always been that way. In this chapter we learn about African American swimmers in the United States, contemplate the possibilities for female swimmers to beat their male colleagues, and pay a visit to the Gay Games.

CONTENTS

Chapter 3
THE LONELINESS OF THE LONG DISTANCE SWIMMER 85

That swimmers spend an incredible amount of time in pools is well known, but to understand why requires diving deeply into sport physiology. Here we encounter parents who set their alarm at 3:45 a.m., a Swede who cannot race wisely, and coaches who destroy their swimmers. And we wonder if a young American has found a shortcut to success.

Chapter 4
ANIMAL KINGDOM 129

On land penguins look rather clumsy, but in their own element they swim up to three times faster than a well-trained human. This chapter investigates what swimmers can learn from penguins, dolphins, and other animals.

Chapter 5
THE FOUNTAIN OF YOUTH 163

What is the optimal age for achieving a top performance? Is it possible to swim fast after thirty? How should you train when you're "over the hill"? We seek answers to these questions from three top-ranking Greek swimmers, in Eastern Germany, and from among the oldest senior citizens in Florida.

Chapter 6

JACKS OF ALL TRADES 205

It is thought that swimmers are just swimmers. In this chapter we discover the exceptions, like the first person who combined swimming and running to go from point A to point B. We also investigate the story behind Island to Island and how many different sports in the Olympics a swimmer can compete in.

Chapter 7

MAN AND THE SEA 243

Ever since Lord Byron swam the Hellesponte in 1810, open water swimming has fascinated us—but it can be hazardous. Through archaeological finds in Egypt and from long distance swimmers who've cheated, we find out how it went for Matthew Webb, the first man who swam the English Channel.

Chapter 8

THE PERFECT BODY 273

Swimmers are often considered to have the most aesthetically pleasing bodies. Here we scan research to tell us what characteristics are particularly favorable to swimmers. We also seek the optimal body for a swimmer, by both trying to identify the right gene pool and going on a treasure hunt for what strength training makes swimmers swim faster.

CONTENTS

APPENDIX   315

Swimming is stacked with statistics. This section contains results and awards that are part of the ongoing history of swimming. It also includes training tools and tips.

THANK YOU!   353

SOURCES   356

INDEX   358

FOREWORD

Mikael Rosén has written a book that takes an internationally collective approach to the history of swimming to offer perspective on where the sport came from and where it is now, so you can be better equipped to help progress it forward. While weaving in his personal perspective, he provides a comprehensive picture of the international world of competitive swimming, and offers inspiration to the grassroots noncompetitive swimming movements happening around the world.

Mikael's extensive education in medicine mixed with years of coaching experience gives him the ability to convey the science of swimming in an easily understandable way. Coaches of all experiences and ability levels will be able to take something from this book to add to their tool kits. Finally, Mikael shares with you his deep of knowledge of the swimming world from being Sweden's Open Water National Coach since 2012.

Whether you are a swimming coach who's spent most of your life roaming pool decks or you are a part-time summer league coach doing your best to inspire the next generation, there comes a time when you need some help and perspective. I have turned to my mentors, colleagues, and friends for guidance when stuck with a difficult coaching dilemma. In your hands you hold the knowledge of one of the best mentors, colleagues, and friends anyone could ever have. Mikael has helped me on many occasions, which has led me to become one of the youngest Division I Power 5 conference head coaches in the NCAA. He takes a clear and relatable approach to help you become a better coach to your athletes, a better co-worker to your staff, an inspiration to the hardworking swimmer, and an understanding resource for the curious parent.

Jon Maccoll, head swimming coach at Rutgers University

INTRODUCTION

The year 1986 was a year of four disasters. The space shuttle *Challenger* exploded, the Soviet nuclear power plant in Chernobyl suffered a catastrophic accident, and the Prime Minister of Sweden was assassinated. It was also the year that my childhood pool burned down to the ground. Much later I was diagnosed with ADD and Asperger's, which is part of the autism spectrum.

Around the same time the swimming pool burned down, I was becoming a sort of Rain Man of swimming. The fire could have put a halt on this development, but instead, my team commuted twice a week for a year. I started to read *Swimming World* magazine and became fascinated by American swimming with the help of loving and devoted parents. Year after year I swam mornings, evenings, weekends, and holidays. As a late-blooming athlete I became a 19-time national champion, and I won second place in the Swimming World Cup, but I did not make Sweden's Olympic team.

It is the inspiring people I met during my swims who keep me going. While swimming and coaching over the last 15 years, I have met people in over 40 countries who have stories to tell. I have been extra lucky to be a Swimrun pioneer and to work with some extraordinary athletes and the tough and ambitious open water swimmers on the Swedish national team.

Swimming bridges not only men and women from different countries and backgrounds, but people of all ages as well. Exercising in a pool or open water has numerous benefits for the body and mind, and boys and girls, and later men and women, train in the same lane.

I hope this book inspires you to embark on new aquatic adventures, meet new friends, and help improve the swimming world. The work you do to expand the pool and open water accessibility in your city will spread.

Don't be a stranger. You can reach me on Instagram: @human_ambition.

Mikael Rosén

CHAPTER 1

BACK
TO THE FUTURE

My technique was perfect and my records will never be beaten.

– Johnny Weissmuller

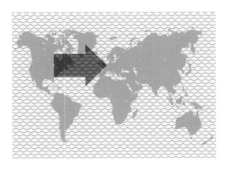

■ **AMSTERDAM, AUGUST 11, 1928.**
Everyone at the arena knew that
Johnny Weissmuller was the
greatest swimmer in the world.
In fact, he'd only lost a single
race during his entire career. This
happened at Weissmuller's first
major competition when, still a
teenager, he was unable to muster
enough power to last 440 yards. He
handled this defeat by simply never
mentioning it, instead coining his
selling slogan: "I never lost a race."

The 1928 Amsterdam Olympics
would be his last competition. At the
time, swimmers and other athletes
were forced to choose between
competing and making money. As
Weissmuller was the best-known
swimmer in the world, three New
York businessmen wearing top hats
and pinstripe suits had successfully enticed him into signing an
advertising contract for their brand
of swimsuits. All Big John had to do
was go to Amsterdam and win the
gold medals in the 100m freestyle
and the freestyle relay race.

The great Weissmuller confi-
dently walked by the Olympic pool
as if he'd done nothing else his
entire life. He stood 6'4" (193 cm)
tall with shoulders as wide as those
of a heavyweight boxer and a smile
that reminded people of the ivory
keys of a piano. Wearing a custom-
made cape over his shoulders,
he joked around with friends and
dazzled his admirers while waiting
for the start signal. He and another
tall favorite, Stefan Baranyi from
Hungary, took up a lot of space
behind the starting blocks. Just like
Weissmuller, Baranyi was born in
the Habsburg Empire, even though
his place of birth (Timișoara) is
now located in Romania. Maps are
frequently redrawn by wars.

Nobody noticed the Japanese
man standing next to these tall
favorites. He was about a head
shorter and had a small beard.

Well-informed audience members looked up in disbelief as the name of the qualified Japanese swimmer was read out loud. Could this slight man really be the swimmer from Japan who'd been portrayed as Weissmuller's biggest competitor for the gold?

Minutes before the start, however, the audience shifted its attention from the charismatic Weissmuller to the Japanese athlete, Katsuo Takaishi. Takaishi warmed up with a gymnastics routine never before seen in the context of swimming: He folded himself over like a pocket knife and spun his arms as if he didn't have any cartilage or restrictive connective tissues. Takaishi had a modest smile on his face and bowed to the audience.

Soon the swimmers took their places on the starting blocks. Then the start signal went off and Weissmuller and Takaishi immediately took the lead. The audience could now witness the masters of two vastly different swimming styles swooshing their way through the pool. The large American arched his lower back and held his head and shoulders high. The smaller Japanese swimmer seemed larger in the water than he did standing next to the pool. He had a lower position in the water, almost below the surface, and cut through the water like a swordfish.

Halfway through the race, the audience gasped in surprise as Takaishi appeared to take the lead. People in the crowd who would have never talked to one another under different circumstances now experienced the miraculous connection people encounter when attending special events. More and more people stood up, and by the end of the race the expensive seats had turned into a mere standing section.

However, halfway into the second and final pool length, the people in the stands realized that there would be no great upset. Takaishi was running on an empty gas tank and was no longer able to keep up with the American. In the end, Weissmuller won in the same great style he liked to emphasize in his tales. He set a new Olympic record: 58.4 seconds. Stefan Baranyi also barely beat the exhausted Takaishi: 59.8 versus 1:00.0.

Katsuo Takaishi became the first Asian male swimmer to win an individual Olympic medal: a bronze medal in the 100m freestyle and a silver medal in the 4 × 200m freestyle relay. Even if Amsterdam was the high point of his career as an active swimmer, his medals were not to be his most important mark on the history of swimming. He was passionate about cracking the code of how to swim faster.

When Takaishi arrived at the next Olympics, he did so as the head coach of the Japanese team. A lot had happened in those four years. The great Johnny Weissmuller didn't participate even though the 1932 Olympics were held in his new hometown of Los Angeles. The King of Swimming had signed a Hollywood contract with Metro-Goldwyn-Mayer to star in Tarzan movies. His career gave him plenty of opportunities to speak on the radio and in newspapers, where he could make unabashed

boasts such as, "My technique was perfect and my records will never be beaten."

As is customary when hosting the Olympics, the Americans prepared a massive show. And there were definitely grounds for optimism. The men's team had won two gold medals, one silver medal, and two bronze medals in the five swimming events of the 1928 Olympics. The United States had also won the relay race. So, just how successful would the Americans be this time, now that they didn't have to take the long boat trip to Europe? During the previous three Olympic games held in Europe (Antwerp in 1920, Paris in 1924, and Amsterdam in 1928), the long trip to Europe meant the American Olympic swimming team had to go ten days without training in the water. Instead, they had to make do with gymnastics and light jogging on the deck while listening to Weissmuller's fantastic stories.

In 1932, the Atlantic steamer *Mauretania* with its four steam turbines and maximum speed of 24 knots would have taken 2,165 passengers living in crowded quarters from New York to Southampton in just five days. However, back in 1928, the American Olympic team had to settle for the SS *President Roosevelt* with a maximum speed of 13 knots. This ship was considerably more modest in terms of comfort, and 16 years later would be used for landing young American soldiers on Utah Beach on D-Day.

Not only did the sinking of the *Titanic* in 1912 give passengers, shipping companies, and ship designers a lot to think about, but in 1921 the United States Congress unanimously adopted a law limiting immigration from Europe. The number of immigrants to the promised land in the West exceeded 800,000 in 1920, whereas only 309,000 hopeful people crossing the Atlantic were allowed entry into the United States during the following two years.

The 1932 Olympics were held at the height of the Great Depression following the Wall Street crash of 1929. The entire world was affected,

and some countries couldn't even afford to send teams to Los Angeles.

Katsuo Takaishi, 1926.

The U.S. had the home team advantage, and was able to muster 474 athletes, versus the 200 to 300 athletes in the three Olympics of the 1920s. In 1932, the U.S. had 26 swimmers, 16 men and 10 women, versus the 22 swimmers (9 men and 13 women) in 1928. Never before in the history of the Olympics had a nation's men's team been this big. The world of swimming was about to witness success!

But the Americans didn't astound the world in the 1932

Olympics—the Japanese did. The entire world of sports witnessed one nation crushing all competition in men's swimming to an extent never seen before. Japan won both the gold and the silver medals in every event except the 400m freestyle, where they won a bronze. They won the relay race in 8:58.4 and set a new world record, beating the previous record by 35 seconds. Japan won all three medals in the 100m backstroke.

So what enabled this overwhelming dominance? Had the Japanese trained harder than the Americans?

One reason was Katsuo Takaishi. After he returned from the 1928 Olympics in Amsterdam, he decided to help other swimmers. And with him as their head coach, the Japanese were in a position to soundly defeat every opponent in Los Angeles.

The Americans were naturally eager to find out the reasons behind the Japanese transformation. Dr. Thomas Cureton at the University of Illinois—also known as the father of athletic physiology—

got to work analyzing the available information. He released a report two years after the Los Angeles Olympics where he identified four key areas that led to Japanese domination:

(1) MENTAL ATTITUDE. The Japanese team had substantial and visible financial support from the government, which resulted in serious and dedicated swimmers.

(2) SWIMMING TECHNIQUE. The Japanese had developed the crawl technique by studying and improving upon the American technique.

(3) FITNESS. The simple, classic Japanese diet of alkaline foods and smaller amounts of meat resulted in the swimmers having greater endurance, which allowed the Japanese to train four times as hard as the Americans.

(4) ANATOMY. The average height of the Japanese winners was a modest 5'7" (170 cm)—small compared to the Americans. The lightweight Japanese floated better than the heavier Americans. They also had more flexibility than anyone had ever seen in the world of swimming.

Prior to the Los Angeles Olympics, Cureton had argued that the body of a swimmer must be kept flat in order to be fast. This was the Weissmuller way. At the 1932 Olympics, the superior Japanese swam while rotating their bodies.

Even though he was of sound mind, Cureton was unable to see the Japanese rotating their bodies as an explanation for the American defeat. In his report, he instead argued that Weissmuller's technique of holding his head high and his shoulders flat was superior. After all, Weissmuller's world records remained in place until 1943–44 when several of them were beaten by Alan Ford (using Weissmuller's technique).

In a *LIFE* magazine interview, Ford revealed the secret behind his success was rotating his shoulders less. Ford and his coaches at Yale University said that the shoulders should be placed so high that they barely touch the water. If, however, the shoulders were to end up in the water, they would work as brake pads. The same also applied to the head, which was also to be placed high. Ford's interview in *LIFE* had a massive impact and resulted in an entire generation of young swimmers making their way through the water in a style reminiscent of amphibian planes taking off.

The Second World War resulted in the 1944 Olympics being canceled. Alan Ford was drafted late in the war, where he served as a second lieutenant in the navy. While serving, Ford lost 20 pounds and smoked two packs of cigarettes a day in order to cope with the horrors of war. He left the navy in the spring of 1948 to resume his swimming and engineering studies at Yale. Half a year later, after having put out his Chesterfields, he won a silver medal at the London Olympics. In 1966, Alan Ford was inducted into the International Swimming Hall of Fame. The festive ceremony was interrupted by loud booing from the back of the room. People turned around to see who was behaving so disrespectfully and laughed when they realized it was Johnny Weissmuller.

In 1935, Katsuo Takaishi published the book *Swimming in Japan*. In it, Takaishi argued that although the Japanese had certainly trained hard, the secret behind their Olympic success was primarily their improved technique.

In order to appreciate Takaishi's revolution, we need to go through the mechanics and physics of swimming.

WATER FOR SPEED AND WATER AS A BRAKE

Swimming is unique among sports, as swimmers are positioned in a liquid that they try to grip in order to move their bodies forward. Water doesn't offer the firm resistance of solid ground, something runners benefit from when moving forward. Water is also 800 times denser than air, so a swimmer tries to minimize the resistance of his or her body in the water.

The form of resistance that's easiest for a swimmer to influence is friction. A shaved and smooth swimmer slides faster through the water compared to a swimmer with a hairy body. The first swimmer to shave his legs is said to have been the Australian Jon Henricks in 1955. The following year, Murray Rose, a fellow Australian, did the same when Australia won five of the seven men's events at the Olympics held in their backyard in Melbourne.

That's why razor manufacturers have had a close relationship with elite swimmers ever since 1956, with one short break between 2000 and

RULES CONCERNING EQUIPMENT

1. Swimsuit

The swimsuit is not allowed to be made out of a material other than textile.

The floating effect of a swimsuit must not be greater than 0.5 newtons in a vacuum. Double swimsuits or two-piece swimsuits are not allowed.

A swimsuit may contain two layers of fabric, but the total thickness cannot exceed 0.8 mm.

A swimsuit can't have Velcro, zippers, or seams forming external patterns.

The swimsuit design can't be of a type that may be perceived as indecent, but there are no restrictions as far as colors or patterns are concerned.

2. Swimming Cap

The cap may not be attached to the goggles.

The cap must follow the contours of the head without attempting to create a sharp, hydrodynamic shape.

The cap is not allowed to have any structure.

The cap must be made out of a smooth, soft material, with a maximum thickness of 2 mm.

Helmets are prohibited.

3. Swimming Goggles

Goggles cannot be attached to the swimming cap.

Goggles are to protect the eyes of the swimmer from water without offering a hydrodynamic advantage.

4. Swimsuit Measurement Variations

Pool: Men's suits are not allowed to extend above the navel or below the knee. Women's suits are not allowed to cover the neck or shoulders or extend below the knee.

Open water: The same rules as those for women's pool swimsuits apply, with the difference that the suits may extend down to the ankles.

5. Wetsuit

In triathlons, competitors usually wear wetsuits, based on the water temperature. The same exemption from international rules also applies to open water competitions in Sweden.

In Swimrun, there aren't a lot of restrictions; for instance, hand paddles and pull buoys are permitted.

6. Other Equipment

Equipment must ust be approved by the International Swimming Federation (FINA) at continental or global championships. The label in the suit indicates if it's approved.

2009. During that period, it was common for swimmers to compete in full-body swimsuits. These suits made them faster, not just by reducing friction, but also because the fabric contained rubber. Thus the laborious pre-competition shaving ritual was replaced by an equally laborious dressing ritual—squeezing into the tight suit could take more than 30 minutes. Swimsuits containing rubber have been banned in competition since 2010, and now suits are not allowed to extend farther down than the swimmer's kneecaps. These changes resulted in the return of the razor manufacturers and their sponsorships. According to *Fortune* magazine, Gillette is said to have sponsored the star Ryan Lochte to the tune of $300,000 during the Olympic year of 2012.

Water resistance is not only affected by the smoothness of the swimmer's body surface, but also by his or her shape, size, and speed; a pointy vessel results in less resistance than a rounded one. This is easy to imagine if we consider the design of competition kayaks.

A large swimmer disturbs more water molecules than a small swimmer. The body surface is the determining factor here—slim swimmers create less resistance than swimmers with more body fat. At the same time, tall swimmers (despite creating more resistance) are better suited for swimming fast because they're able to create more forward-driving force.

$$\textit{Forward-Driving Force} - \textit{Resistance} = \textit{Velocity}$$

In the forward crawl stroke, the swimmer must use their arm and hand as a paddle, pushing water backward to go forward. It's easy to understand that the speed of swimming increases if the arm stroke

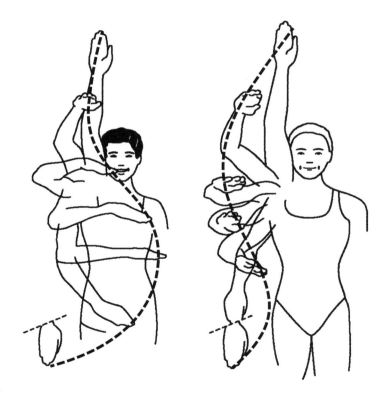

A comparison between Dawn Fraser (left), the best female swimmer of the 1960s, and Sarah Sjöström, who holds a number of world records 50 years later.

frequency increases, given that each arm stroke retains the same length.

Stroke Length × Stroke Frequency = Velocity

Newton's second law of motion illustrates the importance of the swimmer not losing speed:

Force = mass × acceleration
$$F = m \times a$$

The momentary speed varies for all swimmers. The pull of the right hand results in a burst of speed that then decreases while the left hand speed increases. This becomes particularly noticeable in a tired butterfly stroke swimmer who visibly "saws" his or her way through the water. The ability to maintain your speed as much as possible between strokes is called moving inertia and is a variable characterizing the best swimmers. Since the speed after a start or a push-off is much higher than the average velocity during a race, successful pool swimming isn't about creating speed but maintaining the speed taken from the starting block and the walls.

YOUR SWIMMING: THREE CORE EXERCISES

1. The Plank

Get down into a push-up position, and put your weight on your forearms, ensuring your elbows are located directly below your shoulders. Keep your feet as wide as your shoulders. Try to keep a natural arch in your lower back but keep your body straight. Pull in and tighten your abdominals. Hold for 30 seconds. Rest and repeat.

2. Raising Your Back

Lie down on your stomach with your hands against your forehead, palms facing down. Tighten your abdominals. Gently lift your upper body about 1–2 inches off the floor without arching your lower back. Hold for 10 seconds. Rest and repeat six times.

3. Swimming Leg Kick

Butterfly kicks with or without a kickboard strengthen the core for all strokes.

In his book *Swimming in Japan*, Katsuo Takaishi describes freestyle strokes with a kind of precision that's still surprisingly relevant some 80 years later.

Entering the Hand

Takaishi believed that position of the hand entering the water was key to the swimmer's forward-driving force. The hand was not supposed to be stretched all that far forward, but was supposed to grab the water at an earlier stage in order to avoid the lift force created when pushing the hand down far in front of the head. According to Takaishi, the feeling involved in executing this move was absolutely crucial.

THE BENEFITS OF GOOD ROTATION

1. The Right Muscles Are Used

Rotation uses the large, strong, and hardy muscles in your back and chest to move forward instead of the small and delicate shoulder muscles.

2. Longer Strokes

When well executed, body rotation enables longer strokes without the strokes taking any longer to execute. Successfully using your hips helps maintain your swimming speed while avoiding the laborious acceleration between arm strokes.

3. Reduced Resistance

If the shoulder is lifted just above the surface during the recovery, the swimmer's frontal resistance is reduced.

4. Relaxed Recovery

A high shoulder promotes a relaxed recovery instead of looking and feeling as if you're throwing a rock.

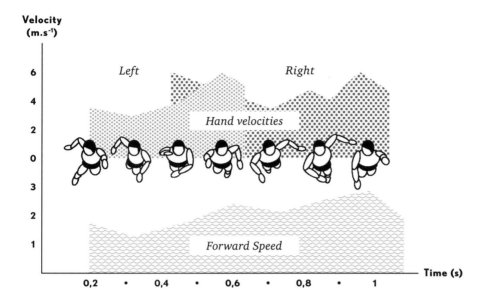

This principle has been important for advances in freestyle swimming during this century. It used to be said that after the arm enters the water, it should be pulled straight down in order to retain as much of the kinetic energy as possible. In recent years, however, swimmers have been pulling farther away from the body, as it's been found that the fastest path from lift force to forward-driving force is farther away. The technique also makes the swimmer better utilize his or her strong and hardy back muscles and use the weaker and more delicate shoulder muscles less.

Body Rotation

Western coaches and experts in the 1950s, as prompted by Thomas Cureton, agreed that the body of a freestyle swimmer should be completely flat in order to avoid unnecessary resistance. They were wrong.

Takaishi saw through the "emperor's clothes" and realized that it was impossible for a swimmer to keep his or her shoulders flat.

Instead, the swimmer created resistance by swaying from side to side, especially when the swimmer was tired. Takaishi found that the shoulders should rotate elliptically—one shoulder is lifted while the other one drops. This movement makes the upper body roll from side to side around its own axis without altering its position. A well-executed body rotation is a terrific way of getting the center of gravity to align with the swimmer's direction in a way that wastes as little energy as possible. The position allows for more natural breathing and is also optimal for the position of the legs in the water. In 1995, researchers at the University of Colorado were able to show that this type of rotation also reduces frontal resistance.

However, rolling from side to side doesn't necessarily result in a better time. In order to enable the force from your arms and legs to move your body forward in the best way possible while wasting as little lateral force as possible, you need strong upper body muscles.

The first to succeed in developing a good body rotation was George Breen, who broke the 1,500m freestyle world record in Melbourne in 1956. He was the first with a time below 18 minutes at the Olympics and set a world record that stood for two years. Unfortunately, Breen couldn't summon the same speed to win the final. Body rotation would have to wait a little bit longer for its great breakthrough—losing the medal was a bump in the road of technique development.

Stroke Frequency and Stroke Length

Body rotation changes which muscles are used. When the body doesn't rotate, only the arms and shoulders do the work. Rotation enables the swimmer to use more and larger muscles, which generates more power and results in a higher speed. The technique elongates the arm strokes.

The considerably shorter Takaishi made fewer arm strokes compared to the imposing Weissmuller. At the same time, Takaishi saw that there was a limit to how much rotation should be used. If the upper body rolls too much, there is a high risk of losing energy laterally or slowing down between arm strokes.

The best method for swimming fast over a given distance is to swim with as long a stroke length and as high a tempo as possible. In theory, this sounds easy enough—making longer arm strokes while retaining the stroke frequency or making more arm strokes per time unit while retaining their length. When swimmers are unable to improve their swimming, the key is found in the rotation of their upper body. The level of rotation is individual as it's very difficult to get the timing right when executing this movement without losing time or energy. It's been shown that long-distance swimmers rotate more than short-distance swimmers and also that good swimmers have a snappier rotation than slow swimmers.

Pull Acceleration

Fifty years before Westerners learned how to use this technique, Takaishi emphasized the importance of finishing a stroke quickly in order to begin a new stroke.

The Japanese started filming their swimmers underwater in the 1930s. Researchers using locally manufactured cameras would stand with their noses pressed up against a window in the pool wall, filming their swimmers.

The Japanese period of glory extended until the 1936 Olympics in Berlin, where Japan won the most medals. Then came the Second World War. Japan was not allowed to participate in the London Olympics in 1948, as they had fought alongside the Germans in the war.

YOUR SWIMMING: FOUR STEPS FOR SWIMMING FASTER

1. Frequency

The best way to become a faster swimmer is to add more swimming sessions to your training schedule. Swimming six times a week is the most effective way to improve your performance.

2. Flexibility

Make sure that you're not held back by your shoulders. Stretching for two minutes a day will show results after a year.

3. Speed

A regular swimmer should master at least four different types of intensity: easy, easy endurance, tough endurance, and sprint speed.

4. Finesse

Improve your technique. Use your upper body to synchronize your arms and legs. The right technique exercises will get you there. Butterfly kicks strengthen your upper body in a way that's helpful for all types of swimming.

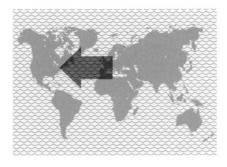

■ **PHILADELPHIA, AUGUST 14, 1976.** The stands were packed at Kelly's pool in Philadelphia. It was four-thirty in the afternoon and the air was hot. It was 91°F (33°C) and the air was trembling.

Behind the starting block for the 100m freestyle race was a tall, slim young man with straight posture, a pronounced chin, and a dark mustache. Someone familiar with British comedy would probably detect a certain resemblance to John Cleese. The blue letters "CJAC" on his orange shirt indicated that he competed for the Central Jersey Aquatic Club. The John Cleese look-alike was in great shape. He spun his arms and looked down the 50-meter pool. The only thing on his mind was the 100m race ahead of him. He'd swum this race before—at least once a day for the past six months.

A downside of the meet was the quality of the pool, far from the standards of the recent Olympic pool of Montreal. The pool in Philadelphia had no wash-through gutter and was only 3 feet (0.9 m) deep in the shallow end. It was very wavy and had just enough room to perform a flip turn without head injury. The Philadelphia Department of Recreation later filled up Kelly's and replaced it with a lawn bowling court.

That week in August was one long, massive celebration of the American Olympic team, which had won every single medal except one at the men's events at the Montreal Olympics a few weeks before. Olympic gold medalists such as John Naber, Peter Rocca, John Hencken, and Shirley Babashoff earned a lot of applause, along with the women's team, which had beaten the fiercely powerful East German team in the 4 x 100m freestyle relay final.

At the races that day, however, there were two other swimmers who brought the sport back to the future: Jonty Skinner and Jesus Vassallo. Jonty Skinner was the name of the John Cleese clone. He stood 6'6" (198 cm) tall and swam for the University of Alabama, where he'd won the NCAA championship in the 100m freestyle a year prior. At that time, the men's college championships (NCAA) was the fastest swimming competition in the world.

However, Jonty Skinner, a South African, had not been permitted to participate in Montreal. Since the South African Minister of Interior, Jan de Klerk, had proclaimed that its Olympic team would only consist of white athletes, South Africa had not been welcome to participate in the Olympics.

With Skinner absent, Jim Montgomery, who trained in the old home pool of Mark Spitz in Indiana, had won the 100m freestyle in great style. He became the first swimmer to complete a 100-meter race with an average speed of over two meters per second. With this speed, he was able to butcher Mark Spitz's Olympic record (51.22), and his 49.99 was a whole 0.82 second better than Jack Babashoff, who came in second—and coincidentally used to train with Skinner in Alabama.

Skinner was thrilled to be standing there at Kelly's pool in the summer heat. He'd been training throughout the whole summer and was in the best shape of his life. As he wasn't allowed to compete in international championships, he'd never before focused on swimming fast in a 50-meter pool. When asked about his swimming, he'd replied, "Whatever the winning time in Montreal, I will swim faster in Philadelphia." Skinner was a pioneer in the use of mental visualization. Time and time again, he'd gone through the race in his mind—what it would feel like, what he should focus on, how he would be able to fight the shocking muscle rebellion that breaks out in a swimmer's body in the second half of a 100m race.

Jonty Skinner's leg kick had never been anything to write home about. Other 100m swimmers typically have a constantly pounding leg kick. Skinner's left foot kicked down once his right hand entered the water, and his right foot went down once his left hand did the same. In between, he let his feet casually rotate around each other—a style he'd developed in his young teens when training under his father, Doug, back home in Cape Town. Other swimmers who've used the same type of kick include Anders Holmertz and today's long-distance champions, Gregorio Paltrinieri and Katie Ledecky. These days, however, practically no one uses Skinner's technique when swimming the 100m freestyle.

The drawback of this two-stroke leg kick is that it doesn't provide all that much forward momentum. Nor is it particularly good at lifting the body, especially if the body is more muscular. Jim Montgomery's 195 pounds were distributed over his 6'3" frame. Jonty Skinner's slim 6'6" body weighed no more than 185 pounds and was therefore better suited to the two-stroke leg kick.

A benefit of using this leg kick is that it saves a lot of energy as long as your feet and legs don't stick out too much. It may also help your balance, which is why it's beneficial if you tend to go wide when returning your arms to the water.

Skinner's technique and mental preparation turned out to be more than sufficient for this race of the year—perhaps even the decade. He crushed the Americans who'd made their way to Philadelphia. Montgomery, the Olympic hero, wasn't there, but Skinner beat his world record (49.99) with a time of 49.44. This was also the first African world record in swimming and it stood until 1981.

Skinner's fierce dream race broke the norm of the dominance of the American men's team in the 1970s. The United States had won 12 out of 13 events at the 1976 Olympics, losing the 200m breaststroke to John Hencken from the United Kingdom. At that time, participating nations were allowed to field three swimmers per event. That meant that there were 33 individual medals up for grabs. The Americans took 25 of these.

Another race that changed the world of swimming in Philadelphia in 1976 may be attributed to Jesus (or "Jesse," as he referred to himself) from the Mission Viejo swim club in Southern California.

At the 100m backstroke event, the heavily perspiring crowd at Kelly's pool saw yet another tall, mustachioed swimmer walk up to the starting block. John Naber had won one silver and three gold medals in Montreal. His specialty was the backstroke, but he was capable of competing in the other styles as well. Next to him stood Jesse Vassallo, who was just 14 years old, had a slight frame, and was a full foot shorter than Naber. Vassallo was one of the most promising American long-distance swimmers who'd made great times at the qualifying races for the 1976 Olympics. His 15:31 on 1,500m freestyle is still the best time performed by a 14-year-old. He was even faster than Michael Phelps, who's at fourth place on this

list with 15:39, and Swedish Anders Holmertz, who's third with 15:37.

Just like Skinner, Vassallo had been prohibited from competing in the Montreal Olympics. By living in the United States, he had broken the rules of the Puerto Rican Olympic Committee stipulating that you had to live in your native country for at least one year prior to the Olympics.

Following his exclusion from the Montreal Olympics, Jesse wanted to try new distances other than the monotonous long-distance races. He had finally settled on the 100m backstroke and he'd ended up next to John Naber in the trials. The young long-distance swimmer had figured out a way of avoiding a problem that had concerned him— being "drowned" by the backwash from the massive Naber. After the start, Vassallo remained underwater and moved like a dolphin, using his abdomen to move forward. Those in the audience who weren't blinded by Naber's star-like appearance had a good laugh at Vassallo's strange style.

In the summer of 1979, the Pan-American Games were held

in the Puerto Rican capital of San Juan. Puerto Rico is an island in the Caribbean belonging to the United States, but with a high degree of autonomy. When Christopher Columbus landed on the island during his second trip, he found it inhabited by Native Americans who referred to it as Borikén. The Spanish named the island San Juan Bautista in honor of John the Baptist, but the name was later changed to Puerto Rico, meaning "rich port." Puerto Rico has participated in the Olympics under its own flag since 1948.

Vassallo was still extremely popular in Puerto Rico, despite the fact that he'd left the country when he was only 11 and he'd chosen to compete for the United States. In 1979, *Sports Illustrated* ranked him one of the ten greatest athletes in the world, together with racing champion Mario Andretti, tennis star Björn Borg, and even Muhammad Ali.

Ahead of the 1979 Pan-American Games, Vassallo's uncle Salvador had spent $6,000 on printing 2,000 bright yellow T-shirts saying VASSALLO in large red capital letters. He handed out these T-shirts to family, friends, and the audience. The people in yellow carried Jesse during the race, all the way to the top of the podium. After "The Star-Spangled Banner" ended, the crowd in yellow started singing the Puerto Rican national anthem, "La Borinqueña." The excitement of the crowd knew no bounds when Jesse waved a Puerto Rican flag. Jesus "Jesse" Vassallo, the son of Puerto Rico who was just 14 years old, was the best swimmer in the world.

As expected, the 14-year-old Vassallo did not make the team in the 400m medley at Kelly's pool that day, but he was still no more than two seconds away from qualifying for the American national team. When he won the same Olympic qualifying race four years later, his time was 4:21. At the 1980 Olympics in Moscow—which President Jimmy Carter chose to boycott as a result of the Soviet invasion of Afghanistan—Oleksandr Sydorenko won the 400m medley with a time of 4:22.

Swimming competitors in the Moscow Olympics were limited to say the least. At the 1976 Olympics in Montreal, 262 men and 208 women from 51 countries had participated. In Moscow, there were only 190 men and 143 women from 41 countries. The United States was missing, along with West Germany, Japan, Canada, and the strong Italian team. The British protested in a polite way by sending a smaller-than-usual team. France and the Netherlands participated, but in support of the U.S. boycott, did not display their flags on the state-run Soviet television. Somalia, Gabon, and Norway also boycotted the games, though this didn't affect the outcome of the events.

So, what about Puerto Rico? Well, German Rieckehoff, head of the island's athletic federation, wanted to send a team based on his conviction that sports and politics shouldn't be mixed. He didn't receive any financial support from the government, but was still able to send the boxer Alberto Mercado, who subsequently became the only American citizen to participate in the 1980 Summer Olympics.

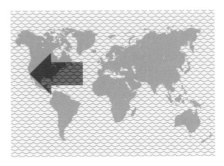

■ **IRVINE, CALIFORNIA, JULY 31, 1980.** Glenn Mills was 18 years old, but he was exhausted. During the past year, he'd been drilled by his young and ambitious coach, Dennis Pursley, in accordance with the Nietzsche philosophy of "what doesn't kill you, makes you stronger." Twice a day, six days a week, he and the other swimmers of the Cincinnati Pepsi Marlins swam 10,000 meters. Mills' specialty was the breaststroke, so he used this style for swimming 30 percent of this distance. Breaststroke is the slowest swimming style. Some days, he swam 20 × 400m breaststroke with six minutes of rest between sets. He was able to do the final

400 meters in 5:10, which is still to this day a respectable time given the extreme amount of exercise.

Mills and his best buddy Greg Rhodenbaugh swam in silence, just like the rest of this group ruled by a friendly but firm hand. During the school year, the morning sessions started at five o'clock. After they completed 10,000 meters in the pool, they did sit-ups and other exercises on land before having a hearty three-dollar breakfast and going to class.

Following the afternoon training sessions, they practiced starts and turns. Instead of going to church on Sundays (his only day off), Glenn Mills stayed in bed, still as a mummy. The only time he got up was to go to the fridge to get something to eat.

During the last two weeks before the U.S. National Championships, the major competition of the summer, the team had swum a little bit less— "only" 6,000 meters a day. Yet Mills walked around yawning and feeling even more tired than before. Coach Dennis assured him that he'd soon

feel better, but nothing happened. As could be expected, the 100m breaststroke was a disaster. Mills had hoped for a medal, but only managed to do 1:05.24 and thus missed qualifying for the final.

The next day, the club's wonder kid, Mary T. Meagher, won the 200m butterfly with a time an astounding five seconds faster than the person who came in second. Her 2:06.37 was more than four seconds faster than Ines Deissler's gold medal race at the Moscow Olympics just a few days before. Mary's record race inspired Mills, and he decided to give it another go. The 100m breaststroke wasn't his best event. It requires more speed during the first length, which wasn't exactly what he'd practiced during his daily marathon sets.

In the 200m breaststroke trials, Glenn Mills came in second after John Moffet, who was from California and also in his teens. At least the race ignited a sense of hope in Mills. However, he was still tired at the start of the final that same evening. In spite of all the times he and his buddy Greg had practiced starts following the evening sessions, his arms and legs were more than just a little worn out. It felt as if he'd jumped into a pool of turquoise paint instead of a pool of water. And to top it off, water was seeping into his goggles.

In breaststroke, most of the power comes from the leg strokes. Mills noticed that his swimming wasn't as fierce and energetic as when he'd been swimming at his best. At 100 meters, he was the last in the field—over two seconds behind leader Nick Navid from the Texas Longhorns.

Let's stop for a moment and talk about psychology. Cognitive psychologists believe there are three ways of managing obstacles: (1) What happened is predetermined and impossible to alter. Besides, learning how to cope with suffering is beneficial. This is *God's Way*. (2) It's someone else's fault: coach Dennis or whoever made the leaky goggles. This is *Your Way*—an approach that ultimately makes you bitter. (3) You take the helm and make

the best out of the situation. The sum of your choices leads to a positive outcome through an "every little bit helps" effect. This is *My Way*.

At the age of 18, Glenn Mills had not read any self-help books—he'd barely read any books whatsoever. The tough training program meant that he didn't study more than necessary. He learned basic grammar, memorized the American Constitution and the most important presidents, and learned enough mathematics to figure out if he'd received the right change when buying breakfast.

Mills had not been able to muster enough energy to go to church, which excluded option one above. Suffering was something he'd already done during practice. He had put so much pressure on himself that his vision had turned all blurry. He'd gotten up at a quarter to four, six days a week, and he'd swum with cramps, sunburn, and goggles that were way too tight. Yet there was nothing as painful as a bad race. Nor was there any time to suffer. Furthermore, Coach

Dennis had impressed upon his swimmers that they were not allowed to blame anyone else for their failures—at least not the coach. Then Mary T. Meagher performed beautifully at the 200m butterfly event.

Back to the race: Glenn Mills now started working his way up the field. His time, 1:08.8, was not a particularly good one for the initial 100 meters. In the stands, Coach Dennis didn't believe that Mills could get a time below 2:20. John Moffet in the lead was swimming toward what looked like a safe victory. Mills knew that he still had some juice left in him and after the last turn he gave everything. He was the only one in the field able to step up his pace, and it looked as if he was about to come in second in the race and get a spot on the American team. If he did, he obviously could not go to the Olympics in Moscow, but would be recognized in a ceremony by the swimming association. This wasn't what was on Mills's mind at the moment—he just swam for all

he was worth. He swam so hard that he was able to catch up with Moffet, who was still not entirely exhausted, but failed to counteract Mills's spurt of energy. At the end, it looked as if they both touched the pool wall at the same time, but the electronics of the time indicated that Glenn Mills had won the race by a mere one hundredth of a second. Qualifying to be a part of an Olympic team without any Olympics to compete in was obviously frustrating, but both Moffet and Mills were still young with a great future ahead of them. The next obvious career objective, the 1984 Olympics in Los Angeles, was still far off in the future. Glenn Mills spent the next four seasons at the University of Alabama, and John Moffet, who was only 16 years old in 1980, ended up at Stanford a few years later.

John Moffet made it to the 1984 Olympics back home in Los Angeles as the world's greatest breaststroke swimmer, after he set a new 100m world record and won the American Olympic qualifying races. In Los Angeles, he hoped for a gold medal, but unfortunately he tore a thigh muscle during the trials. Even though he was in great pain, he swam the final with his leg tightly bandaged. Without any real chance of winning, Moffet managed an easily forgotten fifth place. He left the Olympics with a feeling similar to that of failing your driving test.

Glenn Mills swam a lousy 200m breaststroke at the American qualifying races in 1984. He placed fourth, more than a second slower than four years before, and was unable to join the team. The Olympics is the greatest thing that can happen in a swimmer's career and something that opens doors in America, a country that loves winners. Mills couldn't help going through his career over and over in his head. What if Jimmy Carter hadn't mixed politics and sport? The Olympics being canceled during the two world wars was one thing, but the 1980 situation was nothing but political drama.

Let's return to cognitive psychology. Fortunately, it was not in Mills's nature to dwell on things he was unable to control. At the age of 15, he'd lost his beloved older brother to cancer, something that put his competitions in perspective. Instead of being bitter, he was grateful for his career and all the possibilities, experiences, and friends it had brought him. Today, Glenn Mills works as a swimming consultant, a specialist who helps young swimmers understand how good they can become by improving their technique. In an odd coincidence, his coach Dennis Pursley is now the head coach for the swimming team of Mills's old college in Alabama.

In 1984, Jesse Vassallo was finally able to compete in the Olympics. He had moved back to Florida, where he swam for the college team the Miami Hurricanes. The former teenage star was fast, but not fast enough to win a medal in the 400m medley.

He had shared second place in the butterfly, but then fell back during the breaststroke to end up about a second short of the bronze medal.

Jesse Vassallo didn't compete in the 1988 Olympics in Seoul, but his youngest brother, Sal, did, although he unfortunately didn't make it to the final. However, Jesse's contribution to swimming wasn't over; his dolphin-like underwater swimming technique from the backstroke final in Philadelphia in 1976 had started to influence others.

Someone else competing in Seoul was backstroke swimmer David Berkoff, who'd been a good junior swimmer, even though he was far from being a star. Three years before the Olympics, Berkoff decided to try swimming underwater. By using dolphin-like movements, he was able to swim longer and longer distances underwater while maintaining his speed.

YOUR SWIMMING: HOW TO DO THE BREASTSTROKE

1. Legs

Your legs are what bring you forward. Rebecca Soni, *Swimming World's* female swimmer of the year in 2011, was measured to have a forward-driving force of 100 newtons in her legs, compared to 20 newtons in her arms. Even though not all of us have her leg power, this gives you an indication of just how crucial the leg kick is when doing the breaststroke.

2. Arms

Don't let your arm strokes be larger than they need to be. Anyone overestimating the importance of arm strokes also tends to let his or her arm strokes be too large. Your elbows need to go in before your chest in order to ensure that you're not too wide when the leg kick moves you forward.

3. Find Your Style

A few good breaststroke swimmers, such as Adam Peaty and Rūta Meilutytė, use fast, powerful arm strokes. Others glide more like Megan Jendrick. You may also move your hands above the water like Rebecca Soni.

4. The Head

Look down into the water in front of you as you breathe; don't look up too high.

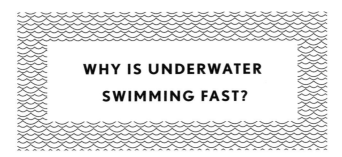

WHY IS UNDERWATER SWIMMING FAST?

Swimming science used to claim that:

- Swimmers can't move forward as quickly using their legs as they can by using their arms.
- The energy consumption involved in a leg stroke is higher compared to an arm stroke as the legs are larger and thus require more oxygen.

The first claim was based on freestyle swimming (where it's still valid), whereas the second claim is still true.

A field of science moves forward by learning from other fields. When a butterfly swimmer swims according to the traditional style, he or she has a leg kick frequency of 44 to 56 kicks per minute. It's difficult to increase this frequency, as swimmers are limited by their ability to increase their arm stroke frequency.

In 1957, Richard Bainbridge at the Cambridge Zoological Laboratory found that the swimming speed of fish (dace and trout) increased in proportion to what he referred to as the "tail beat frequency," which corresponds to the leg kick frequency of a butterfly swimmer. So, what David Berkoff brilliantly practiced in the 1988 Seoul Olympics had already been studied 30 years prior by Bainbridge.

Berkoff used the butterfly kick, but by being positioned on his back, he was able to generate 120–180 kicks per minute. By shaping his arms into a spear (similar to the head of a fish), he was able to swim more like a fish than anyone had seen before.

By using the new technique in the qualifying race for the Olympics, Berkoff was able to beat the world record held by Russian swimmer Igor Polianski. At the trials in the Seoul Olympics, he was even faster: 54.51 was incredibly fast, but the most revolutionary thing was the way he did it.

The Japanese swimmer Daichi Suzuki, who'd started to kick this way underwater in 1984, had slipped under the radar and had made it to the 100m backstroke final, where he and Igor Polianski now flanked Berkoff. Suzuki used to swim 25 meters underwater, but now decided to swim an additional five or six meters. Berkoff swam almost the entire first length underwater and made a lightning-fast turn. However, swimming for such a long distance without breathing results in an oxygen debt and muscle fatigue. This made Berkoff lose all momentum during the last few meters, enabling Suzuki to catch up and win the first Japanese Olympic gold medal in 12 years.

Following the final, the International Swimming Federation (FINA) felt a need to act and immediately decided to limit underwater swimming by, among other things, arguing that butterfly and backstroke swimming had become increasingly similar. The limit for underwater swimming was set to 10 meters, which changed the life of underwater swimmers such as Berkoff and Suzuki. A few years later, FINA redefined the limit to 15 meters. The rule was applied to the backstroke in 1988, to the butterfly in 1998, and later to free-style swimming.

YOUR SWIMMING: TIPS FOR DEVELOPING
YOUR UNDERWATER TECHNIQUE

1. Posture

Kicking is not about generating speed. It's about maintaining
the high speed you get by pushing away from the starting block or the side
of the pool. A good kick is dependent on low resistance and a forward-
driving posture.

2. Flexibility

Having flexible shoulders makes you pointier, thus enabling you to cut
through the water like a swordfish. Flexible hips and ankles result in
a more powerful kick.

3. Fins

Fins are the best aid for developing a good underwater kick. They give you
a good return on investment when used correctly. A serious kicker has three
pairs of fins: standard-sized fins (preferably with an open heel); smaller fins
for a faster, more swim-like kick; and a large blade monofin, which requires
a stronger swimmer. However, diving fins are too long and make it easy to
kick with active knees. The kick should instead be initiated by the hip.

4. Tempo

The higher the frequency of your kicks, the faster you swim. This naturally implies that each kick is equally good. Generally speaking, you want to make small and fast kicks.

5. Strength

Your upper body must be able to provide tempo and maintain your good posture. Your thigh muscles need to be in sync with your upper body. A kick should be powerful going up as well as down, but it's common that the upward kick lacks power and speed. The speed of your toes at the end of the kick is important—think of your upper body as the handle on a whip and of the tip of your toe as the end of this whip.

SCIENCE HELPS SWIMMING GOING FORWARD

Takaishi, Skinner, and Vassallo have all been important to swimming and they represent three great examples of a sport where the format of the competition alters the conditions. They've been the tide that lifts all the boats.

Through history, most successful swimmers have had to watch their competitors try to imitate their styles, regardless of the abilities and makeup of their competitors.

At the beginning of the 1990s, Matt Biondi and Alexander Popov dominated the 100m freestyle—the swimming event that gets the most attention. They were both 6'7" and used a body rotation style when swimming. They both took very long arm strokes and didn't have the same high stroke frequency as previous swimming stars. Furthermore, both Popov and Biondi looked like models, so there's no surprise that every teenager wanted to swim the way they did. Rowdy Gaines, a former world record holder in 100m freestyle, carefully tried to introduce an alternative way of thinking in the magazine *Swimming Technique*: "Not everyone should use long arm strokes. Not everyone can be Popov." Simple mathematics says that if a taller swimmer's arm strokes are as frequent as those of a shorter swimmer, then the taller swimmer has a brilliant opportunity to maintain a higher speed by taking longer arm strokes.

Almost 90 years after Katsuo Takaishi's performance in Amsterdam, it has now been demonstrated that both shorter and taller swimmers can increase their speed by rotating their bodies. Even though Takaishi's observations were correct, and his principles are now used by every current elite swimmer, there's no Nobel Prize in swimming, which is why his deeds have been largely forgotten. The saying, "Tell the truth too early and your words will be ignored; tell the truth too late and everyone will be bored," can certainly be applied to the history of swimming.

8 INNOVATIONS THAT HAVE IMPROVED THE SPORT OF SWIMMING

1. Body Rotation

The Japanese started using this method under Katsuo Takaishi in the 1930s. It was improved upon by George Breen in the 1960s. It's one of the basic aspects in *Total Immersion*, Terry Laughlin's commercial packaging of freestyle swimming for recreational swimmers and triathletes released in the 1990s.

2. Flip Turn

The American swimmer Al Vande Weghe made the first flip turn in 1934. However, for many years after that, swimmers were forced to touch the wall with their hand before turning, which to a large extent offset the benefit of this innovation. Don Schollander won the 400m freestyle at the 1964 Olympics without using flip turns. Since then, flip turns have become the norm.

3. Bodyskin

Men wore swimming briefs for the first time in 1935. Before then, they wore swimsuits. The 1980s brought minimal swimming fashions, but then the swimsuit was relaunched at the end of the 1990s, also for men. This trend culminated in 2009 with full bodysuits made out of rubber. However, swimsuits with floating properties were banned in 2010.

4. Underwater Kicks

Jack Sieg developed breaststroke kicks in 1935. They were subsequently banned, only to be reborn as part of the new swimming style known as butterfly swimming. Jesus Vassallo took kicks underwater in 1976, and David Berkoff and Daichi Suzuki started using them for fast swimming in 1988.

5. Shaving

At the Melbourne Olympics in 1956, the Australian swimmers Jon Henricks and Murray Rose shaved their bodies—and won gold medals. Shaving reduces friction between the body and the water. It also gives the swimmer a better sense of the water, which results in a better execution of the required movements.

6. Swimming Goggles

Persian pearl divers in the fourteenth century used polished tortoise shells to protect their eyes, and Thomas Burgess used motorcycle goggles when he swam across the English Channel in 1911. In the 1960s, swimming goggles allowed swimmers to withstand increasingly longer training sessions in pools with high levels of chlorine. Swimming goggles were first permitted at the Olympics in 1976.

7. Track Starts

When Mark Spitz ruled the 1972 Olympics, he was one of only a few swimmers holding on to the starting block with his hands. The other swimmers spun their arms around the body to then throw themselves into the water in a flat dive. After 1972, more and more swimmers tried to start like Spitz and sort of dive into a small hole. At the 1998 world championships in Perth, swimmers started putting one foot in front of the other, just like in track and field. Since then, the starting blocks have been given a surface with more friction, have been made taller, and also have a steeper slope in order to enable this so-called track start.

8. Strength Training

Until the 1950s, it was believed that all forms of strength training were out of the question, as they made swimmers less flexible and made them sink deeper into the water. These days, however, every elite swimmer uses some form of strength training.

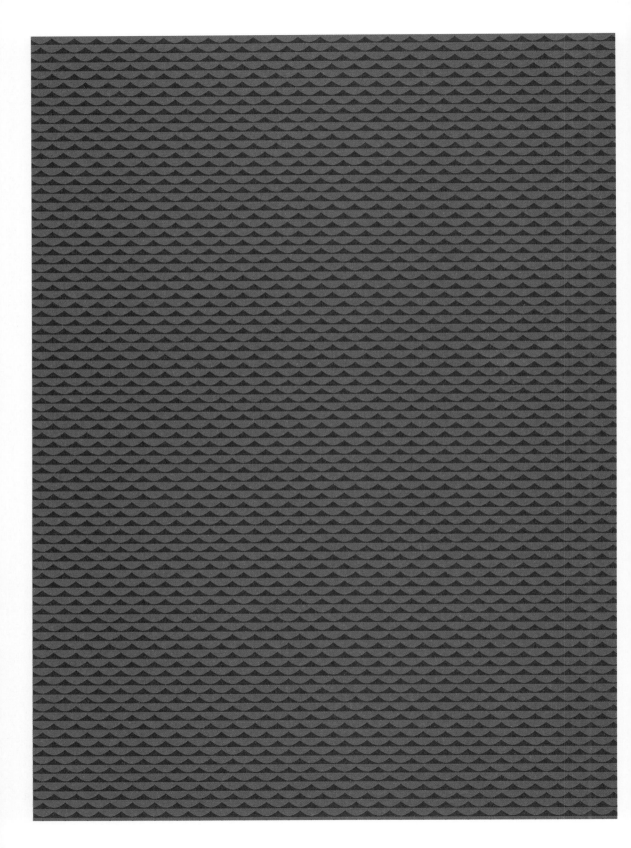

CHAPTER 2

SWIMMING IS
FOR EVERYONE

I'm comfortable saying I'm a gay man and I don't want young people to feel the same way I did. You can grow up and be comfortable and you can be gay.

– Ian Thorpe

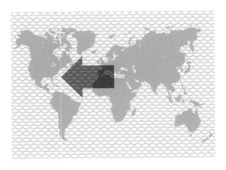

■ **HAMILTON, BERMUDA, OCTOBER 8, 1922.** The world was turned on its head. From then on, the women were coming. One female swimmer had transformed the perception of women in sports. Women hadn't been allowed to compete in the Olympic swimming pools until 1912. In fact, only a few women had been given the opportunity to swim at all.

When the *New York Times* reported on the swimming competition on the Caribbean island of Hamilton on October 9, 1922, it mentioned no less than two world records set by women. Gertrude Ederle had broken the 150m freestyle world record. And an 18-year-old woman named Sybil Bauer, competing for the Illinois Aquatic Club of Chicago, had broken the 440-yard backstroke world record. For those more accustomed to the metric system, a distance of 440 yards is almost exactly 400 meters. Her time of 6:24 didn't mean squat for the businessmen and bankers reading the newspaper, but they probably swallowed their newly cut cigars when they read that Bauer had not only broken the world record for women, but for men as well!

Her teammate Harold Kruger had previously held the record at 6:28, so Bauer's time represented more than just a little bit of trimming—she ensured that his record ended up on the trash heap of history.

Bauer had appeared in the press even before her record. She and her fellow club member, the great Johnny Weissmuller, had served as a main attraction to draw in spectators at competitions throughout North America.

But the record generated new types of articles and was a starting point of what was to become a drawn-out topic of discussion:

Were women going to catch up with men in terms of athletic performance, or even surpass them?

Bauer's record questioned a truth never challenged before, that men were faster than women in short and long running distances. Men in tights with big mustaches lifted iron bars over their heads whereas women were barely allowed to carry their own bags. Men jumped longer and higher. Men threw heavier things farther. While men competed in throwing robust things like the discus, the javelin and the 16-pound iron ball, fragile women had to make do with the sling ball, which was specifically designed for their delicate and sedentary bodies. And they weren't even allowed to compete. Baron de Coubertin, who founded the modern Olympic Games, found female athletes an aesthetic abomination and preferred that women not participate in sports at all.

The newspapers now started to compare the advances of women in sports other than swimming. Even though British golfer Abe Mitchell had hit a tough latex ball 341 yards, Glenna Collett Vare, who was only 18 years old, was closing in fast with her 313 yards. Sure, the Sheffield women's team in field hockey had lost against Philadelphia Field Hockey, but only by a single goal. Early feminist writers started advancing theories that women would even overshadow men in certain sports.

A year and a half later, at a water festival in Miami, Bauer broke her own record by an additional second. The newspaper clips increased in numbers, especially since 1924 was an Olympic year. The headlines concluded that she would be able to beat all men at the Paris Olympics if only she was given the opportunity.

There are no written sources indicating that Sybil herself participated in this debate. She probably did what she liked the most: swimming and studying at Northwestern University. At the Paris Olympiad, she easily won the 100m backstroke with a new Olympic record.

Bauer continued swimming for a few years until November

1926, when she announced her engagement. Her fiancée, the promising sports journalist Ed Sullivan, was based in New York, where he would eventually become a television pioneer with *The Ed Sullivan Show*. However, Sybil Bauer never got to experience this trip to fame. She died of cancer in 1927, at only 23 years old, as the world record holder in all eight backstroke distances.

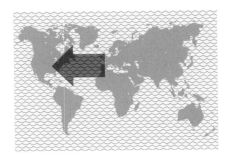

■ ST. LOUIS, MISSOURI, JUNE 21, 1949. At over 90°F (32°C) in the shade in the morning, it was so hot that the air trembled. The Bakelite telephone called out angrily at the house of John O'Toole. The first ring broke the silence with such intensity that he would have heard it even if he'd been vacuuming or visiting his neighbor. He answered the phone and was greeted by a furious man accusing him of being a "n----r lover," adding that he "would have to pay for this." Before eight in the morning, he'd already received three calls with roughly the same message. A shaken John O'Toole called the police, who offered him protection for the remainder of the day.

The newspapers were selling like hotcakes in the hot sunshine. The largest newspaper in Missouri, the *Globe Democrat*, screamed out what was a radical message in the South: "Pools and Playgrounds Opened to Both Races. Negroes and Whites May Hereafter Swim Together in All the City's Nine Pools."

Its competitor, the *Post-Dispatch*, said the following: "Negroes Will Not Be Denied a Swim in Any City Pool."

However, insurance worker John O'Toole had nothing to do with this hotly debated decision. His namesake, the director of the public welfare who had just announced integration at the city pools and whom the calls were actually meant for, was listed in the phonebook under his nickname, "Jack O'Toole."

The Roosevelt Park Pool in Ohio was segregated until the 1960s.

In the afternoon, 200 people were waiting for the fairgrounds pool to open. About 30 of them were black. The group of people outside the women's entrance was smaller and consisted only of whites. The guests flooded in when the gates opened, and they were finally able to cool off in the water a few minutes later. The black men, who'd been given access to the pool for the first time in its 36-year history, kept to themselves.

While people played and goofed around in the blue pool, an estimated crowd of 200 teenagers and young

men had gathered outside the fence. They started calling out threatening jeers. Most of them were armed with baseball bats, iron bars, bricks, or knives. The lifeguards called the police, resulting in seven police officers arriving a moment later to escort the black swimmers from the area.

During the next hour, the young black men, the armed mob, and the police moved around in the neighborhood near the pool. One could sense the impending violence, but nothing happened. By dinnertime, the tensions had dissipated. The mob had dispersed—they had most likely gone home to get something to eat.

Around a quarter to seven that same evening, around 20 young black men were in line to get into the pool. They were told to "get out of here if you wanna stay out of trouble." After some hesitation, they heeded this advice and went up on a small hill offering a view of the swimming pool area.

The white mob reappeared a few minutes past seven, now bigger than before and mostly consisting of white teenagers, but also some adult men.

Rolland, a 20-year-old cement worker, discovered the disappointed black pool guests outside the fence. "There they are. Let's teach them a lesson." A short chase ensued. The black men were surrounded after just a few minutes and a vicious beating ensued. Most of the black men were in their early twenties, but some of them were as young as 13. One of them, Arthur Goodin, took up a knife to defend himself and stabbed Rolland in the thigh.

Everything stopped. The people in the mob looked at each other. It was as if an invisible boundary had been crossed, and the beatings intensified. It didn't abate until the mob caught sight of, and set off after, two black men on bicycles. These two men got away, but a man happened to get in the way of the mob and was beaten so savagely that he lost his ability to speak. While lying on the ground, a 16-year-old boy repeatedly kicked him in the head. The police were eventually able to disperse the mob and the injured victims were taken to the hospital.

The documented injuries were extensive: knocked-out teeth, broken jaws, cracked skulls, incomplete scalpings, broken arms and legs, in addition to countless cuts and bruises.

The unrest led to the mayor of St. Louis closing all pools in the city and creating a working group to resolve the situation. But how could this notion of swimming pools open to everyone be a problem?

CHAPTER 2

THE WHITE SPORT

What happened in St. Louis was nothing new—conflicts concerning the management of public pools were commonplace during the first half of the twentieth century.

The United States was economically successful, and by the beginning of the twentieth century, New York, Chicago, and Los Angeles had turned into global financial centers. However, this great wealth didn't find its way to rural America, in particular, not to the South and states such as Missouri, Alabama, Mississippi, Louisiana, and Georgia.

Blacks were denied the same rights white Americans had, and racism was widespread. The Ku Klux Klan had more than four million members in the 1920s. Fifteen percent of all adult men belonged to the Klan, with a considerably higher percentage in the South. The Klan's slogan of "100 percent American" didn't make any sense, considering the fact that almost every member had at least one grandparent born abroad.

The public pools represented a problem when it came to the notion of white supremacy. The Klan felt confident in mental spheres such as politics and economics, but black men at the public pools showed that the physical superiority of the white race was not a given.

In 1910, Jack Johnson, the son of Texan slaves, defeated Jim Jefferies and became the first black world heavyweight boxing champion. Even though Johnson would lose his title five years later (to a white boxer, Jess Willard), his success had been a threat to white supremacy, especially for people in the Klan.

Back to the public pools. Many feared that the sight of black men, muscular from physical labor, standing next to white insurance salesmen, shopkeepers, and barbers would undermine the belief in white supremacy.

At the beginning of the nineteenth century, approximately 80 percent of the black population in America knew how to swim, versus 20 percent of white Americans. Many slave plantations were located close to lakes and rivers, and a quick bath in nature with some soap was the only chance for slaves to freshen up after a day of sweaty and dirty work.

After the Civil War, white America came to realize that improving people's ability to swim could reduce the number of drowning accidents. As a result, blacks were banned from entering public baths and beaches, and "whites only" signs went up next to public pools. Even though illiteracy was widespread, these were words all black Americans had been taught to read.

White children and teens, on the other hand, could swim and train in municipal pools, at the YMCA, or in a pool at any of the 11,600 country clubs spread across the country. One of these is the Baltimore Country Club (BCC) in the hometown of Michael Phelps.

BCC has three pools: a children's pool, a pool for swim lessons, and a training pool with six lanes. Children have learned how to swim there ever since the pools were completed in the late 1960s. It wasn't until almost 30 years later, in 1995, that BCC accepted its first black members. In order to be approved, the married couple William and Martha Jews had to pay, be recommended by a member, and have their application signed by nine additional members. The fact that country clubs have excluded black members for a long time is something that has also had an impact on American swimming.

People had actually started discussing whether it was even possible for blacks to swim as fast as whites when Chris Silva from UCLA made the U.S. national team in 1983. Silva swam the freestyle distance in the relay team that set a new American record at the Edmonton University Games. Princess Diana asked him out for dinner. He was the first black swimmer she'd ever seen.

During the materialistic 1980s, the charismatic Silva gave private lessons to Hollywood stars. He wore Ralph Lauren clothes, ate sushi, and dated Olympic divers. Life was coming along nicely, but he had a recurring problem: cars.

In March 1988, he received a fine for an unsafe lane change, was caught not using his seat belt and didn't have his insurance information in the glove compartment. A few weeks later, he got a fine for speeding. California has a rule of "three strikes and you're out," so when Chris Silva left the scene of an accident without filling out an injury report, he was banned from driving in the state.

Silva moved to Florida, where he started working at the International Swimming Hall of Fame (ISHOF) to develop swimming for minority groups throughout the country. However, it was only a few weeks before he took his friend's Ferrari Testarossa for a test drive. Just as thrilled about being fast on the road as he was in the pool, Silva tested what the Testarossa was made of. The sports car was speeding like a low-flying airplane down Las Olas Boulevard in downtown Fort Lauderdale. The police report mentions a speed of 90 mph on a street with a 35-mph speed limit. Silva's joyride ended when he crashed into a solid concrete bus shelter. He died instantly, at only 26 years old. Five years after becoming the first black swimmer on a U.S. national team, he was still the only one.

SIX WORLD-CLASS SWIMMERS WITH AFRICAN ROOTS

1. **Anthony Nesty,** Surinam. Olympic gold in the 100m butterfly 1988.

2. **Cullen Jones,** United States. Olympic gold in the 4 × 100m butterfly 2008.

3, 4, 5. **Simone Manuel, Lia Neal, and Natalie Hinds,** United States. Won the first three positions in the 100m freestyle in the 2015 U.S. college championship.

6. **Alia Atkinson,** Jamaica. First black woman to win a world championship gold when she won the 100m breaststroke in 2014.

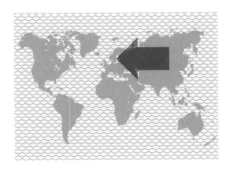

■ **DJURGÅRDSBRUNNKANALEN, STOCKHOLM, SWEDEN, JULY 12, 1912.** Fanny Durack's hand touched the pier serving as the finish line. She blinked twice to get the brown and salty water out of her eyes and quickly looked over to both sides. The other participants in the race were still swimming frantically. She'd won the 100m freestyle by six seconds and her time of 1:19.8 was a new world record. When she realized that victory was hers, she called out and smiled at her friends in the stands, who were shouting and clapping their hands.

Fanny, who grew up near the beach in Sydney, Australia, had

been swimming since the age of 9. The Stockholm Olympics was the first and only time that New Zealand and Australia competed together under the name of Australasia. This was a small matter compared to the fact that Fanny was allowed to compete at Stockholm in the first place. In the Paris Olympics in 1900, women had competed in sailing, tennis, and riding, but they had not been allowed to swim until the Stockholm games.

A total of 27 female swimmers came to compete in the two events of 100m freestyle and 4 × 100m freestyle. Six of them were Swedish and an additional six were British. The United States had not sent any female swimmers. Since there were only four countries participating in the relay event, there was no need for trials. In addition to Sweden and the United Kingdom, Germany and Austria also participated. Australasia had only two women in Stockholm. However, they'd won both the gold and the silver medals in the individual 100-meter race.

Australasia almost didn't send any female swimmers at all. The committee setting up the swim team had thought that sending female swimmers to Sweden was a waste of both time and money. Eventually, however, the wife of a theater director collected enough money to put two female swimmers and their mandatory coaches on a ship to London.

While the young swimmers were still at sea, the theater director's wife managed to persuade the board of the New South Wales Ladies Swimming Association to approve the swimmers, Fanny Durack and Mina Wylie, to participate in the Olympics. They received the good news by telegram as they stopped in Cape Town. Once in London, they spent some time training before it was time to go to Sweden.

The dual victory in the 100m freestyle had given Fanny and Mina a taste for more, so they suggested to the organizers that they would swim two distances each in the relay race. They were so superior that they would have probably won a medal. Individually, they had been a total of 45 seconds faster than the best Swedish swimmers, Vera Thulin and Greta Johansson. Unfortunately, the organizers rejected their request, which meant that the female part of the Australasian team had to watch the final from the stands.

The events in 1912 were still important in terms of equality in sports. This is still a very applicable issue, as in the 2012 London Olympics, women were awarded 30 percent fewer medals compared to men. And even if swimming events tend to have the most even distribution of men and women, there are also differences that are difficult to justify (e.g. that women swam 800 meters compared to the men's 1,500 meters at the Olympics in Rio de Janeiro in 2016).

DIFFERENCES AMONG OLYMPIC GOLD MEDALISTS IN 100M FREESTYLE

	Men	Women	Difference
1912	Duke Kahanamoku, USA 1:03.4	Fanny Durack, Australia 1:22.2	29.7 %
1932	Yasuji Miyazaki, Japan 58.2	Helene Madison, United States 1:06.8	14.8 %
1952	Clarke Scholes, United States 57.4	Katalin Szöke, Hungary 1:06.8	16.4 %
1972	Mark Spitz, United States 51.22	Sandy Neilson, United States 58.59	14.4 %
1992	Alexander Popov, CIS 49.02	Zhuang Yong, China 54.64	11.5 %
2012	Nathan Adrian, United States 47.52	Ranomi Kromowidjojo, Netherlands 53.00	11.5 %

PHYSIOLOGICAL GENDER DIFFERENCES IN PERFORMANCE

The introduction of women to professional swimming took place several decades after men began competing. There has been research on male swimmers since 1905, while the first study on female swimmers came considerably later. In early research on women in sports, we find questions such as, "Is participating in sports dangerous for women?" and "When women train and compete too hard will it affect their ability to have children later in life?"

It is an established and inescapable truth that there are, and always will be, differences between men and women. The only question is how large or small these differences actually are.

Muscle Strength

"Their strength has disappeared. They have become as women." This Bible quote from the book of Jeremiah shows that women have been considered weaker than men for a long time. But are women in fact weaker than men? Superstar crossfitter Rich Froening snatches (lifting a barbell over one's head) a personal best of 305 pounds whilst Zhou Lulu holds the women's world record of 322 pounds.

Our muscle strength is developed during adolescence. Girls on average have 90 percent of the muscle strength of boys at the age of 12 and 75 percent at the age of 16. Women have a lower number of muscle cells—a relationship reflected fairly well in the difference in strength between the two sexes.

On average, women are 40–60 percent weaker in their arms compared to men, whereas the difference in leg strength is only 25–30 percent. This difference is the result of more hormone receptors in the upper body in men; more testosterone makes it easier for men to build muscle in that part of the body. In terms of legs, however, there is no difference in strength per square inch of muscle between men and women. Furthermore, unfit women have a higher proportion of slow muscle fibers compared to unfit men. Women also burn a higher proportion of fat when training, which gives them stamina.

Men have larger lungs and hearts compared to women, even when taking into account that men tend to be larger than women. On average, a woman's lungs hold 1.1 gallons of air, while a man's may hold as much as 1.6 gallons. Lung volume is not a decisive factor in terms of performance; in most endurance sports, the heart's capacity to pump blood is more important. However, swimming is an exception to this rule, as a larger cavity inside the ribs is very beneficial to the buoyancy of a swimmer. The heart's capacity to pump is lower for women compared to men, which is the result of both smaller heart muscles and a smaller frame. Women's hearts are thus smaller, both in absolute terms and in relation to body size.

The hemoglobin count, which determines how much oxygen may be carried in the blood prior to physical activity, is related to an athlete's performance level. The body maintains its hemoglobin value by extracting iron from the food we eat. Men on average have 6 percent more red blood cells than women. This means that women have smaller iron deposits. Women also ingest less iron because they in general don't eat as much as men. Women are on average able to transport 19.0 milliliters of oxygen per 100 milliliters of blood, whereas the corresponding number for men is 21.5 milliliters of oxygen.

Without taking body weight into account, the difference in oxygen uptake between men and women is between about 50 percent (in American studies) and about 30 percent (in Scandinavian studies). If measuring body weight excluding fat, then the difference is between 20 to 30 percent and 15 percent, respectively. After excluding other differences, such as the difference in hemoglobin count, there is still a difference in oxygen uptake capacity of between 12 percent and 15 percent, respectively. The remaining difference is related to lifestyle, which can't be accounted for under equal conditions.

The first time that swimmers were analyzed anthropometrically (comparing proportions of the human body) on a larger scale was during the 1968 Olympics in Mexico City. After having weighed and measured almost all participants in a variety of ways, it was noted that the body composition of athletes in various events differed.

The Seoul Olympics in 1988 was the first time that swimmers were analyzed biomechanically. The results indicated a few differences between male and female athletes. The men were taller, older, and faster than the women. The men also traveled farther with each stroke.

This research continued at the Barcelona Olympics in 1992 when the concept of the magic "9 percent difference" was coined. The male swimmers were 9 percent faster than the female siwmmers. They were also 9 percent older and taller, and their strokes were 9 percent longer. Over longer distances, however, the difference was smaller. Katie Ledecky swimming 1,000 yards freestyle in 8:59 was less than

5 percent slower than Clark Smith's male record time of 8:33. As distances get longer, it seems the male advantages get smaller.

What about other sports? In running, the difference in performance between men and women is 11 percent, from 100 meters up to 10,000 meters. The gap is even greater in sports rewarding explosiveness, such as throwing and jumping sports. In the long jump, the performance difference between men and women is as large as 20 percent.

FACTORS SAID TO INFLUENCE FEMALE SWIMMING RESULTS

1. Anthropometrics (Body Measurements) Body height is a significant factor and women are on average shorter. The wider shoulders and more narrow hips of men also benefit their movement in water.

2. Body Composition Women have more body fat and a smaller proportion of muscles on the non-fat parts of their upper bodies. Increasing upper body strength frequently results in higher speeds. Uncontrolled weight loss may lead to a drop in performance.
A well-thought-out diet plan is important for a man, but critical for a woman wanting to perform optimally.

3. Contraceptives Birth control pills may have side effects such as weight gain, headaches, and dizziness.

4. Iron Deficiency Women need to compensate for their iron loss due to the menstrual cycle in order to perform optimally.A recommended diet (apart from meat, fish, and eggs) consists of chickpeas, pumpkin seeds, lentils, spinach, and many types of beans.

CHAPTER 2

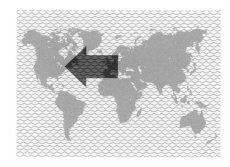

■ **MANHATTAN, NEW YORK, SEPTEMBER 1975.** The sun has started to set. A woman wearing a swimsuit is lying next to a boat in the dark waters of the East River. The men in the boat are trying to communicate with her, but they only receive meaningless syllables in return. When they try to pull her up into the boat, she resists in a way that would have been termed violent had they been police officers. The woman is 26-year-old Diana Nyad—who intended to swim around Manhattan—and the men are operating her boat. Diana is weakened by a virus infection and is now in a position—against her principles—where she has to abandon her dream.

In 1875, Matthew Webb was able to show that long-distance swims could end happily, when he swam from England to France. According to military strategists, you win the battle once you have your enemy surrounded, and swimming around Manhattan was the ultimate analogy. You swim from point A to point B but end up where you started.

A successful swim around Manhattan, the island that has been the financial center of the world for over a century, has more challenges than simply the distance of 29 miles. You also need to be able to navigate the Hudson River, the Harlem River, and the East River. When the first daredevils attempted this swim in 1910, all three waterways were already heavily trafficked. The swim was further complicated by shifting tides in the rivers.

Swedish waters may be cold but they have minuscule tidal effects, and tidal forces are negligible in the northern end of the Baltic Sea. Around Manhattan, however, these forces are pretty visible (although not extreme) and may constitute a challenge when swimming. The tidal currents switch twice a day, which means that the water is still for approximately five minutes before changing direction.

While the National Oceanographic Atmospheric Administration (NOAA) now keeps an eye on all tidal effects in the United States, at the beginning of last century, this task was more difficult. Swimmers hoping to complete this heroic swim threw newspaper pages into the water and watched how they moved in relation to the land to figure out the tidal patterns. The 12-mile swim in the Hudson River constitutes the longest part when rounding Manhattan, and swimming here at the wrong time could be very strenuous.

Eighteen-year-old Robert Dowling attempted the swim in August 1915. He was the son of a hotel baron who arranged accompanying boats. Dowling's plan was to swim from Battery Park up the East River through Hell Gate and onward into the Harlem River. However, he was unable to continue around the entire island as parts of the river were drained of water. His swimming speed for the 12-mile distance in the Hudson River was estimated at approximately 19 minutes per mile. Later NOAA observations enable us to calculate that the tide provided him with half of his speed. This means that his speed in standing water would be 38 minutes per mile, which is quite mediocre by today's standards. A few weeks later, Dowling picked another route and swam all the way around Manhattan in 13 hours and 45 minutes.

Following Dowling's time-consuming swim, other candidates started experimenting with how to use the tide to their advantage. In 1916, Ida Elionsky became the first woman to complete the swim, besting Dowling's time. But it wasn't until 1927, when Byron Summers moved the start to East 136th Street in the Harlem River, that the finish time saw a massive improvement. His 8:56 is a respectable time to this day.

Once she was rid of her fever, Diana Nyad made a second attempt to be the seventh woman around Manhattan. As a child, she'd made a habit out of doing unusual things, and this continued through her adolescence.

Diana was born into wealth in the center of New York City. Her father was a stockbroker but the bulk of the family fortune came from a strange product invented by Diana's mother's grandfather in the mid-nineteenth century. Mrs. Winslow's Soothing Syrup was a mixture containing morphine. "Efficiently puts any man or animal to sleep" was the slogan spread in newspapers, recipe books, and wall calendars at a time when advertising was still in its infancy. Happy parents with small children used it to put their children to sleep and people in the thin-walled apartments of the time were finally able to sleep through the night.

Mrs. Winslow's Soothing Syrup was a big success and the secret recipe was exported to London. The morphine dose was low

enough to ensure that the children probably didn't suffer from any withdrawal, but the parents didn't make the connection between the product and their children's bowel movements: constipation when the morphine was working and diarrhea once the effect wore off. Or perhaps they felt that a good night's sleep was worth the price of additional dirty cloth diapers. This chloroform for babies created a family fortune before the mixture was classified as "bad" by the American Medical Association.

As Diana's mother was well-off, there were no financial obstacles when she divorced her stockbroker husband in 1952, when Diana was three years old. Diana's mother remarried a Greek construction magnate named Aristotle; a name shared with the ancient scientist who was an early specialist in the movement of animal and human bodies on both land and in water. The last name of the mother's new husband, Nyad, was even more fitting. The Naiads (of which Nyad is a singular form) were the mythological

Greek freshwater goddesses. They ruled over rivers, brooks, streams, springs, wells, swamps, ponds, and lakes. As a matter of fact, they ruled all water except for the oceans, which were ruled by their sisters the Oceanids.

The Nyad family moved from New York to Florida, where Aristotle was involved in building a hotel network. Growing up in Florida suited Diana perfectly as she developed an interest in swimming at an early age.

She almost made it to the 1968 Olympic Trials in Los Angeles, until she got sick during preparations. Swimming long and hard with a virus in her body had resulted in a serious case of myocarditis (inflammation of the heart muscle). The illness put her in bed for three months, shattering her Olympic dreams.

Knowing when to train and when not to is essential for the quality of your race performance. Chrissie Wellington, the greatest endurance athlete in the world, has said, "It's better to be 20 percent undertrained than 1 percent overtrained." Choosing not to train is hard in athletic cultures where coaches believe "more training is better training."

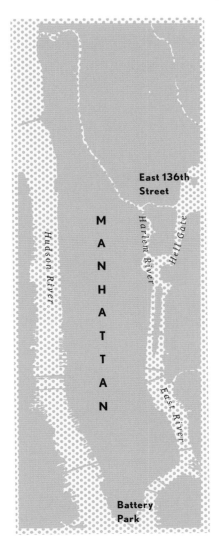

Diana Nyad was expelled from college in her first year after she jumped out of a window wearing a parachute. At her second college, she played tennis and became one of the best in the country in the new sport of racquetball. She still swam as frequently as possible and was introduced to distance events. She ended up becoming a marathon swimmer. Before the Manhattan swim, she completed the Bay of Naples race in 1974—24 miles from Capri to Naples in Italy—so she was certainly ready for the challenge.

Things went better during her second attempt around Manhattan; she made the swim in 7:57, more than an hour faster than the previous best woman. The 5'6'', 127-pound (168 cm, 58 kg) Nyad had swum herself into the absolute center of attention. She was luminous on *Saturday Night Live*, took over the *Johnny Carson Show* as if it was her own, and was asked out on a date by Woody Allen. Swimming had finally gotten a female superstar in Diana Nyad.

Diana accepted Woody Allen's request for a date even though she knew that romance was not in the cards, as she had discovered that she was gay some years before. The fact that Diana was a lesbian didn't put a damper on her popularity.

Nyad decided to take on new projects. She tried and failed to conquer the English Channel three times. But her major obsession was to do something more spectacular: swim the 102 miles from the Bahamas to Florida—without a shark cage—which she did beautifully. Favorable winds and being in the best shape of her life took her across the ocean in 27.5 hours. This swim ended up being her last "competitive" swim. She completed another project when she swam from Cuba to the U.S. in 2013. Nyad was also busy writing columns for Newsweek and the *New York Times*. She published four books and used her sparkling charisma to become a popular lecturer.

There are likely just as few openly homosexual male athletes as there are competitive swimmers who don't find the 200m butterfly absolutely grueling. One of the pioneers was army man Tom Waddell (who placed sixth in the decathlon at the 1968 Olympics) whose persistent work resulted in the first Gay Olympic Games held in 1982 in San Francisco, the city perhaps most associated with the struggle for gay rights.

Another American, Bruce Hayes, had swum in the spotlight during the long relay race of 4 x 200m freestyle at the Los Angeles Olympics in 1984. In the Olympic qualifying races, he had narrowly missed the opportunity to compete individually in this distance. The great swimming star of the games was Michael Gross from West Germany, referred to as "The Albatross" due to his enormous wingspan. Three weeks earlier, at the national team's training camp in Colorado, Hayes was informed that he would be swimming against Gross on the last leg of the race.

In the relay final, with the stands packed, the United States was narrowly beating West Germany until the last distance. The American coaches assumed that the team and Hayes would need to have a three-second lead in order to have a reasonable chance of keeping clear of the German.

Hayes was only 1.5 seconds ahead of Gross at the changeover and the German was able to catch up 50 meters later. In frustration, the American coaches threw off their red, white, and blue baseball hats. Hayes did his utmost not to embarrass himself and American swimming in front of the home audience. The 20-pounds-lighter (9 kg) and nine-inches-shorter (23 cm) American fought on but looked like a small dinghy next to the 6'6" (198 cm) German swimmer.

At the last turn, Bruce Hayes did the unexpected. He responded to the tempo increase of the huge German by letting his legs work even more and was able to reach the side of the pool four hundredths of a second before Gross. The team (which also included deaf swimmer Jeff Float), also set a new world record.

Hayes remembers the last pool length as if in slow motion, and the time immediately after he won is as blurry and confusing as a Monet painting. But he also remembers how humbly the German team congratulated the ecstatic American college guys. After the race, he no longer carried any weight on his shoulders— he'd completed his task and had performed above his ability. He had given the most precious thing he could give to his three teammates and to the United States: an Olympic gold.

Even after Hayes had purged all Olympics-related pressure, he was still weighed down by a secret. He'd realized at the age of 16 that he was gay. The years working extremely hard to get to the Olympics had been a way of hiding and pushing this realization to the sidelines. Greg Louganis, the best diver in the world, was openly gay.

But when other swimmers talked about his amazing performances, they couldn't help adding nasty comments about his sexuality. Consequently, coming out as gay was not an option for Hayes.

There was a lot of progress in terms of equality in the U.S. in the 1980s. Beginning with Wisconsin in 1982, state after state banned discrimination based on sexual orientation. In 1987, 600,000 people gathered in Washington for a massive demonstration for gay rights. But when the third edition of the Gay Olympic Games was to be held in Vancouver in 1990, the International Olympic Committee had not allowed the use of the word "Olympic."

Apart from competitions, the Gay Games also included many seminars. People wore T-shirts saying things like "I don't mind straight people as long as they are gay in public" and bumper stickers saying, "Let's get one thing straight: I'm not." This was an open and inclusive environment where Bruce Hayes finally felt comfortable coming out, becoming the first Olympic medalist to participate in the Gay Games. Hayes won no less than seven gold medals and ended up becoming one of the most important people in the gay movement.

Several top swimmers have followed in Hayes's footsteps and come out during or after their careers. The most famous is Ian Thorpe, who said the following in an interview on the British talk show *Parkinson*: "Today, I have no problem saying 'I'm gay' and I wish that young people shouldn't have to go through what I had to go through, but that they may come out as gay without there being anything weird about it."

TRAINING ONCE A WEEK

Priority objectives:

Improve endurance in your swim-specific muscles

Master different speeds

Improve your biodynamics

Session design:

1) Easy warm-up, preferably using technique exercises

(see Appendix, page 315).

2) Main series for a general increase in aerobic capacity. Add different speeds and take short rests. The Catch-up exercise specifically targets swimming muscles and is preferably combined with heart rate speed.

3) End with sprint speed if this has not been included in the main series.

TRAINING TWICE A WEEK

Priority objectives:

Improve endurance in your swim-specific muscles

Master different speeds

Improve your biodynamics

Session design:

Not as important to do everything in one session. For example, one session may focus on pure endurance while the second workout combines endurance and speed.

TRAINING THREE TIMES A WEEK

Priority objectives:

Increase your top speed

Increase your endurance

Improve your technique

Training three times a week means you can individualize your sessions and get a decent jackpot as a result of your training.

Session design:

1) Endurance sessions with a large portion of swimming at top speed without long periods of rest.

2) Sessions with the main series in intervals, which stimulates breathing and circulation but avoids muscle fatigue.

3) Sessions with the main series stimulating maximum oxygen uptake. Spend the same amount of time resting as engaging in tough activity.

TRAINING FOUR TIMES A WEEK

Priority objectives:

Training four times a week means you can individualize your sessions and get a decent jackpot as a result of your training. Now you want to improve all aspects of your swimming.

Session design:

Start with the three sessions a week design. If you're training for an endurance event, it's a good idea to add an extra distance session. Don't include more than one maximum VO2 session per week (see The Mystic Square on page 348).

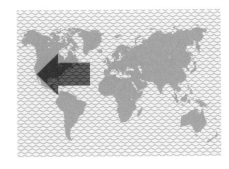

■ LOS ANGELES, CALIFORNIA, 2009. Diana Nyad had just turned 60 when her mother died. The death rattled Diana, who decided to continue the project she'd started in 1978. Nyad realized that she'd need to compensate for the strength of youth by means of an extraordinary training design. She didn't have to go any further than the newsstand to find a program for preparing for a marathon. However, there was less information available for training a 60-year-old woman to swim from Cuba to Florida. The only swimmer to achieve this feat was retired Ohio baker Walter Poenish, who celebrated his 65th birthday in a shark cage swimming between Havana and Little Duck Key in the lower Florida Keys. But Poenish died in 2000 and couldn't share any wisdom with Nyad.

Diana Nyad turned to South African sports physiologist Tim Noakes, but when he couldn't help her, she decided to become her own guinea pig. She started training by swimming 25-minute sessions in the pool of her golf club to build up her shoulder strength. For six months, she engaged in basic training without telling another living soul what she was up to (except the pool keeper at the golf club, who could see her training). Diana gradually increased her sessions to four hours even though she wasn't swimming particularly hard. After some more time, she secretly took off to Mexico where she did test swims for six and a half hours. With this information in hand, she designed a simple but targeted and tough training program. Her training on land included 100 burpees a day, while her swimming sessions got longer and longer—8 hours, 10 hours, some 15-hour sessions. Every Friday, she biked 100 miles to let her shoulders rest.

The weather was not vacation-like in August 2011 when Diana Nyad was set to make a second attempt to swim from Cuba to Florida. She was forced to quit after 29 hours of swimming due to the tough winds, asthma, an aching shoulder, and veering off course.

to succeeding than ever before. Nevertheless, this attempt ended with her getting hauled into the boat after getting through two storms and being badly burned by jellyfish.

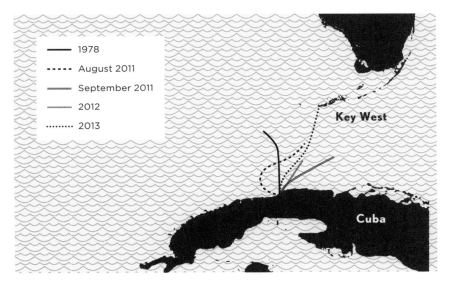

- ——— 1978
- - - - - August 2011
- ——— September 2011
- ——— 2012
- ········ 2013

Key West

Cuba

Diana Nyad's five swims from Cuba

Six weeks later, she tried again. This time, however, her attempt was cut short by aggressive marine life. After 75 miles, 41 hours, and countless altercations with jellyfish, she was forced to quit. By the time she made her fourth attempt, she'd been training for an additional year, and this time she came closer

It would take another year before she made her fifth and final attempt. Diana had made two changes in her training program. First, she swam almost exclusively in the Caribbean, in water as similar as possible to that between Cuba and Florida. Second, she subjected herself to even longer training sessions—14 hours turned into 18 and even 24 hours. She had stopped cycling as it made her legs muscular and heavy. Her shoulders no longer had the same need for rest after she'd polished her technique in order to minimize strain on her shoulder girdle.

On the morning of August 31, 2013, she was also for the first time wearing a full swimsuit for protection against jellyfish. The suit had no buoyancy—it only served as protection against the ocean's inhabitants. Protection is prohibited according to marathon swimming rules, but Nyad's dream was more important than any international ratification.

The conditions were good; the currents were going in the right direction, and her swimsuit protected her from the tentacles of the jellyfish. During the swim, Diana Nyad found time for both reciting Stephen Hawking and hallucinating that Snow White's dwarves were running next to her. Still, after 53 hours of swimming and 35 years after her first attempt, she was able to reach her goal. "Never give up! We never get too old to stop chasing our dreams," was the first thing she was able to say, her mouth swollen from all the salt water.

AMAZING FEMALE SWIMMERS

SYBIL BAUER broke the men's 440-yard backstroke world record in 1922. She beat Harold Kruger's time by three seconds, which led to a discussion on the sports pages about whether the era of men was over.

KIRSTY COVENTRY broke barriers. Nowadays, swimmers come from all over the world, and Coventry from Zimbabwe is a great example. She competed in the semifinals at the Olympics when she was still living at home in Harare. Following this, she moved to Auburn, Alabama, and later won Olympic gold in both Athens in 2004 and Beijing in 2008.

JANET EVANS broke the 400m freestyle world record in 1988 (4:03), a record which stood for 18 years. With her 5'5" (165 cm) frame, she is the only one to have swum this distance at the speed of one body length per second. Had Ian Thorpe with his 6'4" (193 cm) frame swum as fast in relation to height, he would have done so in 3:22 instead of 3:40.

ENITH BRIGITHA became the first swimmer with African roots to win an Olympic medal. She was born on Curaçao and represented the Netherlands when she won the bronze medal behind two East German swimmers in the 1976 Olympics in Montreal. The reason for the East German success turned out to be systematic doping, which puts a sad mark on this story.

DAWN FRASER became the first woman to swim a 100m freestyle race in under a minute, and won the event at the 1956, 1960, and 1964 Olympics. In Tokyo in 1964, she was accused of having swum across a pond at night and of having stolen a flag from the palace of Emperor Hirohito. Even though she professed her innocence, she was suspended from the Australian team for ten years. Her best time swimming the 100m freestyle was 58 seconds—the same time as Johnny Weissmuller, who had dominated the event a few decades earlier.

LYNNE COX, at 15 years old, swam across the English Channel in 1972, faster than any man ever had. In 1987, she crossed the Bering Strait and opened up the American-Soviet border for the first time in 48 years. The swim took two hours and six minutes, and she did it without a wetsuit in 38°F (3°C) water.

DARA TORRES's elite world swimming career lasted between the ages of 14 and 45 (with some breaks). She not only struggled with competitors but also with eating disorders and doubts from the people around her. At 41 years old, she was the oldest swimmer to earn a place on an Olympic team, and at the 2008 Summer Olympics she won three Olympic silver medals and was only one hundredth of a second from winning a gold medal in the 50m freestyle. She won 12 Olympic medals in all, four each of gold, silver, and bronze.

CHAPTER 3

THE LONELINESS OF THE LONG DISTANCE SWIMMER

Older runners tend to go for longer races. It's the opposite in swimming because your body can't handle the endurance.

– Kirsty Coventry

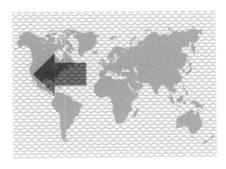

■ **WHITTIER, CALIFORNIA, DECEMBER 1997.**

Why So Ungodly Early?

Classes at West Whittier High started at 8:00 a.m. Other students at the school could simply set their alarm clock to 7:00 a.m. This happened to be the same time that Mike and Brian Soria also got up—from the swimming pool at the Industry Hills Aquatic Complex. This facility (which no longer stands), served as the location of the diving scenes in the movie *Back to School*, where Rodney Danger-field plays a businessman in his 50s going to college. (Hint: he spends more time partying and diving than studying.)

Even if Mike and Brian were frequently too tired to keep up with classes and sometimes skipped doing their homework, this wasn't due to any partying. In addition to their nurturing mother, they also had Coach Rick at the Industry Hills Aquatic Club (IHAC).

Rick Walker possessed one of the thickest black mustaches one could imagine, and he also had a training program that was difficult to grasp. The youths in his group were between the ages of 13 and 18.

Each session was at least two hours long, and the morning sessions hardly contained enough rest for saying hello to one another. Swimming for 8,000 to 9,000 meters meant that Rick's hoarse voice was already calling out "Ready . . . Go!" at 5:00 a.m. The four morning sessions were complemented by six afternoon sessions including 7,000 to 8,000 meters of swimming.

This meant that the group swam between 75,000 and 85,000 meters a week. Long

night. Going to bed and getting up so early may be unusual these days unless you're a baker or delivering newspapers. So why did the Sorias pay $150 a month for this seemingly unpleasant intrusion into their lives? The answer is: the expensive American college system.

Future President Nixon left Whittier at the age of 21. After graduating from the same high school as the Soria brothers, he received a scholarship to study law at the prestigious Duke University on the East Coast. Most American colleges have sports teams; many also have a swimming team. A full athletic scholarship pays for housing, food, insurance, and books. It will also pay for tuition, which constitutes the largest expense of a college education in the United States. The amount varies between different universities, but an annual tuition of $30,000–$35,000 is not unusual.

weekends and holidays didn't mean a vacation, just more swimming. On Christmas Eve in 1997, Mike and Brian swam 15 × 1,500m (i.e., 22,500 meters). They were joined by swimmers like Kevin Clements, who later won the U.S. championships in the 200m medley. At the beginning of the new year, they could look back at a ten-day period containing over 200 kilometers (124 miles) of swimming!

On weekdays, the brothers were fast asleep by eight o'clock at night. So, for them, midnight was literally in the middle of the

The Soria parents had not gone to college. The best chance their boys had of leaving Whittier was not an academic scholarship (like Nixon), but doing their hard work in the pool in the hopes of an athletic scholarship. There are more than 300 colleges in the United States giving out scholarships to young and talented swimmers. Since Coach Rick and Industry Hills annually sent several swimmers to universities, the Sorias found it reasonable to invest $150 a month in their sons. They had no idea whether Coach Rick's training program was optimal, but the concept was working, and that was sufficient to justify the insane amount of meters swum in the pool.

WHY SO LONG?

How do you justify training for 20 hours a week for a competition that only lasts for 20 seconds? The physiological part of this answer requires a somewhat deeper analysis.

Since the 1960s, world-class swimmers—with only a few exceptions—have swum for 20 hours a week or more. This also applies to those competing in short distances, such as 50m and 100m. But why? Swimming 100 meters takes less than a minute and 50 meters takes a little over 20 seconds. Most people can accept that open water swimmers about to swim 10 kilometers in two hours need to swim long distances in training, but why should sprint swimmers swim until their skin gets wrinkly? And why does our skin actually start to look like a prune when we've been in the water for a long time? The science of swimming contains many questions for curious minds. In order to avoid the question of prune-like skin interfering with your working memory, let's get it out of the way.

The longer the training sessions in the pool, the more wrinkles humans get. The reason for this has been a mystery for a long time. It used to be the consensus of researchers that your fingers got wrinkled due to osmosis (that the skin absorbed water).

Later research has shown that the "pruning" effect occurs when blood vessels in the fingers contract, which results in the skin folding. This is controlled by our autonomic nervous system, which also controls the beating of our hearts, our breathing, and many other things beyond our conscious control.

Tom Smulders, researcher at the Institute of Neuroscience at the University of Newcastle, has gotten to the bottom of this problem and has found an answer to the mystery.

Smulders placed balls made out of lead and heavy weights at the bottom of a water-filled container. He then let his 20 test subjects move the objects using their thumb and index finger. At the first attempt, their hands were dry without wrinkled fingertips. But before the second attempt, subjects had to keep their hands underwater for 30 minutes. The experiment clearly showed that moving the objects with wrinkled fingers was much faster and easier.

Humans have always lived close to water. In the past, we often looked for food in rivers and lakes. To get a better grip on flexible and slippery prey, our body over time developed a response to extended exposure to water: our fingers get wrinkly.

"This facilitated our use of tools in wet conditions; for example, primitive hunting weapons like harpoons," explains Smulders.

Why swimmers train so much is a more complex issue. As usual we get our answer in small type from the always-reliable authorities of history and science.

Arne Borg was the Swedish Johnny Weissmuller—gold-medal-winning, good-looking, and cocky. He traveled across the world to show off. Once, on a visit to Germany, he dove into a canal to fish out a deutschmark coin someone in the large crowd had been asked to throw into the water.

Borg dove in and was gone for a long time. When the crowd started to fear that all hope was lost for the Swedish athlete, he resurfaced. But instead of a deutschmark coin, he brought up two 50 pfennig (penny) coins to the surface. "That's not a deutschmark," the audience heckled him. "Now you've surely failed." "No, I've already gotten change!" was Borg's immediate reply.

In 1927, the Stockholm native beat the 1,500m freestyle world record by three minutes. His best time was 19:07.2, which would remain the world record for 11 years.

Swimming 1,500 meters in 19 minutes gives you an average time of 1:16 per 100 meters. The current world record of 14:30 corresponds to an average of 58 seconds. This, along with Arne Borg's split times in 400m freestyle at the 1928 Olympics—1:02, 1:17, 1:17 and 1:27—not only show some shortcomings with regard to how he planned his races, but also that he wasn't trained for the distance.

Feel free to compare Borg's record with the 1,500m records of some American 12-year-olds: 16:44 (Nicholas Caldwell) and 16:48 (Isabella Rongione). Only a small part may be explained by differences in conditions such as water temperature, swimsuit, pool ropes, and goggles, developments since the time when Arne Borg was a brassy athlete some 90 years ago. These 12-year-olds would still make him look like a turning buoy over longer distances, despite the fact that they're not that much faster in a 100m race.

In order to make this clearer, let's look at the keys for physical performance from different perspectives. In a well-trained athlete, all components in the physiological performance appear to work somewhat better. Scientists have yet to identify every reason for this, but we know quite a bit when it comes to the following three points:

(1) A well-trained swimmer has a higher cardiac output and a lower heart rate at a given load compared to a less-well-trained swimmer. He or she also has a higher capillarization of his or her blood vessels, is better at utilizing absorbed oxygen, and consumes less oxygen when using his or her muscles.

(2) He or she has an increased skeletal muscle strength in the relevant working muscles.

3) He or she has better coordination in his or her special event and thus masters an energy-efficient movement pattern.

Early competitive swimmers did little to no training. British Charles Steadman, the swimming champion of the 1840s, revealed in his 1867 book *Swimming* that he never trained. The water didn't attract him, but he did like to impress other British aristocrats.

Over time, people started competing over set distances, which led to competitive swimmers trying to break records. This is why they and their coaches were always looking for ways to improve their times. Arne Borg, the long-distance king of the 1920s, got his endurance training primarily by playing water polo. But he also engaged in more organized swim training. For instance, we know that while preparing for the 1928 Olympics, he swam the 8 × 200m as fast as he could. Warming up or other forms of swimming were out of the question, and it's very likely that he had a cigar or something cheaper to smoke after his workout.

In the decades following Arne Borg, training was revolutionized with the help of research. Swimming coaches and researchers spent a great deal of time studying how runners trained, and the methods they developed were a mixture of science and trial and error.

One could argue that the overload principle sums up the scientific discoveries over the years. Two researchers unaffiliated with swimming laid the foundation for this research. One was an orthopedist who rehabilitated soldiers injured in war; the other was a Hungarian chemist living in exile in the United States.

The physician Thomas DeLorme managed the long-term recovery of badly injured soldiers who'd survived their dreadful military service in the Second World War. DeLorme experimented with a new type of training for rehabilitation: the war veterans were to lift heavy weights ten times, rest, and then repeat the exercise for an additional two sets. At the next training session, they were to put additional weights on the barbell. DeLorme noticed that when the war veterans lifted weights close to their maximum capacity, things happened to their muscles which made them adapt the next time they lifted weights.

The discovery of the overload principle not only led to strength training becoming more accepted but also to the general phenomenon of getting accustomed to extreme conditions. Strength training always involves anaerobic work as the oxygen uptake is never sufficient. Overload means a workload in excess of what the body is accustomed to or, more precisely, work when the oxygen uptake is insufficient for the needs of the body. This, in other words, is why strength training is anaerobic, as the oxygen uptake is never enough. The overload principle tells us that increases in muscle size, muscle strength, and endurance depend on an increase in work intensity during a specified time frame. Muscle growth (hypertrophy) only occurs when the muscle works harder than usual. That's why swimming longer sessions is not sufficient—you must also occasionally increase your speed to get the optimal effect of your training. Training according to the overload principle leads to the following:

(1) ADAPTATION. When the body is overloaded time and time again and gets accustomed to the increased demands, it results in a body that's better prepared the next time around.

(2) FAILED ADAPTATION/OVERTRAINING. The body fails to recover from the load or get accustomed to the increased demands. The result is a lower level of performance, which may be perceived as more or less chronic. Unfortunately, during times of high training loads, it's a fine line whether you get downtrained and adapt or become overtrained.

ADAPTATION IN DIFFERENT TYPES OF TRAINING

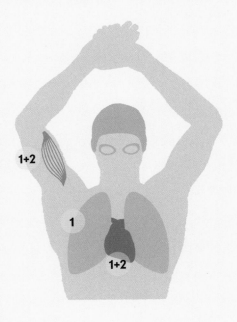

(1) AEROBIC TRAINING
results in the adaptation of circulation, respiration, and muscles.

(2) ANAEROBIC TRAINING
results in the adaptation of circulation and muscles.

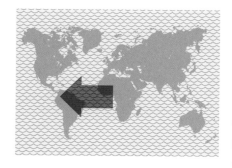

■ CALI, COLOMBIA, 1975.

A teenager standing 6'2" (188 cm) tall with glasses, protruding ears, and a contagious, boyish smile climbed to the top of the podium. Shy and skinny, Tim Shaw, from Long Beach, California, was the best swimmer in the world. Only 17 years old, he now received his third gold medal at the swimming world championships, this time held in South America.

Tim Shaw is the only person who's ever held the world records in 200m, 400m, 800m, and 1,500m freestyle. He didn't break any world records in California, but he still dominated the freestyle events. He won the 400m with a three-second margin and the 1,500m by over ten seconds. In 1976, he was given the James E. Sullivan Award, which is awarded annually to the best amateur athlete in the United States. Also in the running for this award was decathlete Bruce Jenner (now Caitlyn Jenner). Others who've received this award include running star Wilma Rudolph, Mark Spitz, Carl Lewis, Florence Griffith-Joyner, and Michael Phelps.

It was 1975 and Tim Shaw was on top of the world of sports. Everyone expected him to be the king of the 1976 Olympics. Today, not even the most dedicated fans of sports statistics know who he was— so what happened?

Coach Dick Jochums had come to Long Beach when Tim Shaw was 13 years old. The training group only admitted seven swimmers without "talent." But what these swimmers lacked in talent they made up for in the ability, will, and singlemindedness to submit themselves to tough training sessions week after week, Shaw in particular.

Shaw's training in preparation for the 1976 Olympics in Montreal would be tougher than anything the young world champion had ever experienced.

Jochums loved Shaw like his own son; he later said that Shaw was on his mind more than his own children. The desire to create history at the Montreal Olympics resulted in Jochums pushing Shaw to an extreme degree. After the world championships in Colombia, they only took a few days off before traveling to the qualifying races for the Olympics in Long Beach.

Longer and longer training sessions at an increasing pace initially led to spectacular results. Shaw swam faster than he had the year before. Jochums continued to push his favorite swimmer more and more—until he was destroyed. Driven by his desire to dazzle the world, Jochums had flown too close to the sun. Shaw, suffering from overtraining, lost 20 pounds and got weak, anemic, and depressed. Jochums reluctantly started designing shorter sessions, but it was too late—the damage had been done.

Shaw had planned on breaking three world records at the U.S. Olympic qualifying races but was barely able to make the team in one single event: the 400m freestyle. He had the third-best time in the trials for the 200m freestyle, but his body gave up on him in the final and he ended up fifth. This led to Shaw qualifying as a substitute in the 4 x 200m freestyle relay team. In his number-one distance of 1,500m freestyle, the world record holder ended up eighth and last in the final. His time was almost 20 seconds slower than his own world record. Adding insult to injury, he lost his world records in both the 400m and the 1,500m freestyle to his biggest rival, Brian Goodell, who also hailed from Southern California.

Once in Montreal, Shaw managed to win two medals—a gold and a silver. This would have been a success for most people unless they'd been named the world's greatest athlete the year before. His gold medal came in the 4 x 200m freestyle while wearing his warm-up clothes on the stand. In the 400m freestyle final, he managed to keep up with Brian Goodell for seven out of the eight lengths but had nothing left to offer when his one-year-younger rival picked up the pace.

Jochums has said that "everything I've learned about coaching, I learned on Tim Shaw's body." History shows that he learned a few things. Eight years later, during the 1984 Olympics in Los Angeles, Jochums' protégé George DiCarlo won the 1,500m freestyle event while breaking an American record that would last for 15 years.

Tim Shaw also participated in the 1984 Olympics, winning a new silver medal. However, this win came not in swimming but with the American water polo team—they came in second without having lost a single game. This time, his training had looked completely different, and he was smiling much more than he had in Montreal.

OVERTRAINING

Overtraining was not a familiar concept in the 1970s and, as discussed above, it manifests as a lack of progress. The easier it is to measure the training, the more noticeable the symptoms. Other symptoms are the need for longer recovery, weak muscles, and poor technique. Medical symptoms include an increased resting heart rate, swollen lymph nodes, declining blood lactate levels when exerting yourself, and increased susceptibility to infections.

There are a number of factors that may trigger overtraining. Most scientists consider a lack of energy one of the most common causes.

For a swimmer training a lot and with great intensity, it's absolutely crucial to get enough food. That's why world-class swimmers eat a lot. It's been said that Michael Phelps may wolf down as many as 12,000 calories a day. Skipping meals and not eating enough is a risk factor in terms of overtraining.

Heavy training, together with a great deal of psychological and physiological stress, could lead to the body producing too much of the stress hormone *cortisol*. Cortisol levels that are too high may compromise the body's immune system, which may result in fatigue, illness, and injuries.

An unbalanced autonomic nervous system may also lead to overtraining. The autonomic nervous system consists of two parts: the sympathetic and the parasympathetic. The sympathetic system is the one activated when we're exposed to a fight-or-flight situation. The parasympathetic system is activated when we're relaxing and/or digesting food. Too much intensity may overload the sympathetic nervous system and too much volume may overload the parasympathetic nervous system. In both cases, the *hypothalamus* region in the brain is affected. The hypothalamus controls things like blood pressure, body temperature, metabolism, and sleep. These are all important functions you need to have running efficiently if you want to be a successful athlete.

Central fatigue refers to a situation where an imbalance in the brain constitutes a significant contributor to overtraining. A scientific consensus believes that not enough carbohydrates after a heightened dose of training and high-intensity competition leads to low glycogen levels, which in turn leads to an increase in the level of free tryptophan. The tryptophan crosses the blood-brain barrier, subsequently increasing the amount of serotonin in the brain. Abnormally high serotonin levels cause fatigue, melancholy, and ultimately, depression.

However, knowing the exact cause behind overtraining is not all that interesting once you're afflicted. A quick guide to avoiding this ordeal is therefore in order. In most cases of overtraining, the athlete is under the illusion that more training is always better. Regardless of whether it's necessary, the athlete feels he or she needs to train frequently, and long and hard.

It's possible that training frequently, long, and hard will be sufficient to reach a certain level of performance. Meanwhile, research clearly shows that this is not the way to get the most out of your body. A common model in endurance sports is that more than 75 percent of the training should be low intensity and that no more than 10 to 15 percent should be high intensity. This both ensures that you avoid overtraining and that you are able to engage in intense training when your body is sufficiently rested.

YOUR SWIMMING: RISK FACTORS FOR OVERTRAINING

Characteristics	You believe that more is better.
	You set unreasonably high goals.
	You develop eating disorders.
	You're stressed about your job, education, money, and/or family.
	You take breaks in your training, but only reluctantly.
Sports	You're at a higher risk of overtraining in the following sports:
	• Endurance sports (triathlon, running, bicycling, multisport)
	• Sports with several events (triathlon, multisport, modern pentathlon, decathlon)
	• Sports with non-individualized training

Training	Increases in volume and/or intensity that are too fast
	A lack of a scientific approach when designing training programs
	Non-varied training
	"Now-or-never season"—for example the Olympics or an optimal age group season
	Not being noticed by the coach
	Changing training climate (high altitude, temperature, and humidity)
	Not writing a training diary
	Being trained by a former elite athlete

DIFFERENT TYPES OF TRAINING

Starting in the middle of the 1950s, swimming coaches have developed four different types of training sessions that are used worldwide: over-distance training, interval training, repetition training, and sprint training.

Over-Distance Training

Over-distance training (now called simply "distance training") is the most time-consuming type of training. The swimmers simply swim longer distances than the ones they are to compete in (i.e., a 200m swimmer may swim 1,500m without stopping), either with low intensity or with as high an intensity as possible. The objective of distance training is to:

- Increase your heart and lung endurance.
- Persistently repeat correct swim strokes.
- Develop self-confidence, the logic being if you can handle longer distances when training, competition seems more manageable.

Distance training constitutes up to 95 percent of the total amount of training for an endurance athlete. These days, this type of training is often managed by measuring heart rate. If it's less than 60 percent of the

The pace clock helps the swimmer maintain the right intensity.

athlete's maximum heart rate, the effect is marginal, and if it's higher than 80 percent, the swimmer tends to get too tired to be able to work out for as long as he or she needs to in order to reach the desired effect.

Interval Training

Interval training means that you swim a number of set distances with controlled rest periods in between. The rest period should be long enough to partially—but not fully—allow the body to recover from the effort. The acronym used for the variables of interval training is DIRT: Distance. Interval. Rest. Time.

The benefits of interval training include:

- The swimmer learns how to relax when swimming fast.
- The swimmer works on efficient coordination.
- The swimmer's muscle strength is developed.
- It has a fast effect.

The less positive effects of interval training include:

- It has a higher learning curve, and the swimmer runs a greater risk of illness, overtraining, or metabolic injuries.
- More joint strain and increased risk of injury.
- It requires more care and control to be carried out correctly. (Distance training is easier to perform.)

Repetition Training

Repetition training simulates competition by working faster than or at the goal speed over periods shorter than the competition time. In an ideal repetition training session, a swimmer reaches their maximum heart rate. In between repetition sessions, the swimmer rests until their heart rate has fallen to somewhere between 100 and 110 beats per minute. Woldemar Gerschler was the coach most influential in developing repetition training. He coached the runner Rudolf Harbig, who set the world record in 400m (46.0), 800m (1:46.6), and 1,000m (2:21.5) before the Second World War.

Gerschler successfully used the "trial and error" approach by making sure he learned from his mistakes. Contrary to the previously used training regimen for runners, he shortened the length of the intervals and let the athlete wait for his heart rate to go down to 120 beats per minute before initiating a new repetition.

The nice Gerschler didn't hold his tongue—on the contrary, he was happy to share his knowledge. On one occasion, he bumped into James "Doc" Counsilman, a cutting-edge American swimming coach. Together, they came up with the next evolution in interval science; using individual heart rate management to produce even better results.

Almost 50 years after Woldemar Gerschler's experiments involving intervals, his theories were confirmed by Russians Viru and Urgenstein when they released their research on 3,000 athletes just a few weeks before Gerschler died in 1982. High-intensity interval training stimulates the relevant muscles more and enables the nervous system to have more precise control over movement patterns as well as an appropriate intensity.

Sprint Training

Sprint training means swimming short distances at maximum speed. Even if the swimmer's speed were to decrease after 10 to 15 seconds, it was still considered a sprint if the swimmer did four 100-meter runs with 10 minutes of rest in between.

YOUR SWIMMING: ANALYZE YOUR SWIMMING

In order to get a better understanding of your swimming, separate it into seven compartments. By means of a *good posture*, you want to improve the movements in your *arm strokes*, your *leg strokes*, your *breath*, and your *upper body*. Additionally, good *flexibility* is an important building block when you want to optimize your swimming. You also have to master the different intensities and find your optimal *pace*.

POSTURE:

The head is the best controller of your posture. A head that's placed too high puts strain on your neck and pushes down your legs. Try to keep your spine and your head straight.

ARM STROKES:

Symmetry: Symmetrical swimming reduces wear on your body and increases your chances of moving through the water without leaking energy. Your right arm stroke shouldn't be too different from your left.

Hand Entrance: Don't enter your hand in the water in front of your head, as this initiates lateral forces resulting in energy leaks from your coveted optimal direction. Furthermore, it puts unnecessary strain on your shoulder, which might lead to persistent inflammation. Enter your hand in front of your shoulder so that your large pull muscle, the *latissimus dorsi*, does most of the work. In this position, you reduce the risk of injury and are in a position to increase your speed.

Stretching: When your hand enters the water, it should be stretched out to benefit your stroke length. But it mustn't be over-stretched. This could lead to your hand ending up higher than your elbow (which should be avoided).

Anchoring: As soon as possible, pull your hand and forearm parallel with the direction you're traveling in. In swimming circles, a successful anchoring is referred to as "having a high elbow."

Pull: Pull shoulder-wide with a relatively shallow elbow. Don't cross the center line with your hand.

Finish: Your hand leaves the water. This should be a movement where you avoid any stops in your rhythm. Finish with an outward tilt.

Return: This part of the arm stroke should be relaxed.

UPPER BODY:

Lead from the hips: Hip torque is important if you want to swim fast. If you're able to use your hip to link your movements together, then your swimming will become more powerful and efficient.

Timing: Your hips should set the pace, followed by your arms and legs. This makes it easier for you to get the different parts of your body to "come together."

Outcome: Good swimmers rotate their hips more than average ones.

Power: A good swimmer is characterized by a sharply and rapidly rotating hip.

LEG STROKES:

In the best-case scenario, only 20 percent of your forward-driving force will originate from your legs. Nevertheless, it's still important to control your legs in order to avoid two negative effects: (1) Putting biomechanical strains on you by not being positioned tightly together and thus increasing your resistance. (2) Working too hard and draining your energy.

An overly intense leg kick may easily become counterproductive.

BREATHING:

Symmetry: Your breathing shouldn't steal extra time from your arm stroke rhythm. Your breathing motion should be carried out easily and quickly.

Position in the water: A good breathing motion should be carried out without raising your head.

FLEXIBILITY:

Shoulders: Having flexible shoulders is important for the swimmer. Being stiff inhibits mobility, water position, and movement economy. Most people who've not been swimming for a long time need to put in some work to regain flexibility in their shoulders.

Hips: Having hip flexors that are too stiff will impede your position in the water as well as your ability to successfully use your hips.

Ankles: Elite swimmers have very flexible ankles, which don't work well with running and cycling.

PACE:

Intensity: A serious swimmer needs to master four levels of intensity: easy, easy endurance, tough endurance, and sprint speed. Training at all speeds is good for your coordination.

Stroke length and stroke frequency: Experiment to find your stroke length, then try to retain this stroke length while increasing your frequency. This will make you swim faster.

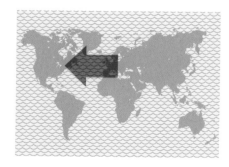

■ **MONTREAL, CANADA, JULY 31, 1976.** The alarm clock went off in the second-floor bedroom at a quarter to five. The 69-year-old jumped out of bed and bounded down the stairs. He opened the refrigerator and took out a glass of cold orange juice he'd pressed the evening before. He gulped down the juice and noted that it was 77°F (25°C) outside. "This will be hard on the marathon runners," he said out loud to himself with a voice that didn't betray any particular accent. The start for the Olympic marathon was to go off at 5:30 that same night. He went down into the basement, took off his bathrobe, and plunged into the 30-foot (9-meter) swimming pool that occupied almost the entire basement floor. He complained a little that no one from his native Hungary was to participate in the marathon race. He was satisfied with the Olympic results of some of his countrymen, but not with the individual winners in javelin throw, fencing, and gymnastics. No, he was proud that Hungary had won the water polo tournament. They hadn't crushed their opponents in any of the games, but had received criticism from Hungarian journalists for "only" having beaten Italy 6–5 and Romania 9–8. But after having tied Yugoslavia in the final game, Hungary's sixth gold medal in water polo was a fact.

He swam 20 lengths before grabbing the plastic ball that had been bobbing around next to him temptingly and threw some shots against the wall over the short side of the pool. "And in the last minute of the game, Hans Selye of Hungary wins the game and becomes a national hero!" he called out excitedly. Fifteen minutes later, he was riding his bike on his way to the University of Montreal.

Hans Selye worked between 10 and 14 hours each day, seven days a week. He'd done so for a long time.

He had arrived at the University of Montreal in 1945, where he studied how the body and mind react to extreme conditions. At most, he supervised 40 researchers and managed 20,000 laboratory animals. What was of interest to the world of sports was his research on the differences between various types of stress. He referred to negative stress as "distress" and positive stress as "eustress."

Australian Forbes Carlile linked the research of Hans Selye on positive and negative stress to the different types of training previously described. Carlile decided in the 1930s to combine his research on human physiology with his interest in swimming. Both his vision and science led to him finding the optimum temperature in competition pools and inventing the pace clocks we see near pools worldwide, among other things.

Carlile's winning formula took training (and the subsequent results) to new levels, which led to him being appointed the swimming coach for Australia in advance of the 1948 Olympics in London. His students had been swimming 11 sessions a week since a young age. Each session lasted two hours, and rather than increasing the length of the sessions, or adding more sessions during the week, their development was measured in the distance swum by the swimmers each session. This stimulated highly efficient strokes, in combination with an energy-efficient technique. This in turn led to great results on both long and short distances.

Based on his own research and based on Hans Selye's ground-breaking research on positive and negative stress, Carlile developed an all-new training approach. It appeared as if his swimmers could swim even faster if, after following a long adaptation process, they were given a period of less work. If they swam shorter distances, less hard, or even missed a few sessions, they performed much better than what people used to think possible. Forbes Carlile had discovered what we refer to today as "tapering."

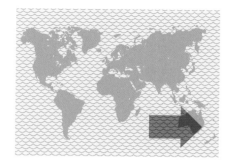

■ **SYDNEY, AUSTRALIA, 1972.** Shane Gould, one of Carlile's swimmers, simultaneously held the world record on every distance from 100m to 1,500m. Swimming had become increasingly popular "down under" ever since Frederick Lane had won two gold medals at the Paris Olympics in 1900. Australia has produced many male world record holders and Olympic medalists: Murray Rose, John Konrads, Mike Wenden, Stephen Holland, Duncan Armstrong, Kieren Perkins, Michael Klim, Ian Thorpe, and Grant Hackett. Continuing the trend started by Dawn Fraser in the 1960s, Shane Gould was to become the greatest Australian female swimming star.

The Gould family lived in Fiji when Shane was a little girl. She was able to muster a decent dog paddle by the age of 3. Shane's father, Ron, who wanted her to become a swimmer, introduced her to the sport and drove her to and from all training sessions. And things turned out the way Ron had hoped. At the age of 13, Shane started to train for Forbes Carlile, who gave everything he had to make Shane the best female swimmer in the world—and succeeded in doing so.

Shane liked Carlile's research-based approach and dedicated herself to his training. At the age of 15, she won five medals, including three individual golds at the 1972 Olympics in Munich.

Naturally, her training volume was extraordinary. After her alarm went off at 4:20 a.m., she fed the family dog, brushed her teeth, grabbed the bag she'd packed the night before, and was driven to the swimming pool by her father. After more than two hours of swimming, she went to school, completed a new mammoth session in the pool, did her homework, and went to bed early. This is what it looked like day after day, week after week, month after month, year after year until Shane was 17, when she put her swimsuit in the drawer for good.

Shane married a man who wanted to save her from stardom and preferred her to be a wife and mother rather than a swimmer. He got what he wanted—for a while. After 22 years of marriage and four children, they divorced and Shane took up swimming once again. In 2001, at the age of 45, she beat several world records in her age class. Her time on the 200m medley was faster than the world record in the 1960s. She was once again Shane Gould, the swimmer. She also showed that Carlile's training model wasn't outdated; on the contrary, his physiological principles are to a great extent used even today by long-distance swimmers.

NEW TIMES, NEW METHODS

The American and Australian training personalities we've discussed here also received support in a Swedish study from the 1980s. This study found an almost spookily linear correlation between time spent training and marathon race results. Completing a marathon race in under three hours required running for 45 to 50 miles a week on average. The study also showed that the global elite—almost without exception—ran 105 to 135 miles a week.

Distance training appears to have a lower aerobic effect compared to interval training, at least for those already in great shape. However, distance training is better for movement economy, something we established in previous chapters as being the most important parameter for swimming fast over all distances. Moreover, most swimmers find that a solid base of many long training sessions makes them better at handling shorter, high-intensity sessions.

The terrain of swimming and training methods has changed a lot since the 1970s. More nations than ever before now make it to the podium. Almost all championship medals in the 1970s were won by Americans, Soviets, and East Germans. Today we find medalists from Norway, Zimbabwe, South Africa, Brazil, Tunisia, Trinidad, and South Korea.

Apart from that, there are also more distances to compete in today. A new distance was introduced in the program for the 1988 Olympics in

Seoul: one length, 50m freestyle. Naturally, everyone swam 50 meters from time to time, and every good swimmer in 100 meters was also able to compete in half the distance. At the same time, the new distance also attracted a bunch of odd birds.

One of the first specialists in 50 meters was Dano Halsall. He competed in three Olympics for Switzerland, which he chose to represent instead of his father's native Jamaica. Halsall had muscles fit for a body builder, a shaved head, and a gold chain weighing half a pound (227 grams) around his neck.

Halsall was an impressive figure—standing 6'3" (191 cm) tall, weighing 200 pounds (91 kilograms), with shoulders as broad as those of a heavyweight boxer. After races, he liked to indulge in a cigarette. While his competitors, used to distance training, warmed up by swimming for 45 minutes, Halsall jumped up and down on the diving board for 30 seconds and did three sets of push-ups before gliding through the water for 200 meters.

One of his hallmarks was his kangaroo-like jump from the starting block. In 1985, he followed this jump with swimming so fast that he broke the 50m freestyle world record with a lightning-fast 22:52. He left conventionally trained swimmers behind, such as Robin Leamy, whose world record Halsall broke. Sure, Leamy was 6'1", but he weighed only 175 pounds (79 kilograms). Rowdy Gaines, the world record holder in 100m freestyle, weighed only 160 pounds (73 kilograms).

Today, swimmers compete in 50m in all swimming styles at the world championships, the European championships, and so on. In the stripped-down Olympic program, however, there's only room for 50m freestyle. This distance differs physiologically from the others. It takes a good swimmer between 20 and 30 seconds to swim 50m, regardless of swimming style. In longer distances, the working muscles need oxygen to maintain their contraction speed. The faster a movement pattern is carried out, the faster the consumed oxygen needs to be replaced with new oxygen. When Olympic gold medalist Nathan Adrian swims 50m, he doesn't breathe at all. Over 100m, he only breathes on every other arm stroke.

Even the traditional training models have been challenged. A model referred to as Ultra Short Race-Pace Training (USRPT) is based on the notion that all work in the pool needs to be of high quality. The technique and physical effort of the swimmer should exactly resemble how the swimmer swims during races. Instead of swimming long distances much slower than competition speed (20 × 400m), it's recommended that swimmers do more short distances (50 × 25m), with no resting period exceeding 23 seconds. The swimmer gets help from the coach in terms of deciding the speed for the 25m lengths, as well as establishing criteria for how he or she should breathe and how many arm strokes per length is considered reasonable. When the swimmer is no longer able to handle one of these variables, then he or she aborts the series, recovers, and tries a new training series.

Brent Rushall was the one who dared to break the old sacraments in the religion of swim training. Rushall got his PhD under James "Doc" Counsilman at the University of Indiana in the 1960s and wrote his first article in the field of sports psychology in the magazine *International Swimmer* in 1965. Over time, he's shifted his focus from psychology to physiology, where he's studied the impact of the nervous system on top-level athletic performance. He has written around 60 books on a variety of subjects.

Brent Rushall sees two major physiological benefits to adopting USRPT: (1) It creates correct neuromuscular patterns. Traditional distance training causes fatigue, saps the swimmer's glycogen supply, and prevents the nervous system from operating the same way it does during races. When using

USRPT, swimmers always work with race-like movements. There is enough time for the swimmer to rest. The shorter active time enables a fast recovery for the body.

(2) Proponents of USRPT believe that the method is suitable for both short- and long-distance swimmers.

A third benefit is that young people training according to USRPT don't have their lives ruined by all the time they have to dedicate to training. By adopting USRPT, they also have time for school and friends.

YOUR SWIMMING: AVOIDING SHOULDER INJURIES

Technique: Entering your hand in the water in front of your head puts too much unnecessary strain on your small shoulder muscles. Instead, enter your hand in front of your shoulders and let the back muscles take the heat—they won't let you down.

Training: Don't increase your amount of training too quickly.

Accessories: Swimming with fins may reduce the strain on your shoulders by up to 30 percent, which may be a decisive factor.

Flexibility: Improve your flexibility. A flexible shoulder handles the requirements of swimming better than a stiff one. Regularly stretch your shoulders.

Strength: Balance out your strength among the small muscles of the shoulder. Work on improving your shoulder strength on a regular basis. Strength exercises are rarely spectacular, but they're exactly what you need as a swimmer.

CHAPTER 3

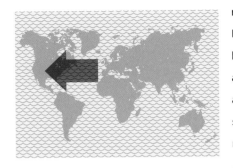

■ **LAWRENCE, KANSAS, FEBRUARY 2016.** USRPT has a handsome poster boy in phenom Michael Andrew. In addition to his unorthodox training program, he had been home-schooled by his strict parents. When Michael was 14, his parents surprisingly signed a sponsorship contract, which meant that he could never receive any scholarships or swim for a college team. His mother, Tina, was clear: "Michael does not need to be seduced by sex, drugs, and silly ideas from liberal professors." The only other American swimming star who'd chosen not to be a part of the college system, instead opting to become a professional swimmer, is Michael Phelps.

Michael Andrew was born in 1999 to South African parents who'd recently moved to the United States. His mother, Tina, is 6'1" (185 cm) and had appeared on TV in the 1990s as the American Gladiator known as Laser. His father, Peter, who served as a diver in the navy and now coaches Michael, is also tall. As a result of good genes, Michael at the age of 14 was 6'5" (196 cm) and wore size 13 shoes. His broad shoulders and narrow waist gave him the classical look of a swimmer even back then.

His father met Brent Rushall at a swimming coach conference when Michael was 10 years old. He eventually bought into the USRPT model hook, line, and sinker. Michael's training had largely been carried out in the family's custom-built garden pool measuring 13 × 82 feet (about 4 × 25 meters).

Swimmers of the same age and caliber as Michael swim more than 10,000 meters per training day, whereas Michael is content with no more than 3,000 meters with a complete focus on perfect technique at a high speed. So, is he any good? And how long is he able to swim based on this training volume? And doesn't he gain weight easily? As everyone knows, swimmers eat like boa constrictors!

Michael Andrew's development hasn't shown the slightest sign of slowing down ever since he became a pro at the age of 14, despite the fact that he hit puberty at an early age. He's broken several of Michael Phelps's age group records. His best times at the age of 18 are 21.75 in 50m freestyle, 52.57 in 100m butterfly, and 59.82 in 100m breast-stroke. These times were made in Olympic-sized pools (i.e., twice as long as the pool he's accustomed to). One would think that his comparatively modest training

volume wouldn't be sufficient for a demanding distance such as the 200m medley. But even here, Michael Andrew has been successful, and his 1:59.86 as a 16 year old was exactly 1 second better than Michael Phelps's result at the same age.

The younger Michael is set on becoming the best swimmer in the world but needs to continue his strong improvement in order to make it onto the U.S. Olympic team. From a physiological point of view, it's interesting to note how basically the only swimmer to use the USRPT model throughout his entire career is also one of the most promising new names in the world of swimming.

YOUR SWIMMING: PLANNING YOUR TRAINING

Regardless of which type of training you submit yourself to, it's a good idea to think it through. It's a common cliché that you must believe in what you do, whereas history invariably shows that doing it right is even more important.

No one had more faith in himself and his methods than the dominant swimmer of the 1920s, Johnny Weissmuller. When the great Tarzan was at his best, he did 58.6 seconds on 100m. The Olympic

favorites Nathan Adrian and Sarah Sjöström have done this distance
in 47 and 52 seconds, respectively. Jack Groselle was 60 years old
when he swam the distance in 57.79 seconds in the summer of 2014.
Conditions have naturally improved since the 1920s, but the main factor
behind this development is first and foremost training theory. Current
swimmers have a better technique, are better at looking after their health,
and swim using scientifically designed and largely proven methods.

To get the most out of your training, you need a training
plan—a logically designed system guiding the training process
and letting you achieve a desired objective in a controlled manner.
A training plan contains both short-term and long-term objectives.

ALL THOUGHT-OUT TRAINING PLANS
CONTAIN THREE AREAS

1) Timeline: The plan may be for four years or only for the season. It
may also include shorter periods, commonly divided by weeks.

2) Measurement (toward a goal): Some form of a final goal, like
winning an Olympic gold, swimming the 100m freestyle in under
a minute, finishing the Vansbrosimningen in under 40 minutes, or
completing an Ironman triathlon in under 10 hours. A good plan
also contains intermediate goals. Different race results point toward
you being on the right track toward your final goal. The third
measurement method is training goals. These may be things like
getting stronger on land or having enough energy to swim longer
with a certain stroke length.

3) Contents: The plan needs contents: how often, how long, and how hard you need to train in order to achieve your goals.

Goals are the most difficult to determine as they require a good measure of self-knowledge. In the elite endurance circles, it's common that people have goals that aren't based on reality but on their imagination. However, this doesn't necessarily mean that they're impossible, just that the person setting the goal doesn't have a clue as to whether it could be done. If the goal is possible, assessing how long it takes to get your body ready is also difficult—and this is before uninvited distractions cloud your precise and detailed training plans.

More than six months before the qualifying races for the 2008 Olympics, Bob Bowman, Michael Phelps's coach, was standing in his kitchen making a yummy vegetable soup when he received a phone call from a hospital emergency room: Michael had broken a bone in his wrist. The Bowman-Phelps team had declared earlier that same fall that Michael was aiming to win eight gold medals in Beijing. Ever since, sponsors and journalists had been as intrusive and disruptive as the plaster Phelps now needed. "I'm clumsy on land," said Phelps as he explained how he'd lost his balance when getting into a car and landed on his hand.

The fracture meant a blown-up bridge on his perfect road to Beijing. As soon as Bowman came to his senses, he started reasoning the way he'd been taught to do when studying psychology at the Florida State University: How are we going to deal with the problem at hand? How long will it take to make it go away?

Putting a cast on Michael was out of the question as this would keep him out of the water for six weeks—an ice age for an ambitious swimmer. Instead, they decided to insert a small rod into his wrist, which would keep him out of the water for 10 days until the stitches had healed. During those 10 days, Phelps cycled a total of 30 hours on an exercise bike they'd put next to the pool. This kept him sufficiently in shape to win his eight golds in Beijing.

YOUR SWIMMING: CREATE YOUR OWN TRAINING PLAN

Regardless of your approach to training, it's common to divide the season into four phases based on your main goal: basic training, race-preparatory training, race-specific training, and recovery.

(1) Basic training: Basic training prepares the swimmer for the real training. The main purpose here is to avoid injuries. Studies on college swimmers show that swimmers are affected by four injuries for every thousand hours of training, on average.

Endurance training may be balanced and there are many options. However, it should prepare the heart for the requirements in swim training. Running, water polo, and soccer are used in some training groups, even if the latter involves an unjustifiably high risk of injury for uncoordinated swimmers with flimsy ankles.

Strength training may be carried out in a variety of ways and should use the entire body. Your upper body needs to be strong enough to be your power plant, and your shoulders should be prepared so that your swimming doesn't cause strains or injuries. Around 90 percent of swimmers age 13 to 25 have experienced shoulder pain. Your lower back and knees are other danger zones. Swimmers should pay extra attention to the small muscles that are not used all that much, so as not to create an imbalance and subsequently risk ruining the season.

(2) Race-preparatory training: Race-preparatory training focuses on transferring the effects of basic training into something even more useful. The swim training here becomes increasingly important even if alternative forms of training are still present.

The objective could be to swim faster or maintain a given speed over a longer time period. These two objectives go hand in hand most of the time. The swimming volume differs between different athletes: a sprinter may swim as little as 30,000 to 40,000 meters a week, but a long-distance swimmer such as Axel Reymond, European champion in open water, swims 120,000 meters a week.

It takes 4 to 12 weeks before your progress is significant enough to make it worth your while to enter the next phase, which may be a new training cycle (after a short recovery period) or a race-oriented phase.

(3) Race-specific training: Race-specific training uses an increasing amount of the training to remind you of the main goal of the season. Movement patterns and body processes need to be calibrated to how they should manifest themselves at the time of the race. Some form of fast swimming is done every day. The timing of how you enter and exit your turns needs to be as tight as a swimming cap. Practice races or simulations take place at an increasing rate.

The competition season ends with the main event where you need to be prepared to give everything you've got to feel like a wrung-out dishrag afterward.

(4) Recovery: In order to continue your development, you need a mental and physiological period of rest. This doesn't mean that you need to be completely passive, but during recovery, the load on a top athlete needs to go down by 60 to 70 percent. However, the longer this period is, the greater the risk that it will take even longer to get back into shape during the basic training period. Being absent from the training pool for two to three weeks is common among world-ranked swimmers.

Some swimmers are in a good mood in spite of all the training.

WHICH TRAINING MODEL IS BEST?

Physiologist David Costill at Ball State University in Indiana has studied the effect of training for years. He compared two groups of swimmers over a period of 25 weeks. For the first 9 weeks, the groups trained the same amount (once a day). For the 6-week test period, he had one group swim twice a day. For the last 10-week period, both groups swam once a day. The group training twice a day didn't perform better than the group training once a day during the test period, and this is regardless of whether you looked at results or analyzed the physiological metrics of the swimmers. In this study, extra training didn't have any effect whatsoever.

In another study, he compared swimmers training 10,000 meters a day to swimmers training 5,000 meters a day over a four-year period. He didn't see any significant improvement in performance there either. Both groups improved by 0.8 percent.

Costill's conclusion was that a training volume that's too large is only useful for preparing a swimmer to withstand a large training volume. The swimmers who suffer the most with large volumes of training are the ones unable to maintain their stroke length. Studies show that swimmers who make it to the Olympics are good at preserving the distance they travel with each arm stroke cycle, regardless of their level of fatigue or pace. Keeping the training optimal is a challenge for swimming coaches as different swimmers in the same group may require different types of training to see the best progress.

The USRPT model has become a frequent topic of discussion among swimming coaches around the world; many argue for it and many argue against it. Both camps include both well-informed and emotional arguments. Perhaps the optimal training model is to be found somewhere between distance training and USRPT.

Michael Andrew's 30,000-meter weeks to get below two minutes on the 200m medley are hardly a method that suits everyone. At the same time, there are significant variations among open water swimmers. Andreas Waschburger, from Germany, and Axel Reymond, from France, who both swim 100,000 to 120,000 meters a week, were beaten by Greek swimmer Spiros Gianniotis and Dutch swimmer Ferry Weertman at the 2015 world championships. The Greek and the Dutchman both swim 50 to 60 percent of the German and French swimmers' distances, but at a much higher speed.

A very noticeable piece of evidence that there are paradigm shifts in the world of swimming is that an Australian youth club, the Carlile Swimming Club, now trains according to the USRPT model. Yes, it's Forbes Carlile's club—the guy who asked 13-year-olds to swim 22 hours a week back in the 1970s. Old Forbes might be turning in his grave. Until his death in 2016, Carlile served as coach emeritus in the club, working side by side with his wife, Ursula, on the love of their lives: swimming.

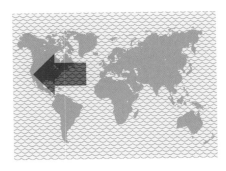

■ BACK TO WHITTIER. So, what happened to the Soria brothers we got to know at the beginning of the chapter? Did the uncompromising distance training program of Coach Rick bring a return on investment so that Mike and Brian were able to leave Whittier and get a college education?

The youngest brother, Brian, was short and so slim that he floated down into the water from the starting block when he dove in. That meant that 50m freestyle wasn't his thing as he lacked both power and fast muscle fibers. However, his skills were the most beneficial on 1,500 meters, where his 15:43 won him a full scholarship to Kansas University. Tuition, food, housing, and books were paid for four years.

Mike had a similar set of genes in that he was also better at longer distances. His 15:58 in 1,500m freestyle was sufficient to land him a scholarship at the University of Las Vegas (UNLV).

Today, Mike is a police officer and lives in California with his wife, Juanita Trujillo, who's the mayor of the small town of Santa Fe Springs, not far from Whittier. Juanita Trujillo became the youngest female mayor in the history of California when she was elected.

EIGHT SWIMMERS WHO'VE TRAINED LONG AND HARD

TRINA JACKSON competed in the 200m butterfly at the 1996 Olympics. During the preparatory camp for the national team, she alone (among both men and women) was able to compete in the 80 × 200m with a start every 2:30. Jackson swam in shorts. Slovakian Richard Nagy managed to do 100 × 200m at the same starting time in 2016. He, however, wore swim briefs.

AXEL REYMOND prefers to swim 25 kilometers and won the European championships in 2014. The Frenchman has also swum as far as he could in an hour, completing 5,859 meters. This means an average of 30.8 seconds per 50 meters.

ANNA OLASZ missed the Olympics in both 2012 and 2016 by the smallest margin possible but came back and won the world championship silver in 25 kilometers two days after her last Olympic failure. She trains at a higher speed than most men. One training series of hers is 50 × 100m with an average of 1:03 per 100 meters and a new start every 1:10.

ERIK VENDT was the first American to do the 1,500m freestyle in under 15 minutes. In his last year in high school, he swam 30 × 1,000 yards (914 meters) with a start every 10 minutes. This meant that his training session lasted five hours.

JANET EVANS had world records in freestyle and won the 400m medley at the 1988 Olympics. Her sessions were long and furiously paced. It wasn't unusual that she beat the best results in the world that year when training. Once, she swam 1,500 meters in 16:15, and then continued with the 6 × 400m medley, where her average time was just over five minutes per 400 meters.

TOM DOLAN had the 400m medley world record for a long time. A classic training series of his was 24 × 400m, with 6 x 400 in each swimming style, and where each 400 meters was done faster than the previous one.

MIREA BELMONTE won two Olympic medals in London in 2012. She's also the woman who'd swum the farthest in an hour with her 5,592 meters. She has also done 3,000 meters in 31:58.

STEPHEN HOLLAND competed in the 1,500m freestyle at the 1976 Olympics and, at the age of 17, won the bronze with 15:04. One of his training sessions consisted of swimming 10 × 500m, striving to go below 5:10 on the last 500 meters. However, only doing 5:11 meant that he had to do the last 500 meters over again—48 times (!)—before he managed to get below 5:10. This resulted in his session stretching over 24,000 meters, of which 19,500 were at maximum effort.

Note: All training times were made in a 50-meter swimming pool unless otherwise specified.

CHAPTER 4

ANIMAL KINGDOM

Be a shark.
You've just got to
keep moving.
You can't stop.

– Brad Pitt

PENGUINS OF
MADAGASCAR

Penguin 1: *Seriously! Does anyone even know where we're marching to?*

Penguin 2 in line: *Who cares?*

Penguin 3 in line: *I question nothing.*

Penguin 4 in line: *Me too.*

Penguin 5 in line: *Me too.*

Penguin 1: *Well, fine. We'll just fly to the front of the line and see for ourselves. Kowalski, Rico—engage aerial surveillance.*

Penguin 2: *Sure! Let's go. Come on.* [The penguins flap their wings and jump.]

Penguin 2: *Skipper, we appear to be flightless.*

Penguin 1: *Oh, well, what's the point of these?*

(From *Penguins of Madagascar*, 2014)

Penguins are in many ways fascinating animals. Their distinctive appearance and odd behavior have given rise to the fictitious band of penguins from *Madagascar*, and also to characters such as the emperor penguin Mumble in *Happy Feet* and the Swiss clay animation figure Pingu, who never fails to make both adults and children laugh.

Penguins differ anatomically from other birds. Their feathers more resemble the fur of seals. Their skin secretes an oil that protects them against cold temperatures in the water and on land. Penguins are characterized by a long upper body with a very flexible spine and short legs—their knees are actually positioned inside their bodies. They are unable to fly, both because they lack hollow bones (found in other birds), and because they weigh between 45 and 90 pounds (20 and 40 kilograms).

Penguins are clumsy on land, but are definitely more flexible in the water, in which certain species spend up to 75 percent of their lives. Their skeleton, which is unusually heavy for birds, acts as a "weight belt," ensuring that they don't float up to the surface. Scientists have documented that penguins are able to stay underwater for up to 20 minutes. They are near-sighted on land, as their vision has been adapted to work in water so that they may catch fish, which constitutes the bulk of their diet. Their ability to swim is crucial—not just for getting food, but for avoiding becoming the prey of predators. Penguins swim four times as fast as we do. The Adélie penguin, for instance, moves at up to 65 miles per hour (105 kilometers per hour) without the assistance of a starting block. They are also able to accelerate underwater to breach the surface and "fly" up to 10 feet (3 meters) above the water surface to accurately land on an ice floe.

The long bodies of penguins are perfectly streamlined. Strong chest muscles help the harder wing perform flapping motions, which effectively pushes the penguin's body through the water. By twisting their way forward, they are able to press a larger area of the wing against the water. The joint attached to the wing resembles the human shoulder joint and offers a variety of possible movement patterns. This enables penguins to change direction surprisingly fast.

Still, all of these stunning traits don't explain why penguins are able to swim so darn fast. In 2006, an Irish research group studied the air bubbles that penguins leave behind in the water. Until then, the air bubbles were believed to be the result of the penguin releasing air through its beak.

However, the research group's study on emperor penguins found something different—the small air bubbles originated from their plumage. Before emperor penguins jump into the water, they ruffle their feathers, and once below the surface, the water pressure leads to the air getting "stuck" inside the feathers.

The bubbles you see are the result of a little air at a time escaping the plumage to act as a sort of lubricant to reduce the friction between the penguin and the water. This kind of air insulation has been well known among ship builders for a long time, but it was just discovered that penguins also use this technology. The difference is, ship builders don't want any air in the propeller, whereas penguins push their body forward with their wings outside the air bubbles. Calculations show that penguins are able to double their speed in the water thanks to these air bubbles. This phenomenon is hard for the competitive swimmer to replicate, though underwater exhalation creates bubbles that travel along the chest to give a fraction of the same effect.

THE EVOLUTION OF SWIMMING

Most competing youths are told that they swim like a fish, but what's really the case? Fish and other animals move through water with stunning variation. Animals moving in or above water may be divided into different categories:

(1) Runners, such as insects and lizard

(2) Rowers, such as crustaceans

(3) Surface swimmers, such as ducks and geese

(4) Fish, which use their entire body to move

(5) Octopi and jellyfish, which move by jet propulsion

When swimmers like Michael Phelps and Sarah Sjöström swim fast to win their races, they use some of the same mechanisms as animals.

Fifty-two million years ago, all the land masses were connected into the supercontinent of Pangaea, and there was only one ocean: Tethys. At that time, there was a dog-like mammal walking around near the ocean. Paleontologists refer to this ancient dog as *Pakicetus*. It set itself apart from other mammals in that it was able to catch fish in shallow water. *Pakicetus* had a cavity in its jaw, which enabled it to hear well underwater. It also had pretty decent eyesight below the surface.

Fast-forward a few million years and *Pakicetus* has undergone an evolutionary change to become *Ambulocetus*, a kind of sea lion that hunted by swimming in the water as well as moving on land. Several additional million years later, it had developed into *Rodhocetus*, which moved slowly on land, but was a good swimmer thanks to its strong and flexible tail. *Rodhocetus* subsequently evolved into *Dorudon*, which in turn developed into today's humpback whale.

The prehistoric dog's name, *Pakicetus*, means "whale from Pakistan." So, the five-foot-long (1.5-meter) prehistoric dog has evolved step by step into a 50-foot-long (15-meter) whale weighing a nice 36 tons.

Such a fast rundown through prehistoric times makes it tempting to believe that good swimmers in general—and butterfly stars like Sarah Sjöström and Michael Phelps in particular—are whales at an early stage. They're slightly larger than average, much more flexible in what could be compared to the tail of *Ambulocetus*, and they spend about as much time in the water as *Rodhocetus*.

Evolution means development. Not necessarily developing into something better but developing in order to adapt to prevailing conditions. Evolution requires what is known as genetic variation. Phelps and Sjöström are not just carefully trained with a long-term perspective by Bill Bowman and Carl Jenner. They also have a set of genetic factors rendering them better suited for breaking swimming world records compared to virtually everyone else.

We have already established that swimmers are tall and flexible. They also possess a type of protein synthesis allowing them to easily build relevant muscles made up of the right kind of fiber. The kind of muscles necessary for creating the force that propels them forward quickly in their favorite distances of 100 and 200 meters.

Mastering a complex movement such as a flip turn requires the swimmer to quickly go through a number of steps. These are steps controlled by different parts of the brain, which must be able to communicate with each other. The brain consists of gray and white matter. In the white matter, signals travel between the brain cells along pathways called axons, which are insulated by a material called myelin. People with multiple sclerosis (MS) lose this myelin over time. At the other end of the spectrum, scientists have become increasingly certain that a common denominator for successful athletes, musicians, and dancers is that their axons are exceptionally well-insulated by myelin.

There have most likely been other talented swimmers with the physique and ability to develop skills at the level of Sjöström and Phelps who dropped off along the way. This may be the result of environment, motivation, or some other limiting factor. However, the fast-forward theory is rejected by established research, which also requires selection for Phelps and Sjöström to be intermediate stops for a life form adapted to living underwater.

Selection is based on the strongest traits being passed down from generation to generation. One example of selection is that healthier kids:

- become sexually mature at an earlier age (and may thus produce more offspring);
- survive long enough to have kids of their own;
- get bigger and are therefore better at defending their kids;
- are able to mate with more individuals from the opposite sex.

If there is a sufficient number of traits separating two different populations not interacting with one another (for example, species on the island of Mauritius, which got separated from India when Pangaea split), a new species is formed.

The genes of the swimmer parents Göran Sjöström and Debbie Phelps have obviously been quite excellent, but in order to speak of a selection process, swimming would need to be key for survival. Furthermore, the creation of a new species is also a very slow process, which may be discouraging for those wanting to be eight feet tall with webbed fingers and fins instead of feet. In spite of this disappointing fact, we may still learn much from animals when it comes to swimming.

Fish, birds, reptiles, mammals, and insects are all swimmers, but for various reasons. Dolphins use swimming for all forms of movement. Ducks swim to locate food and frogs swim to avoid attackers. Salmon have to swim to mate and bears like to cool off and enjoy themselves, just like us. Some animals swim on the water surface whereas others swim below. Not many animals are good swimmers, including dogs, which move both slowly and awkwardly when placed in water. In other words, the variation is significant.

Matt Biondi

One of the most graceful aquatic animals around is a mammal. In the spring of 1988, before he went on to win seven Olympic medals, Matt Biondi went to the San Diego zoo to swim with dolphins. Not because

The butterfly is said to be the toughest stroke. The kick is similar to how a dolphin kicks.

some sponsor wanted images of the two species swimming together, but because he wanted to watch and learn from the smooth and efficient movements of the dolphins. The 6'7" (201 cm) tall California native wasn't just an outstanding freestyle swimmer (breaking world records in the 50m and 100m freestyle), but also a fantastic butterfly swimmer, where he was a favorite to win the 100m at the Seoul Olympics.

Henry Myers, who competed for the St. George Dragon Swimming Club in Brooklyn, had started experimenting throwing his arms over the water surface back in 1933. However, it wasn't until the 1950s that butterfly became an established style. Back then, it hardly resembled the graceful way that dolphins swim—butterfly swimmers back then used the breaststroke leg kick. This style used to be a pain in the neck and was mostly seen as some kind of trial to show others what you were made of. The best butterfly swimmer in the training group might have been somewhat of an oddball but was nevertheless able to show that he or she could take a beating and was thus accorded a high level of status in the swim squad.

It wasn't until the 1990s that it became commonplace to swim parts of the butterfly race underwater, which resulted in a huge advantage. First, you were able to avoid the tough resistance of the water surface. Second, you were able to increase the speed of your kicks and thus your overall speed.

Matt Biondi had a vision in which he was told that underwater swimming could make him go faster, but he wasn't sure whether he had enough guts to use it in a race setting at the 100m butterfly Olympic final. In the final back then, racers used two underwater kicks at the start and when turning. Two kicks is about what you need to even resurface. Eight years later, the established standard was to use eight or nine kicks at the start. Anyway, in the starting field at Seoul where the competitors made so few kicks, Biondi took off and had a big lead after a length. His 24.53 was sixteen hundredths of a second below the world record and everything looked fine for the huge American.

Nevertheless, 100 meters of world-class butterfly swimming represents a massive effort. The physiological explanation behind this is that as the arms pull simultaneously, the momentary speed increases and decreases at a higher rate compared to freestyle. The speed is the highest at the last part of the arm stroke, then decreases when the arms are returned, followed by a new acceleration during the next arm stroke.

The acceleration up to the top speed means that resistance increases fourfold, which is the main reason why butterfly swimming requires so much energy. Water is approximately 800 times denser than air and creates a great deal of resistance in freestyle where the swimmer is still able to maintain a more even speed. In butterfly the resistance may thus become extremely difficult to handle.

Butterfly swimmers who are extra tired tend to amuse other swimmers and coaches on the sidelines, who like to chuckle that the swimmer has "got a piano on his back." Professor Björn Ekblom at the Swedish School of Sport and Health Sciences in Stockholm has described the process experienced by the swimmer carrying a piano as, "A lot of bodily functions are temporarily shut off. Your vision gets blurry, you don't hear, and you're unable to think clearly. Meanwhile, a lot of other functions are affected, such as the respiratory center and your heart's ability to pump."

What's usually blamed for this is lactic acid, also known as lactate, as it is said to make the muscles so acidic that they stop working. However, this is not the case, as more recent research has shown that muscle fatigue has nothing to do at all with lactic acid.

We know that there is muscle fatigue similar to a functional collapse in sports where athletes work very hard between 30 seconds and a few minutes. Håkan Westerblad at the Royal Karolinska Institute (the medical university that awards the Nobel Prize) has contributed important research in this field. His predecessor at the same university, Jöns Jacob Berzelius, showed in 1804 that a tired muscle contains more lactic acid than a rested muscle. A rested muscle has a pH level of 7.05, where a muscle of a swimmer that has performed an intense race may be as acidic as a pH level of 6.5.

This example teaches us the difference between causality and correlation. The fact that lactic acid is present in all muscles exhausted by a workout is a correlation. If this exhaustion had been the result of lactic acid, then it would have been a causal relationship. In the 2010s, however, Westerblad was able to show that muscle fatigue could be the result of a number of factors, none of which are lactic acid. When physiologists study lactic acid, they see lactate ions and hydrogen ions, where the former have turned out to have only a negligible effect on muscle function. An increased amount of hydrogen ions—a decreased pH level in the muscle—may surely affect some muscle functions, but not to any significant extent. Instead, they have seen a strong correlation between phosphate ions disturbing and impairing muscle function during exhaustion, especially when the glycogen level in the muscle is low.

So, why is it so common to measure blood lactate in athletes? Have coaches failed to understand anything whatsoever?

A dolphin is capable of swimming much faster than a human.

Measuring the level of lactate in the blood is easy. One can see a clear correlation between fatigue and a high concentration of lactic acid. The explanation for this is that the muscles work so hard that there is not enough oxygen to push them further, which is when lactate comes in as somewhat of a substitute. The more tired the muscles are, the more lactate that is needed. The lactate level in the blood thus reflects the effort but has nothing to do with why the muscle is not performing as well.

Back to the Olympic pool in Seoul. It's very likely that Biondi had started to get a high level of lactic acid in his blood halfway through the race. His arm strokes became heavier and heavier, and his lead was shrinking. But Andy Jameson, the British swimmer with the best time in the trials, wasn't the one gaining on Biondi. It was the swimmer in lane three, Anthony Nesty. He was from Surinam, which had been a Dutch colony until 1975. It was only the year before that the young country had held its first democratic elections, and it was now on its way to winning an Olympic gold. In the end, Nesty won over Biondi by a whole one hundredth of a second.

The American dream that Biondi would win seven gold medals, just like Mark Spitz did 16 years before, had been shattered two days prior to the 100m butterfly final. As it turned out, Biondi had already been beaten in the 200m freestyle race by Australian sensation Duncan Armstrong and Swedish young buck Anders Holmertz. Biondi's seven total medals still made him the most decorated male athlete of the games, alongside track and field athlete Carl Lewis, who won the 100m race after Ben Johnson from Canada had been disqualified.

At the beginning of the 1990s, underwater kicks, both in backstroke and in butterfly, represented a paradigm shift in the quest to swim faster. Apart from freestyle swimming, underwater kicks represent the fastest way for a human to travel through water. Fast freestyle swimmers, such as Frenchman Florent Manaudou and Ranomi Kromowidjojo from the Netherlands, perform underwater kicks for 10 to 12 meters after the start. Shinri Shioura carries on the tradition of Japanese innovation as he kicks almost the entire allowed 15 meters when swimming the 50m and 100m freestyle.

Compared to the dolphin, however, humans don't stand a chance. Thanks to their faster upward and downward thrusts, enabled by tail muscles better adapted to this task, dolphins swim five times faster than us humans.

YOUR SWIMMING: FOUR STEPS FOR A GOOD BUTTERFLY

1. Use fins This style is based on good body movement. Fins give you a good return on investment and they help you notice when your kicks are correct. They also help to maintain good technique.

2. Save your breathing The rookie butterfly swimmer tends to lift his or her head too high when breathing. This has a negative effect on his or her position in the water and results in his or her swimming becoming unnecessarily heavy.

3. Match your kicks The leg kicks give you an extra boost when you need it the most. Kick once when entering your hands, and once when lifting them out of the water when finishing the pull. Learning how to time this right may be a long and difficult process.

4. Maintain your technique Start with short distances and a good technique. If you work too much with a poor technique, then you force your shoulders to work too much, thereby increasing the risk of injury.

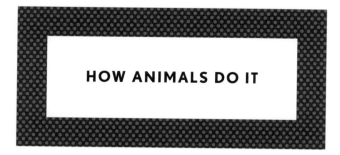

HOW ANIMALS DO IT

The person who has received the most publicity for having walked on water is Jesus Christ. According to the Bible, his disciple Peter also walked on water, as long as his faith in Jesus Christ was sufficiently strong (Matthew 14:22–33). There have been others who've either stood or walked on water. Seneca relates how the Greek god Hercules "crossed the seas by foot" and Buddha has been described as "walking across the river Ganges as if it were solid ground."

However, there is no evidence that Jesus—or any other person for that matter—has successfully walked on water. Nevertheless, some bugs and lizards manage to do so. How is this possible? And do we humans have something to learn from them in terms of shaving off time in future Olympic games?

Water strider (or Gerridae) are a family of insects you may see running across the surface of small and tranquil bodies of water. They need to run quickly or else they sink. Their weight makes them sink down a bit, which increases the surface of water pressing against them, which in turn increases the lifting force.

What enables them to walk on water is their tiny weight. The surface tension of water at 68 degrees is 0.073 newtons per meter. A nursery web spider weighs about one gram and may therefore be carried by the water surface of 0.001/0.073 = 0.014 meters. A person weighing 155 pounds (70 kilograms) would need feet measuring more than half a mile (0.8 kilometers) in circumference. This means that it's impossible for a human to run across the water in the same way as a water strider.

Basiliscus (meaning "little king") is a South American genus of lizards known for running across water surfaces on their hind legs. Weighing a full 4.6 ounces (130 grams), they're too heavy to be able to use surface tension to remain afloat. These lizards run across the water surface at a speed of 3.4 miles per hour (5.5 kilometers per hour) and are thus able to run almost 5.5 yards (5 meters) before they sink (and then start swimming).

Three factors enable the little king to run on water:

(1) First, its feet strike the water at a very high speed, approximately 3 meters per second. Its steps pull the water back and Newton's second law of motion shows us that force is equal to mass times acceleration. Impulse is force generated over time and the lizard's fast step provides it with approximately one fifth of the force needed for lifting its weight. Its hind limbs are relatively large with webbing between the toes, which enables the lizard to float by creating a larger surface area and an air pocket underneath its feet.

(2) Second, its foot drops down a little bit when stepping on the water. Before the water envelops the foot, a small air-filled cavity is formed on top of the sole. Since the foot is pulled up from the water after only six hundredths of a second, the air cavity doesn't get filled with water. The atmospheric and hydrostatic pressure interact and contribute one third of the force needed by the lizard to run across the water.

(3) Third, the lizard's steps constitute a forward-driving force on the water, which is more than sufficient for it to be able to run across the water as long as it maintains its high speed.

Ducks, penguins, chameleons, snakes, and many other animals swim with the tops of their bodies above the water surface. Ducks use their feet to propel them near the food they want. Penguins use their wings as a lifting surface when they swim. Chameleons use both their front and hind legs when swimming, and snakes slither across the water.

Swimming animals use their extremities in two different ways: to get either a forward-driving force or a lifting force. Ducks stretch out the webbing in their feet and then create a forward-driving force by pulling them back through the water, whereas penguins flap their wings just like their flying relatives. Ducks thus use the same physics as paddle steamers, and penguins generate a lifting force like a propeller. Flying animals need to put in a lot of effort just to remain in the air. However, swimming animals, whose body density resembles that of water, don't need to spend all that much energy on maintaining their vertical position and may thus focus on moving forward.

All animals swimming on the surface create waves by forcing water to the side so that a V-shaped backwash is created. Waves pushed forward are called bow waves. The slowest waves travel at 0.5 miles an hour (0.8 kilometers per hour) with a wavelength of 0.67 inch (1.7 centimeters). Shorter waves are flattened by surface tension and longer waves by gravity. This means that waves related to swimming are driven by gravity.

Creating kinetic energy in waves requires mechanical work, so there is always resistance when a body pushes water forward. This resistance is what causes bow waves. Swimming at the surface has been particularly important when calculating the energy efficiency of different ways of moving through water.

In the book *Energetics of the Little Penguin*, a team of Australian zoologists describes how the penguin's metabolism is affected when the little rascal is moving through the water. They let a few penguins swim in a narrow pool and measured their energy consumption. At rest, it was 6.3 watts per kilo of body weight and 8.4 watts when swimming underwater at a speed of 0.72 meter per second. When the penguin swam on the water surface at the same speed, its energy consumption increased to 12.2 watts. When measuring otters, the energy cost for swimming on the surface increased even more (up to 70 percent), due to the force used when creating the bow wave.

This research also showed that swimming close to the surface was demanding. In order to avoid the resistance from the surface, underwater swimming needs to take place at a depth of at least 2.5 body diameters. This insight is used by more and more swimmers for maintaining speed following the start and when turning.

The results of the penguin researchers also show the inefficiency of traveling faster than your displacement speed. Speedboats traveling faster than their displacement speed use a hydrodynamic lifting force—their bows lift (plane), thereby reducing resistance from the bow wave. A smaller portion of the vessel's body under the water surface has a significant impact when it comes to reducing water resistance. Ducklings also manage to plane for shorter distances, reaching speeds of up to 4.5 miles per hour (7.2 kilometers per hour). One might think that ducks paddling with first the left foot and then the right one would end up in a wobbling movement with high levels of lateral energy leakage. However, thanks to the position of their feet, close to the center line of their body, they're able to avoid strenuous sideways wobbling.

Snakes are able to move easily on the surface of the water because they're flat. The end of a snake's body resembles a rudder and makes it easy for them to maintain their course. According to the Swedish National Herpetological Association, there are three types of snakes in Sweden: the European adder, the grass snake, and the smooth snake. The adder is the most notorious due to its venom, and the least common is the smooth snake, which is paradoxically capable of eating adders. They can all swim even though the adder is clumsier and keeps its head above the surface like a periscope. In fact, the Latin name of the grass snake, *Natrix natrix*, means "swimmer." It was given this name by Carl Linnaeus himself (the great botanist, zoologist, and creature namer), who found that it was frequently positioned in water.

Another exciting species is the backswimmer. Not the ones competing at the Olympics, but small insects in Sweden, of which there are five species. Backswimmers are small creatures, no more than half an inch (1.3 centimeters) long and with long hind legs, which they use for movement while lying on their back. They prefer to swim just below the water surface, which is made possible by them first sucking air into their abdomen. They are the fastest on the surface, where they hunt for insects, tadpoles,

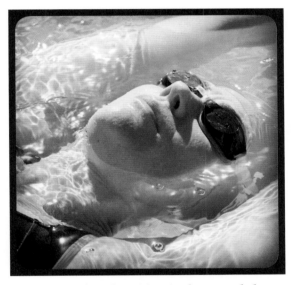

Having a relaxed position in the water helps the swimmer.

YOUR SWIMMING: SEVEN TIPS FOR AN EFFECTIVE BACKSTROKE

1. Swim shallowly

Keep your head, hips, and heels at the surface to reduce resistance. This may sometimes result in a feeling that water is washing over your face, but this is just something you need to get used to.

2. Use your legs

Backstroke is a style where you benefit from having an active leg kick the whole time. Kick from your hip instead of letting your knees do the work.

3. Ten to two

When your arm enters the water directly in front of your head, it creates lateral forces. If your arm enters the water a little bit away from your direction of travel, then you're able to pull yourself forward faster.

4. Adapt your arms

Keep your arm straight over the water surface and bend it below the water surface.

5. Rotate your body

Due to anatomical reasons, you need to rotate your body more when doing the backstroke compared to freestyle. This lets you get a good grip with your arm stroke. The challenge is doing so without your head bobbing around. A common stroke drill to correct this is swimming with a hockey puck on your forehead.

6. Breathe frequently

Breathing once per arm stroke cycle will help make your swimming more stable.

7. Navigate

If you're indoors, you may use the ceiling to maintain your direction. This is harder outdoors, but if there are no clouds, then you may get good at keeping your direction based on the outdoor light.

and small fish. In fact, backswimmers are the multisport athletes of the animal kingdom, as they are also capable of flying (with their bellies turned downward).

Animals using their extremities as oars must "row" at a speed that's not only faster than their body but also faster in relation to the surrounding water. The 0.67-inch- (1.7-centimeter-) long water beetle acilius is such a rower and moves at a speed of 1.1 miles per hour (1.8 kilometers per hour). This might not sound all that impressive, but if acilius were to increase its size by a factor of one hundred to 70 inches (178 centimeters), then it's not unreasonable to imagine that its speed would increase proportionately. Acilius swims with its second and third pairs of legs, which are covered with hair much like the branches of a spruce tree. One might think that a hairy leg wouldn't be all that helpful, that the water would flow through the hairs, but this is not the case. On the contrary, only a very small amount of water flows through them. When pulling, the hairs stand out to create as much of a forward-driving sur- face as possible, and when acilius sneaks back its legs to do a new stroke, the hairs disappear. Large "oars" are more beneficial than small ones, as it is more energy efficient to pull more water less frequently than the other way around.

Newton's second law of motion tells us that it's crucial to maintain existing momentum. Even though acilius has two pairs of "oars," it still loses momentum between strokes, and it isn't particularly streamlined. A higher stroke frequency would reduce the costly need to increase speed in between strokes, but at the same time, shorter strokes would result in its "oars" being opened too frequently, which would reduce speed. Since it's not possible to alternate between the front and rear pairs of "oars," as they would collide, the one remaining option for acilius to swim more efficiently would be to alter- nate its strokes and use one side at a time, like a cross-country skier. Unfortu- nately for the beetle, this is not an option, as its shell does not allow for any type of rotation without it heeling from side to side. Fortunately, on the other hand, its shell works as a hull, effectively maintaining the beetle's direction when swimming, as if it had abs of steel.

WHAT'S THE OPTIMAL FREQUENCY?

Our arms serve as our oars. Just like for acilius, our speed in the water depends on the length and frequency of our forward-driving strokes. The swimmer is able to increase his or her speed in three ways:

- Maintaining stroke length and increasing stroke frequency
- Maintaining stroke frequency and lengthening the strokes
- Making longer arm strokes and increasing stroke frequency

So, which one of the three options is the best? It naturally depends on your present level and what level you aspire to reach. Increasing your frequency is probably the fastest way for you to beat your friends to the floating sauna. If your swimming is poor, if you swim in a wetsuit and you don't want to exert yourself in your triathlon, then it may instead be a good idea to use longer arm strokes. If, on the other hand, you have a serious and long-term desire to take your swimming to the next level, then you need to do both.

When French swimmer Yannick Agnel won the 200m freestyle at the London Olympics in 2012, he made 32 arm strokes on his second length (i.e., 16 cycles). He completed the length in 26.0 seconds, which means Agnel made an arm stroke every 0.72 second and performed 42 arm stroke cycles a minute, and each cycle carried his body forward by 2.6 meters. This is about the frequency and stroke length you need in order to match an Olympic champion.

Swede Mikael Nelker is a serious triathlete who is in the elite group of non-professionals in Ironman competitions. By utilizing a watertight metronome, he was able to swim 50 meters in 34.9 seconds, giving him a stroke length of 2.1 meters. This means that Nelker's stroke length was 80 percent of Agnel's, while his speed was at 74 percent. So, if Nelker would want to offer Agnel some competition, he needs to work on increasing his frequency without shortening his stroke length. This is complicated by the fact that triathletes don't swim enough to be even close to their full potential. Luckily, triathlon competitions are not determined by the swimming, even though a weak performance when swimming may result in a worse position for the rest of the race.

FREQUENCIES OF ELITE SWIMMERS OVER DIFFERENT DISTANCES

WOMEN	Seconds/ Arm stroke	Arm stroke/ Second	Seconds/ Cycle	Distance/ Cycle
50m freestyle	0.46–0.50	60–65	0.92–1.00	1.80–2.00
200m freestyle	0.56–0.63	48–54	1.12–1.26	2.10–2.20
800m freestyle	0.70–0.77	39–43	1.40–1.54	1.70–2.10
Open water	0.50–0.60	43–50	1.00–1.20	1.50–1.80
MEN	Seconds/ Arm stroke	Arm stroke/ Second	Seconds/ Cycle	Distance/ Cycle
50m freestyle	0.45–0.54	56–67	0.90–1.08	1.90–2.20
200m freestyle	0.60–0.64	43–51	1.20–1.28	2.25–2.45
1,500m freestyle	0.65–0.79	41–42	1.30–1.58	2.30–2.60
Open water	0.60–0.70	43–47	1.20–1.40	1.60–1.90

Swimming Like a Fish

No animals are capable of swimming faster than fish. While a human's top speed is around 2 meters per second, tuna fish are able to swim at almost 21 meters per second. There's been extensive research on how fish swim. However, there have only been a very small amount of studies on how swimmers could mimic the way fish swim in order to swim faster.

Most fish move by using their whole bodies to create wave-like movements. Some fish use only their tail fin to create water swirls similar to those created by a skilled butterfly or backstroke swimmer kicking underwater. The tail fin first turns in one direction before changing direction at lightning speed. As the lateral forces cancel each other out, a forward-driving force is created.

Swimming coach Terry Laughlin has highlighted a concept he refers to as Total Immersion, which proposes that we should try to move forward using as little energy as possible instead of working as hard as possible. He argues that even if we don't have the same anatomy as fish, we may still pursue the ease in which fish move in the water. The first step for a born-again Total Immersion swimmer is to minimize his or her frontal resistance by extending his or her body in the water, using the hand as a breakwater. The next step is to swim like this length after length, and then in step three, increase his or her frequency without losing too much stroke length.

Future research on how animals move in water (especially how they reduce frontal resistance), could be valuable for a better understanding of the physics of swimming.

THE PHYSICS OF SWIMMING

Identifying and describing the physics of swimming is extremely difficult, as the swimmer influences the water, which in turn influences the swimmer.

The physics of swimming refers to the process during which an object changes its position in the surrounding medium, be it water or air. The majority of research has studied movements in the water, and not the parts of the swimming cycle carried out above the water surface.

Speed

Speed is the velocity at which a swimmer changes his or her position per unit of time. Speed is a scalar unit and may be measured with a single number. Swimming speed is commonly measured in meters per second and may be measured instantaneously or as an average over a distance or time. The easiest way of measuring speed during a race is to start the clock when the race starts and stop it when the swimmer reaches the finish line.

Velocity

Velocity is described as speed in a particular direction, and is also measured in meters per second. The fastest swimmers reach velocities of 2.4 meters per second, like when Caeleb Dressel, Bruno Fratus and Nathan Adrian swim 50m freestyles in around 21 seconds. Velocity (instantaneous velocity) is a vector, as it has both magnitude (speed) and direction. Isaac Newton's three laws of motion say that the velocity of an object is constant if it is not influenced by any external forces. For the swimmer, it's important that the velocity goes in a particular direction—the one representing the shortest distance between point A and point B. The difference between speed and velocity is that with velocity, direction matters.

Average Velocity

Average velocity is usually referred to as average speed. Average velocity is equal to the length of the traveled distance divided by the time interval. With regard to flows, one may talk about the average velocity at a certain time.

An example: when Sarah Sjöström broke her 100m butterfly world record by doing 55.48 in Rio in 2016, she split her first length in 26.01 seconds and came home in 29.47 seconds. The average velocity for the entire race was 1.80 meters per second. The average velocity during the first length was 1.92 meters per second, which slowed down to 1.70 meters per second during the second length.

Two factors determine why swimmers are unable to maintain the same velocity during an entire race. The previous example concerning Matt Biondi illustrates one: muscle fatigue. The second factor is the swimmer's start. In a world-class start, the swimmer sets off at about 3.5 meters in 0.4 second which means he or she breaks the water surface at a velocity of 8.7 meters per second. Newton's first law of motion tells us that a body in motion will strive to keep this motion. Still, there's no way for the velocity not to drop to below two meters per second. The reason for this is the resistance caused by the density of the water.

Acceleration

Acceleration specifies how the velocity changes per unit of time. Acceleration may be positive and indicate an increase in velocity, or negative, which indicates a reduction in velocity. Acceleration is relevant at both the start and during changes in velocity during the swimming cycle.

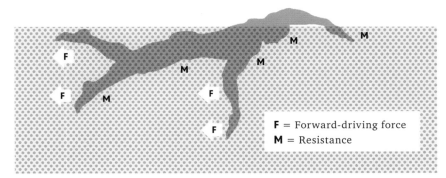

F = Forward-driving force
M = Resistance

The forward-driving force of the freestyle swimmer comes mainly from the movement of his or her arms under the water surface. To a large extent, the resistance depends on how deep in the water the body is situated.

Force

Force is produced, produces motion, or produces shifts in the motion of bodies. A forward-driving force causes motion as well as resistance-impeding motion. The concept of force was introduced by Isaac Newton, who formulated his three laws of motion:

(1) A body at rest tends to stay at rest, and a body in motion tends to stay in motion with the same direction and speed, unless acted on by an external force.

(2) When force acts on an object, it will make the object accelerate. It takes more force to move a heavy object than a light object. This is written as force = mass × acceleration.

(3) For every action (force), there is an equal and opposite reaction (force), meaning that the operating forces between two bodies are always equal and moving in opposite directions.

Center of Gravity

The center of gravity is the point at which an object's weight works the most. In sports, the center of gravity changes more or less depending on how much the athlete moves his or her extremities, which happens constantly in swimming.

Mass

Mass indicates how much matter a body contains. Mass remains constant.

Weight

Weight is the magnitude of the gravitational force pulling a body down. Mass is constant, but weight changes depending on location. This means that your weight changes if you're on the moon or in water.

The swimmer's weight in water is affected by his or her body composition. An average young adult man consists of 7 percent minerals, 15 percent fat, 18 percent protein, and 60 percent water. Bones, muscles, and blood are heavier than water. Fat not only protects against the cold, but it's also the lightest component of our bodies.

Virtually all elite swimmers weigh somewhere between 3 and 12 pounds (1.4 and 5.4 kilograms) in the water. Female swimmers are lighter than men in water as their bodies contain more fat. When the National Collegiate Athletic Association (NCAA) measured the body composition of active athletes in 17 sports in 2015, they found that the fat ratio was 9 to 12 percent for men and 14 to 24 percent for women. Male swimmers were located at the middle of the scale in comparison to the other sports whereas female swimmers belonged to the group with a higher proportion of body fat.

In the 1990s, researchers at the University of Miami tested whether extra fat could make swimmers faster. Ten young men and ten young women swam 2 × 50m wearing a triathlon suit. During one of the 50m runs, they were given three-pound inserts similar to body fat to place on their stomach, thighs, chest, back, and behind. Wearing this padding, the swimmers were able to float better, but also became slower; their average time for the weighted swim was 27.4 seconds

THE WEIGHT OF THE BUILDING BLOCKS OF THE BODY IN RELATION TO WATER	
WATER	0.997 g/cm^3
Blood	1.04 g/cm^3
Bone	1.5–1.9 g/cm^3
Skeletal muscle	1.06 g/cm^3
Fat tissue	0.91 g/cm^3

BODY COMPOSITION	
COMPONENT	Percent of body weight
Bone	16.65 +/− 1.34%
Muscle	45.27 +/− 3.29%
Fat tissue	10.22 +/− 2.92%

Based on measurements from 39 top Spanish athletes in 2015

compared to 26.8. The reason was the increased frontal resistance of the body, in combination with the swimmers not being accustomed to swimming with their new "body."

Momentum

Momentum is the product of an object's mass and velocity. Momentum may be perceived as a measure of how difficult it is to change an object's state of motion, which is determined by its mass and speed. A natural consequence of Newton's first and second laws is that a reduction in speed or mass results in less momentum and vice versa. Momentum is a preserved quantity in the sense that the total momentum of a closed system (one not influenced by external forces) cannot be altered. Momentum is particularly relevant for sprint swimmers, who want to maintain it by making a good start. The fact that water is 800 times denser than air means that a good position in the water is critical.

Inertia

Inertia is a complicated concept that becomes most noticeable in swimming in the form of the friction between the swimmer and the water. Inertia is short for the "principle of inertia" as it was described by Newton in his first law of motion. The term "inertia" is also used to qualitatively refer to an object's ability to resist changes in speed, which is determined by the object's mass. Swimmers wear smooth swimsuits and shave their body to minimize friction.

Moment of Inertia

Moment of inertia is a measurement of resistance with regard to accelerating a body's rotation. The body rotation of a freestyle swimmer needs to shift from arm stroke to arm stroke. Strong and stable upper body muscles, together with a well-timed movement, is the best way of overcoming the moment of inertia that's produced when changing the direction of the hips.

Angular Velocity

Angular velocity is a measurement of how fast an object is rotating. If a point on the rotating object is located at a distance of r from the axis of rotation and moving at a velocity of v, then one may calculate the angular velocity as v/r. The unit for measuring angular velocity is "radians per second."

Other measurements used for angular velocity are speed and frequency of revolution (i.e., the number of revolutions of a rotating object per unit of time). Speed of revolution is often expressed as revolutions per minute (rpm), whereas frequency is normally expressed as events per second (hertz).

Angular Momentum

Angular momentum is sometimes referred to as rotational momentum. For a rotating body, a change in angular momentum—and thereby also of the body's state of rotation—is related to the momentum of external forces affecting the body. For a body rotating around a fixed point, the angular momentum is determined by the point of the body's distribution of mass relative to said point and its angular speed. A flip turn is a textbook example of how to optimize the angular momentum in order to save time.

Viscosity

Viscosity is used to indicate how dense and slow-flowing a liquid is. Swimmers in a pool generally have to travel through 80°F (27°C) water containing some chloride and negligible amounts of salt.

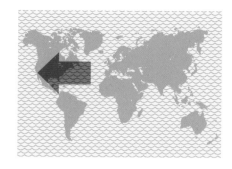

■ **SAN BENITO, CALIFORNIA, 2009.** Jamie Hyneman and Adam Savage hosted the television show *Mythbusters*. The point of the show was to use scientific methods to determine whether rumors and myths are true. They tested things like whether a frozen turkey falling off a kitchen counter is able to crush a small pet or whether it's possible to waterski behind a cruise liner.

This time they found themselves in what could be described as the wilderness between San Francisco and San Jose to test whether it's possible to swim as fast in syrup as in regular pool water. The fact that syrup is 500 times thicker than water speaks in its favor as it's possible to generate more forward-driving force in it. Unfortunately, the resistance is also 500 times greater.

Finding the answer to this quandary appears to contain no benefit whatsoever for humankind, but has nevertheless fascinated people ever since the seventeenth century. When Isaac Newton wrote his book *Principia Mathematica*, he argued that viscosity plays a role in how fast an object is able to move through a liquid. His contemporary competitor Christiaan Huygens disagreed, forcing Newton to compromise in his book, as well as include Huygens's theory.

The syrup experiment had been carried out once before—in 2003 in a pool at the University of Minnesota. In order to carry out the experiment, the experimenters had been forced to apply for 22 different permits, including being allowed to flush crazy quantities of syrup into the municipal water system.

The Mythbusters team had constructed two simple but accurately measured 25-yard pools with the help of an excavator, chipboard, styrofoam, and treated fiber cloth. One of the pools was filled with 1,400 cubic feet (40 cubic meters) of water and the other with the same amount of syrup mixture. Both Adam and Jamie swam. Adam was a few tenths of a second slower in syrup than in water whereas Jamie got worn out so quickly that his swimming didn't live up to any scientific standards whatsoever. The fact that Jamie was in poor shape was nothing new, which is why they called Olympic champion Nathan Adrian.

The swimming of Adam Savage and Nathan Adrian in their roles as Mythbusters produced the following results:

(1) The denser the syrup mixture, the lower the speed. (2) The more experienced the swimmer, the more he or she has to gain by swimming in pool water. (3) The decreased visibility in the syrup mixture may have affected the direction of the swimmers and hence their speed. (4) Both of them felt that it might be possible to swim as fast in syrup as in water if they were to train more. Nathan Adrian said that his current technique was unsuitable for syrup.

Using Animals as Mentors

Humans are unique swimmers, but may still learn from their animal friends. The physics behind water striders walking on the surface shows us that it's unnecessary to spend time on walking or floating on top of the water. Rowers teach us the importance of having a stable upper body linking our movements together, whereas fish teach us to be streamlined in the water.

So what about the penguins of Madagascar? Despite the fact that they're fun to watch, there's much to learn from their movement patterns. Having strong upper body muscles to drive the body forward in a streamlined position is exactly what fast swimmers try to accomplish (except breaststroke swimmers).

Perhaps the most exciting aspect of the discovery of the penguins' layer of air creating less resistance is the realization that there are additional future groundbreaking discoveries to be made in human swimming research. Swimming styles will be refined. Records will be broken—even the absolute best.

	Species: Marlin Top speed: 75 mph (121 km/h) Standard size: 15 feet/1,650 lbs (457 cm/748 kg)
	Species: Octopus Top speed: 25 mph (40 km/h) Standard size: 2 feet/40 lbs (61 cm/18 kg) Comment: Uses jet propulsion to move around
	Species: Human (Caeleb Dressel) Top speed: 5.4 mph (8.7 km/h) Standard size: 6.5 feet/220 lbs (198 cm/100 kg) Comment: 50m freestyle in an Olympic pool. Without the start, the speed would be lower.
	Species: Seahorse Top speed: 0.006 mph (0.01 km/h) Standard size: 1 inch/0.02 lbs (2.5 cm/0.009 kg) Comment: The slowest swimmer in the ocean is never in a hurry.
	Species: Dolphin (bottlenose) Top speed: 22 mph (35 km/h) Standard size: 10 feet/550 lbs (305 cm/249 kg)
	Species: Penguin (gentoo) Top speed: 23 mph (37 km/h) Standard size: 2 feet/18 lbs (61 cm/8 kg)
	Species: Otter Top speed: 5 mph (8 km/h) Standard size: 4 feet/90 lbs (122 cm/41 kg)
	Species: Pike Top speed: 15 mph (24 km/h) Standard size: 3 feet/9 lbs (91 cm/4 kg)

CHAPTER 5

THE FOUNTAIN
OF YOUTH

The water doesn't know how old you are.

– Dara Torres

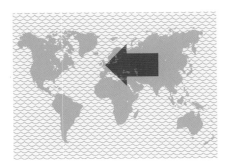

■ BARNET, LONDON, NOVEMBER 24, 2009. Three Swedes are on their way to the Barnet Copthall indoor pool, located a bit northwest of the subway system of central London. The tallest of the three is there to compete in a race and the other two—we will refer to them as The Professor and The Boxer—are more focused on central London's culinary experiences. The Tall One is only set to swim in one race, and how long could that take? Sixteen minutes or so?

Once the three friends find their way to the swimming pool, they realize that the competition will take longer. No less than 63 swimmers are to complete 1,500m. The Professor starts calculating how long it will take before they can return to Soho, Hammersmith, and Earl's Court to get a nice meal.

The competition pool has eight lanes, which means that swimmers enter the pool eight at a time. Every 1,500m takes about 20 minutes for the fastest swimmer. This results in three races per hour. However, not everyone is able to swim the distance in 20 minutes—most swimmers need about 30 minutes. The Professor's mathematical calculations indicate that the trio won't be able to reach the center of London until about 10:30 p.m. Are the kitchens even open at that time? The Professor, who appreciates well-prepared food, in horror imagines himself standing next to a fast food joint eating soggy falafel in a dry pita.

The competition is open to both men and women. One of the competitors in the first heat is a large woman using a mobility walker for support. She jumps into the water from the starting block to happily reach the finish line 39 minutes later. The vast majority of swimmers competing in masters swimming don't care about their relative speed compared to the other competitors.

Somewhere in the middle of the competition, The Professor, The Boxer, and The Tall One notice something: a woman born in 1931 is going to swim! Jane Asher isn't the oldest swimmer on the list, but the time she has reported is surprisingly fast: 23 minutes, or 46 seconds per 50m. The Tall One and The Professor start doing some math and reach the conclusion that the swimming skills of Jane Asher in relation to other, predominantly younger swimmers, means that she would be close to the first quartile finishing an Ironman swim. This at the age of 78. Astounding!

Some messy planning of the heats means that the three friends don't know which lane Jane Asher will swim in. Nor does a visual inspection of the physiognomy of the swimmers provide them with any clues, despite the fact that they're not that far away. After the start, however, there's no doubt as to who's the star in the race.

Jane Asher holds every world record in freestyle swimming for women in the age class of 70–74,

as well as in her current class of 75–79. In swimming circles, she is known as "the Royal Highness Lady Asher." Flanked by two splashing and snorting mustachioed men, she travels through the water in a graceful and seemingly energy-efficient manner. Still, the walruses next to her take off for the first few lengths, even though Lady Asher is

Jane Asher and the author

able to catch up with one of them after only 400 meters. While they're now punished for their tough starts, Lady Asher has found a smooth and reasonable pace after 50 meters. She's able to catch up with the second walrus after 800 meters. After 60 lengths, Lady Asher reaches the finish line, even though she doesn't care about the result: "I do this for my own sake. I swim in order to feel that I'm able to control my body and for the good feeling of having completed a race or a training session. And that's what everyone else should do."

You might wonder where the term "masters swimming" comes from. You'd think that "veteran" would be a better description for competitions for senior athletes, but "veterans" is already in use for people returning from U.S. military service. That's why the term "masters" is used, though it doesn't signify that the competitors were champions at the height of their careers.

Initially, the people attracted to masters swimming were the athletes who were ambitious when they were young, and senior swimmers who'd finished their careers. But was it really the love of swimming that attracted them? An older swimmer, who felt he'd reached the age where he no longer needed to cover his thoughts in pretty wrapping paper, said, "Well, half the contestants just want to go to the banquet and screw their old teenage flings."

Regardless of whether the candid veteran was right, there is a range of benefits associated with training in general and with swim training in particular, at least as you get older.

WHAT HAPPENS TO OUR BODY AS WE GET OLDER?

It's a well-documented fact that our body changes as we get older. Scientists know the mechanisms behind some, but not all changes. Getting older means that we lose an inch or so in height, get drained of liquid, get fatter, and our bones get lighter and more fragile. In addition, the functional system of our body collapses in an inevitable and—for those of us enjoying our lives—very sad way. The databases are full of research emphasizing this tragic message that reminds us of the volatility of life.

It's said that after we reach our peak around 30 to 35 years old, we lose approximately 10 percent of our capacity each decade—around 1 percent a year. Toward the end of life, this deterioration seems to increase. We shrivel up at a greater speed until we're nothing but memories for those surviving us.

Throughout history, there have been many people who've tried to solve the seemingly unavoidable problem of death. People not only put their faith in an afterlife but also, in recent decades, pay companies to freeze them. Unfortunately, the prospects for a successful future thawing are small for the 200 people frozen at the Cryonics Institute in Michigan, as being frozen means massive damage to every cell that makes up our bodies.

So, if we're unable to avoid death, then we may at least find ways of keeping ourselves as strong and vital as possible while still alive. Avoiding toxins, taking care of our personal hygiene, and exercising regularly have all proved effective to postpone poor physical health into the future. With regard to regular exercise, complex questions follow on how to avoid unnecessary wear on your body and how best to improve your situation at a given time and age.

But let's start by looking at how medical research describes the aging process between the ages of 35 and 60.

THE SKIN loses elasticity while its layers get thinner and more vulnerable. This means that both small and large wounds heal more slowly. The immune system may thus need to work for a longer period, which subsequently reduces your performance level as the immune system consumes energy that could otherwise be used for performance. Furthermore, the number of working sweat glands is reduced, which results in your body's cooling system not working as well as it used to.

THE HEART becomes more rigid in some parts, as do your blood vessels. Furthermore, the cells of the heart muscle contract with less and less power. This means less oomph in your heartbeats and the amount of oxygen available to your working muscles is reduced. A reduced maximum cardiac output is a strong contributor to deteriorating athletic performance, even when it comes to short distances.

It's frequently said that the heart starts aging significantly around the age of 55 to 60, but your performance level may start to go down when you're 25. Endurance training five days a week stimulates the production of the good cholesterol that keeps the walls of your blood vessels elastic. The best way to mitigate the aging process in your heart is continuity, so never stop exercising.

YOUR LUNGS become less elastic and your chest wall becomes more rigid. This doesn't affect your total lung volume, but it does affect how much oxygen may be sent out to your muscles and how much carbon dioxide you're capable of exhaling. It also makes it more difficult to clear your lungs of mucus and your cough reflex becomes less precise.

YOUR KIDNEY FUNCTION deteriorates due to your glomerulus shrinking. The glomerulus is a sort of cluster of blood vessels that filters blood, with the excess filtrate being made into urine.

YOUR STOMACH AND INTESTINES don't produce as much gastric acid, your mouth doesn't salivate as much, and your GI tract doesn't "knead" the food you've eaten as well, meaning your body finds it increasingly difficult to absorb nutrients, and might make you constipated more often.

YOUR BONES become weaker with an increased risk of fractures. This is a factor that's both good and bad for swimmers of an advanced age. It's good as the risk of breaking bones is low when swimming, even extremely low if you exclude the risk of slippery floors. It's bad insofar as swimming isn't a weight-bearing exercise that slows down the process of the bones getting weaker. That's why weight training is a great complement for those over 50 wanting to engage in swimming as their main type of exercise.

YOUR MUSCLES are reduced in size and function. Skeletal muscles are replaced by fat and connective tissue. Your metabolism goes down because muscles work and fat and connective tissue rest. As a result, your tolerance for glucose is reduced, which may in turn lead to diabetes.

A reduced sense of balance is closely related to muscle loss, according to muscle researcher Håkan Westerblad at the Karolinska Institute in Stockholm. He says that old people who've experienced falling accidents often complain that they've become light-headed in their old age. Westerblad's research shows that falling accidents are to a large extent explained by those tripping having lost muscle function in their legs and that their feet, knee, and hip joints are unable to counteract a fall the way they used to.

The change in our muscles is among the most dramatic in the aging process, but also the easiest to prevent or slow down. The muscle fibers we lose as we age are type 2 (i.e., fast-twitch muscle fibers). Training in general and strength training in particular enable a fit person to retain or even increase his or her muscle weight, especially in someone who's never exercised before. With the right training, the difference in ratio between slow and fast muscle fibers goes away completely or becomes very small.

YOUR IMMUNE SYSTEM produces fewer white blood cells, which makes you more susceptible to infections as well as less capable of getting rid of them.

YOUR NERVOUS SYSTEM loses function, which means that your sense of balance gets worse and your reaction time gets slower.

YOUR JOINTS deteriorate as you get older. Rheumatism, gout, and different types of arthritis are often found in older people. Your joints get less flexible and tend to hurt.

YOUR EYES deteriorate, which is not that troubling in a well-marked pool, but may cause a great deal of trouble when swimming in open water, where you need to see well both to perform well and to be safe and oriented in the right direction. Fortunately, there are prescription swimming goggles available on the market.

So, what contributes most to the age-related decrease in performance level are your heart, lungs, and muscles. Of these, muscle reduction is the easiest to slow down through activities like strength training. You may exercise your heart to some extent, but it's not possible to do all that much to improve lung function.

It's a fact that the body ages, and some athletes have a hard time accepting age-related reduction in performance level. It may be painful to realize that you're not as fast as you were in your youth, the time when you had not yet gained your lovely life experiences such as emotional crises, parenthood, and knowledge. With the exception of the most closed-minded, we become better people in all aspects as we age, except for one area—the physiological.

Just how fast we deteriorate is a subject of discussion. "The Royal Highness Lady Asher" is a brilliant example of someone getting better with age, but there are others who've also performed impressive feats in their "old age." Jamaican athlete Merlene Ottey ran 100m in 11.68 at the age of 50, and 50-year-old South African Titus Mamabolo ran a marathon in 2:19. Rich Abraham swam the 50m freestyle in under 25 seconds at the age of 60, the same age as Laura Val when she swam the 400m freestyle in 4:55.

Before the qualifying races for the 1968 Olympics, 36-year-old marathon runner Hal Higdon tested his maximum oxygen uptake at the Dallas labora-

Swimmer and masters coach Marty Hendrick trains every day.

tory of physiologist David Costill. It was found that Higdon's body was able to absorb 67.6 ml/kilo per minute. This measurement had admittedly fallen a bit when it was measured again 14 years later, but thanks to regular and thought-out training, it was still at an impressive 63.7 ml/kilo per minute.

David Costill is one of the most revered physiologists in the world. He has written the massive book *Sports Physiology* together with Jack Wilmore, and has published more than 400 articles in the area of performance physiology, as well as a large study on dehydration (1970). In marathon races, it used to be that you weren't allowed to drink before arriving at the 10 kilometer mark. Drinking was just as banned as doping. This ban resulted in runners commonly having body temperatures in excess of 109°F (43°C). Moreover, they could drop 11 to 13 pounds (5 to 5.9 kilograms) of body weight due to dehydration.

Costill made a valiant effort as a runner, but despite the fact that he ran 60 miles a week for many years, he was unable to complete a marathon race in under 3:15. He'd swum as a young man, where his best result was completing a 1,500m freestyle race in 23:21. Thirty years later, at the age of 52, he did 19:42 on the same distance. Costill's reverse development shows that an aging physiology might not hinder a person as much in swimming, where technique can help.

That swimming is well suited for retaining the powers of youth is highlighted by Dr. Jim Miller, who is the head of medicine for USA Masters Swimming. Dr. Miller, who was also in charge of safety at the open water swimming during the 2015 world championships in Kazan, summarizes the positive effect of swimming in four terms: balance, body position, temperature, and humidity.

The way the water exerts pressure on the body is good in itself, a bit like massage. Balance (or rather lack of balance) isn't a major issue for swimmers. In the pool, you eliminate fall-related bruises, fractures, or sprains, which tend to happen more frequently for those increasing in age who choose to exercise on land. Furthermore, swimming and other forms of water-based exercise are gentle on joints and are thus recommended for patients suffering from arthritis.

Practicing your sport lying down is not particularly common in sports other than swimming. A soccer player in a horizontal position is either in severe pain or is showing off his or her acting talents. When lying down, your blood is distributed more evenly in your lungs, which optimizes the ability to deliver oxygen and to remove carbon dioxide from the blood more quickly. This horizontal position also relieves unnecessary strain on your bones due to you only weighing between 3 and 12 pounds (1.4 and 5.4 kilograms) in the water.

High humidity in pools has proved beneficial for many people suffering from asthma-related problems. High humidity makes secretions in your lungs, body cavities, and mucous membranes thinner and easier to get rid of.

The pools and bodies of water in which we choose to swim are frequently temperate. Most swimming pools have a temperature of 80°F (27°C) (up to 88°F [31°C]), but are not recommended for aggressive endurance programs. They raise the body's core temperature, resulting in a risk of heat stroke.

So, what's a suitable temperature for open water competitions? There is no definitive answer—it depends on many factors. The following variables may play a role in the safety of the swimmer:

- Water temperature
- Air temperature closest to the water surface
- Whether the sun is shining and how strong it is
- The type of swimwear the swimmers are wearing. Are they wearing a swimsuit or swim briefs? Open water suit with long legs? Wetsuit with long sleeves and long legs? Wetsuit with short sleeves and short legs? What's the thickness of the wetsuit? What material is the wetsuit made of?
- The swimmers' headwear (swimming cap or a rubber hood)
- Swimming stroke (breaststroke or freestyle)
- Length of the race/how long the swimmer is in the water
- The swimmer's body temperature before the race

- Whether the race begins in the water or land. If water, for how long are the swimmers positioned in the water before the start?
- The swimmer's percentage of body fat
- Energy generated by the swimmer during the race. If the swimmer is able to maintain a high level of intensity, then his or her metabolism may offer heat during the race.
- Level of experience swimming in open water and/or experience in the current water temperature

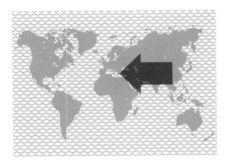

■ **HELLENIC AMERICAN COLLEGE OF ATHENS, GREECE, NOVEMBER 2015.** It's an early morning in Athens during the warmest fall in living memory. Even though it's the middle of November, the temperature refuses to go below 68°F (20°C). One good thing is that the warm nights allow the large number of refugees staying in the city to be able to sleep without freezing.

We're outside despite the heat, at the newly constructed swimming pool of the Hellenic American College. It's the first competition of the season and the expectations for achieving good times have been toned down. The big topic of discussion on the tightly packed stands is the men's 1,500m freestyle.

Steve Prefontaine, in the biopic *Without Limits*, is quoted as saying his favorite distance of 5,000m is "13 minutes of pain." It is the toughest challenge in running: the pace is too high to allow for any type of rest, but the distance is long enough to offer plenty of opportunities for doubt and for anaerobic activities to give way to the intensely uncomfortable grinding feelings. The 1,500m freestyle for swimmers is the equivalent of a 5k for runners; the distance takes about 15 minutes for the specialists and is not comfortable for more than the first 300 meters, at best.

Swimmers are placed in lanes according to the formation of a flight of birds. The swimmer with the fastest sign-up time gets the lane in the middle, where he or she is flanked by the swimmers with the second- and third-best times. This morning, The Champion was set to swim in lane 3. The Champion, Spyridon Gianniotis, grew up on the island of Corfu with a British mother and a Greek father. Named after the patron saint of Corfu, Spyridon (called Spiros) left the island at the age of 16 to train in Thessaloniki, finally ending up in the city that holds half of the entire population of Greece: Athens.

After the Athens Olympics in 2004 and the sensational win in the European championships in soccer that same year, Greek sports had been on a downward slide. Sure, the basketball team beat the American dream team at the 2006 world championships, where LeBron James and company were ground down by the well-coordinated

Greeks. However, by 2015, individual Greek sports were sadly reduced to a number of decent rowers and Spiros, who'd become the most accomplished and popular Greek swimmer over time after winning everything except for an Olympic medal. After he won the world championships in 10 kilometers open water in both 2011 and 2013, The Champion not only received the award for the best athlete in Greece, but prompted a surge in swimming interest. At the London Olympics in 2012, the 10 kilometer race was held in the Serpentine in Hyde Park, where Spiros, after nearly two hours of swimming, missed a medal by a margin of just five seconds.

During the Greek economic crisis, Spiros had been advised on many occasions to use his British passport to open up a bank account in the UK instead of keeping his money in the insecure Greek banks with their restrictive rules concerning withdrawals. He didn't do it—how would that benefit his beloved Greece? The Champion's combination of upright attitude and personality has made him immensely popular. People stop him on the street and admire him like the god Poseidon, who was able to tame the waves.

The Champion has turned 35, and in competition contexts he considers himself to be more or less the same age as the ancient ruins in Athens. He trains full time with only a few distractions. After having placed seventh at the 2004 Olympics, he was offered a position in the Greek navy, which means that he receives a salary as long as he gets top results; if the results start to take a downward turn, he may still remain as an officer. The Champion also owns a share in a gambling business and has built a 17-meter pool where he and his wife teach kids how to swim.

Back to the pool at the Hellenic American College. There, in lane 4, The Kid is also set to swim. The Kid's name is Dimitrios Negris, and he's only 17 years old, but already at an international level in the 1,500m. He's been given a ride by his mother, who still refers to him as her little boy and accompanies him to races to make sure he eats his sandwiches.

At the junior world championships in Singapore, The Kid came in fifth in the 1,500m freestyle. His 15:18 was only four seconds slower than winning American Taylor Abbott. Just like The Champion in lane 3 and The Workhorse, Antonis Fokaidis, in lane 5, he also trains for Coach Nikos Gemelis in the large club of Olympiakos with its red and white colors.

Fokaidis is 26 years old, the age at which endurance swimmers tend to peak, if you look at lists of results, study progression curves, and talk to coaches. This is an age where the training volume has had enough time to increase to an optimal level without muscles, joints, and mentality getting so tired as to affect performance. Nor has life become as complicated as it may get later with mortgages, picking up and dropping off children, or taking care of sick parents.

The Workhorse belongs to the category of athletes who, despite an almost mind-boggling amount of training and daily bodily abuse, don't get all that much in return for their efforts—at least not in money or recognition. Five years earlier, he had won the gold medal in the team event at the European championships. This is an event that resembles the team time trials in cycling where three swimmers swim five kilometers together and where the third swimmer's finish time is also the finish time of the team. The teams usually consist of two men and one woman where the woman drafts behind her teammates swimming through the water. Back then, The Workhorse had competed on the same team as The Champion, who'd been the one in the team to answer questions from journalists.

The three swimmers had looked upon the competition as a training race of lesser importance. With only an hour left before the start, they're still sitting around joking. The still somewhat shy Kid's eyes wander back and forth between the two experienced swimmers in the national team, almost as if he's watching a game of tennis. However, with only 30 minutes left to go, the atmosphere shifts as the swimmers, after having put on their almost unbelievably tight competition swimming briefs, turn into focused introverts. The Kid puts on a yellow swimming cap. The Workhorse is wearing the white swimming cap of Olympiakos with its red club logo. His teammate, The Champion, is wearing a swimming cap with his name, "S. GIANNIOTIS," written in capital letters underneath the Greek flag.

And they're off! To the experienced eye, they don't seem to possess a particularly good starting technique or explosive style. It would be a waste of a lot of training time trying to save half a second in a race that takes 15 minutes, or an open water race that takes one or two hours. The experienced eye may also notice that all three men have a high position in the water and that they swim with a relatively high arm stroke frequency. The Champion has the highest rate of everyone.

Nor are their turns all that impressive. All training in Greece focuses on competitions in 50-meter pools, like in the Olympics. Simple arithmetic tells us that those races involve half as many turns compared to races in 25-meter pools, like this one. A powerfully completed, elongated turn is faster than one where the swimmer glides for a shorter distance and starts to swim at an earlier stage after the turn. However, such turns may be difficult for swimmers with a high arm stroke frequency, as their swimming might get jerky. Turns that are executed too well may thus disturb a swimmer's harmony, and not all swimmers are able to manage them even if they're faster.

The Kid has the best technique of the three. It looks sharper even if he's not as strong as his older competitors. The Kid's body is straight and symmetrical, and he uses his arms in a biomechanically beneficial manner. Coach Nikos says that this is because he's been coaching The Kid since he was 10 years old. The Champion, on the other hand, lets his head go all over the place and his swimming is not as symmetrical as it was when he was 20. Yet, already after a few lengths, both The Champion and The Kid have left The Workhorse behind by a few meters.

Swimming the 1,500m freestyle in a swimming pool, and doing it in a way that gets the best time of the day, is to spend at least a dozen minutes with aching muscle fatigue, burning air pipes, and thinking that there are things in life that are much more pleasant. It's not even all that nice once you reach the finish line.

The Champion looks back at the time when his training was at its best. Now, as an open water swimmer, he knows all the tips and tricks for using as little energy as possible in order to save it until it's time to position yourself before the final sprint. Here, in a pool race over 1,500 meters, there are no opportunities like those in open water swimming to position yourself "on someone's feet" and save energy. Here, the swimmers have each been assigned a lane, and if they were to change lanes for some reason, they would immediately get disqualified.

We're now halfway through the race and The Kid is leading over The Champion by about two meters. This is when The Champion starts letting some negative thoughts sneak into his mind. He's on antibiotics after a toothache, and he now starts to feel weak and is losing the rhythm he knows is the correct one. He actually thinks about getting up from the pool, to stop and simply not complete the rest of the race. What if he gets worse after the race? What if he loses a full week of training? He could always blame the antibiotics when Coach Nikos inevitably demands to know what the hell he's doing.

After 200 meters' worth of doubts, The Champion gives himself an imaginary slap on the face and pulls himself together. If he's to lose against The Kid, who was born the same year The Champion swam his first world cup competition in Malmö, then he'll do so standing tall. He's always been a man of dignity. With eight months left to go before his final race, he has to maintain his darn dignity. The Champion shifts into a new gear. Even though he's unable to find the same flow he recalls he used to possess in his best performances, there are only 400 meters left to go. Just 16 measly lengths out of the 60 that were ahead of him at the start.

The Kid has started too hard. Not too fast, but as a result of being positioned between The Champion and The Workhorse, his swimming has been tense. He tried a little bit too hard at the wrong places in the stroke and tried a little bit too hard in the turns. Not even a trained eye is able to see that something is wrong. The only one who sees it is Coach Nikos, who's got a feeling. Coach Nikos is not one of the most science-oriented coaches, but he knows his swimmers better than his own wife. He knows exactly how they react to each training session and he's able to read their body language. His philosophy is to never leave his swimmers, which is why he never goes on vacation. His job is a calling and if he doesn't give everything he's got, how is he supposed to demand that his swimmers do so? All that remains of the race is 400 meters and The Kid increases his intensity. But The Kid also sees that The Champion is about to catch up, which makes him tense up even more.

On his other side, The Workhorse has found some new energy after having started off at a calmer pace compared to his competitors. He let The Kid get away, and when turning at the shallow end of the pool, he saw The Champion. With 400 meters to go, The Workhorse hasn't emptied his revolver like the other two. He pushes a little harder during the turns while moving toward the side of the lane that's the farthest from The Kid. And there he goes. After 60 lengths, The Workhorse is the first to finish. His time—15:21—is his best time ever in a 25-meter swimming pool, an unusual format for Greek swimmers.

Nevertheless, The Workhorse still has quite a bit left to meet the standard required for him to qualify to the Olympics. But this is also the first race of the year and Coach Nikos has not given any of his three protégés any rest before the competition. In the week before, they swam around 65,000 meters. This is certainly less than many other top swimmers, but one of the characteristics in Coach Nikos's training programs is that the purpose of almost all sessions is to reduce what is generally (and partially incorrectly) referred to as the lactate threshold.

The afternoon sessions on Wednesdays are a bit shorter—1 to 1.5 hours with some leg kicks, a little lighter swimming and somewhat shorter top-speed intervals. Basically all other sessions consist of 1 to 2 kilometers of warm-up, followed by a hard series lasting 30 to 60 minutes, followed by a cooldown to prevent the swimmers from feeling like geriatric patients when they return to their next session. The objective of the main series always revolves around keeping the average speed as high as possible, such as swimming 40 × 100m at around 1:01. More muscular swimmers, or swimmers who've not adapted to this type of training, would not be able to handle the sessions of Coach Nikos.

AT WHAT AGE ARE SWIMMERS THE FASTEST?

Experiencing the unglamorous everyday life of The Champion, The Kid, and The Workhorse raises a few questions. Science tells us that it's a physiological fact that performance starts to deteriorate at the age of approximately 35. However, for those wanting to optimize their performance, putting a wet finger up in the air to know which way the wind is blowing is not enough. More and better formulated questions need to be answered:

How long must The Kid train before he reaches his full potential?

Since things start to deteriorate when you turn 35, does that mean that The Champion is already on his way down? If not, how long will he be able to maintain his terrific shape?

Does the moment of decline differ among different sports? What determines whether this moment differs from one athlete to another?

How do you get as good as possible? And how do you stay on top for as long as possible?

Does general health advice like eating more vegetables and having less stress in your life apply here too, or are top performances the result of different factors?

It is known that people who exercise moderately are able to increase their performance until their 90s. Is it also possible to increase performance after the magic age of 35 for those with a better background in training?

And as an extra dimension for all questions: do the effects of time affect the two sexes differently?

The first question is the easiest to answer, so let's start there. Swimming was more or less a sport for youth for a long time. In the 1970s, most swimmers ended their careers before turning 25. The American boycott of the Moscow Olympics in 1980 meant that several swimmers who would have otherwise ended careers after the games instead decided to stay on for an additional four years with their eyes set on the 1984 Olympics in Los Angeles. Cynthia Woodhead, Tracy Caulkins, Mary T. Meagher, Craig Beardsley, Rowdy Gaines, Bill Barrett, and Steve Lundquist all qualified for the fictional Olympic team of 1980 and then proceeded to the Olympic qualifying races in 1984. Breaststroke swimmer Lundquist, who won gold medals in Los Angeles, referred to the gang as "the gray beards." Their average age: 23.

Forbes magazine estimated that Ryan Lochte made over one million dollars in sponsorship revenues during the Olympic year of 2012. At the beginning of the 1980s, however, there were no sponsorship programs, so when the college scholarships ended when the swimmers were around 22 or 23, the swimmers lacked the funds necessary for housing, travel, and the copious amounts of food swimmers wolf down between training sessions.

The undeniable emperor of competition pools, Michael Phelps, was only 15 years old when he came in fifth at the Sydney Olympics in 2000, and he broke his first world record before he'd even turned 16, a time he's beaten by a significant margin since then. The same applies to every distance in which Phelps has competed on a regular basis; his best times come at the age of 23 to 24 (see following table). That's significant for a world-class swimmer, but not in comparison with the steep development experienced by "ordinary" teenage swimmers.

Swedish swimmer Simon Sjödin didn't swim nearly as fast in his teens, but he's considered a late bloomer. At the age of 16, he only had the thirte-

MICHAEL PHELPS'S DEVELOPMENT FROM PUBERTY ONWARD (1999–2016)

Age	100m freestyle	200m freestyle	100m freestyle	200m butterfly	200m medley	400m medley
14		1:55.37	55.78	1:59.02	2:06.50	4:24.77
15				1:56.50	2:06.91	4:25.97
16		1:51.73	52.98	1:54.58	2:00.86	4:15.20
17		1:48.90	51.88	1:54.86	1:58.68	4:11.09
18	49.05	1:45.99	51.10	1:53.93	1:55.94	4:09.09
19		1:45.32	51.25	1:54.04	1:57.14	4:08.26
20		1:45.20	51.65		1:56.68	
21		1:45.63	51.51	1:53.80	1:55.84	4:10.47
22	48.42	1:43.86	50.77	1:52.09	1:54.98	4:06.22
23	**47.51**	**1:42.96**	50.58	1:52.03	1:54.23	**4:03.84**
24	47.78	1:43.22	**49.82**	**1:51.51**		
25	48.13	1:45.62	50.86	1:54.11		
26	48.08	1:44.79	50.71	1:53.34	**1:54.16**	
27	48.49	1:44.05	50.86	1:53.01	1:54.27	4:09.28
28						
29	48.45	1:48.20	51.17		1:56.04	
30	49.66		50.45	1:52.94	1:54.75	
31			51.00	1:53.36	1:54.66	

Note: Numbers in bold indicate the best times.

SIMON SJÖDIN'S DEVELOPMENT FROM PUBERTY ONWARD (2000–2016)

Age	100m freestyle	200m freestyle	100m freestyle	200m butterfly	200m medley	400m medley
14			1:08.51		2:31.44	5:14.94
15					2:27.18	5:15.88
16		2:06.50				
17			1:03.30	2:14.08	2:16.91	4:49.14
18			57.99	2:08.63	2:09.82	4:36.61
19	53.30	1:55.81	59.01	2:05.70	2:09.24	4:41.29
20		1:57.12	55.00	2:01.13		4:53.81
21		1:54.74	54.48	2:00.52	2:07.46	4:33.12
22	51.80	1:56.84	53.96	1:57.75	2:09.06	
23	**51.00**	1:50.27	**52.27**	**1:57.01**	2:02.19	
24	51.72	1:53.71	53.00	2:00.11	1:59.72	4:21.52
25	51.58	1:52.77	53.15	1:59.66	2:00.22	4:20.96
26		1:54.86	53.73	2:00.42	1:59.44	4:24.21
27			53.26	1:59.18	1:58.02	4:21.74
28		**1:50.08**	53.64	1:58.32	**1:59.14**	**4:19.68**
29			53.40	1:57.22	1:58.10	4:26.50
30		151.0	52.53	1:56.46	1:59.41	

Note: Numbers in bold indicate the best times.

enth best time in a local race. There were probably not many people in the audience who saw him as a future world championships finalist. And even if he kept making steady progress in the background, he remained uneven for a long time. Questionable results such as 2:20.01 in the 200m medley at the age of 19 was nothing to call the newspapers for. Nevertheless, Simon Sjödin now belongs to the European elite and has both competed in the world championship and won medals in the European championships, where his best time was 1:58.02. Phelps and Sjödin, now both in their 30s, got their best times after they turned 23. It's thus reasonable to assume that most swimmers are able to improve some variables at least until they turn 30. Reaching your full potential as a swimmer requires a seemingly unfathomable time investment in training, the majority of which is spent in the pool. If the skin had a greater ability to change in terms of genetics, then we'd perhaps see the fourth generation of elite swimmers developing scales, and legs that resemble the tail fin of a mermaid.

There doesn't seem to be any difference between boys and girls in terms of height, weight, and lean muscle mass before puberty begins at the age of 12 to 14. After puberty, however, girls have somewhat more body fat compared to boys, which is the result of the hormones estrogen and testosterone. Fetuses that will develop into men secrete testosterone in their testicles. When the young boy is born, the brain's pineal gland shuts down the testosterone factory. The differences in body fat remain at a low level until puberty when the testicles once again start producing testosterone.

The testosterone makes boys produce more proteins, which build bones and muscles. A 14-year-old boy typically grows a whopping 4 inches in a year. Malnutrition may interfere with puberty and is one of the reasons why some groups of people are shorter on average. The estrogen that girls start producing to an increasing extent in puberty makes their hips wider, their breasts larger, and helps their body store a little bit of extra fat. These are critical characteristics for humans in terms of survival and evolution of the species, but they also mean that men are the winners in the biological lottery when it comes to swimming and other physically demanding activities.

The hormonal roller coaster in adolescence results in men being on average 5 to 7 inches (12 to 18 centimeters) taller than women. Adult men on average weigh 30 to 40 pounds (13.6 to 18 kilograms) more and their body fat is 6 to 9 percentage points lower compared to women. Given that their training is similar, and that testosterone is not added in any unnatural way, men are stronger than women. Muscle mass for men increases from the onset of puberty until they are approximately 22 years old, whereas women reach their maximum level at the age of 16 to 18.

In light of research on adolescent physical development, it's therefore likely that The Kid has yet to reach the age for top performances. Even if the natural growth process is individual, The Kid probably still has five years of steady increase of his potential to look forward to, assuming his training program is correctly designed. If his movement along the developmental staircase resembles that of Michael Phelps, then he should—if everything goes according to plan—be able to reach a high international level. If he instead progresses similar to Ryan Lochte, then The Kid has a top-level, world-class career to look forward to.

The most important variable in swimming is a good technique. Studies show that not even superior physiological skills make one swimmer faster than another. Being strong, tough, and able to persevere are good traits, but they have no function if they can't be used in the water. In the 100m breaststroke, top athletes like triathlon Olympic champion Jan Frodeno or crossfit phenomenon Rich Froening would lose by at least 15 to 20 meters to 12-year Carly Geehr when she posted a time of 1:09 on the distance in a 50-meter pool.

Generally speaking, one might argue that there are two types of training programs in youth sports: the East German model and the soccer model. The East German and the soccer models are in agreement concerning the need to teach motor skills from an early age. Comprehensive research shows that the best period for learning movement patterns in order to carry them out accurately, powerfully, and in a relaxed manner at different speeds is between the ages of 6 and 17.

But that's where the similarities end. The focus for East German swimmers was on large volumes at a speed that was mostly aerobic and more or less of the same intensity. It was only after the swimmers had gained a good technique that they were allowed to swim longer, and then longer, and longer.

When we look at Zlatan Ibrahimović, Lionel Messi, and Cristiano Ronaldo during a game, we get a good idea of what the soccer model entails. On the field we see them use the full movement spectrum (standing still, walking, jogging slowly, and proper endurance running) in order to be at the right place when starting their maximum run to get a chance to score and finish with clinical precision. If, on the other hand, they had remained at an East German threshold speed the entire time, then they wouldn't have any energy saved to make a difference in the result of the game.

Soccer fans love to discuss the stunning performances of their favorite players, how incredibly fast or tough they are. When considering the large selection of people playing soccer, it must be that the ones able to reach the top are the fastest and toughest. Or is it? When sprint coach Håkan Andersson simultaneously coached both his track and field youths and a Swedish top-level soccer team, he noted that the adult soccer warriors were often relatively slower than his 13-year-old track and field talents.

Michail Tonkonogi at the Swedish School of Sport and Health Sciences is a professor in medical science who's studied the training of youths for many years. He argues that endurance training for children under the age of 13 is unnecessary. It doesn't make a difference, at least not when it comes to improving endurance. When an adult is engaged in endurance training, both heart rate and blood pressure go up. Children's hearts are not sufficiently large and their blood vessels are more elastic, so their blood pressure does not increase to the same extent, which in turn means that their heart muscle is not put under the same amount of strain despite a faster heart rate. Tonkonogi recommends various forms of playful youth training that vary in both tempo and movement patterns to improve the children's coordination, speed, strength, and ability to handle muscle fatigue. This is also the best training approach for improving the oxygen uptake as much as possible at that age.

An additional reason for being careful with the East German model is that it has been found that an overly monotonous grind may wear down the children's brains. This is due to the fact that children's blood sugar rate is lower compared to adults and thus more sensitive to further reduction brought on by persistent endurance efforts. But anyone who still wants to cling to the East German model could argue that it would be difficult to maintain a good swimming technique if you played water polo instead of swimming back and forth in the pool.

After good technique, the second most important variable for a swimmer's performance is muscle strength. This also explains why most swimmers increase their performance level the most at the time when their muscle strength also increases the most (i.e., up to the age of 18 for women and 22 for men). This naturally takes individual variations into account.

So, what about young people and strength training? There are those who fear that starting strength training too early might be harmful, and there are those who argue the opposite. Tonkonogi represents another position. "Without a reasonable doubt, strength training does have an effect on youths," he argues, "In just a few months, we see a 14 to 30 percent increase in strength, which is the same growth seen in adults. However, what's improved is mainly the connection between nerves and muscles, which means that there is no risk that we will see children who, after a period of strength training, start to resemble body builders."

As we've discussed previously, the age between 6 and 17 is the best for adopting a desired movement pattern, and this applies to strength training as well. The main argument for selling gym memberships at parent-teacher association meetings is still the injury frequency among youths. Research shows that children playing soccer suffer injuries at a frequency 1,500 times higher than those involved in strength training.

In order to understand the overall picture concerning strength training, it's important to know that the strength of a muscle is proportional to its size or, more accurately, the size of its cross-section area. For the beginner, the increase in strength during the first 6 to 8 weeks is mostly the result of the body adapting to new movements, so-called neural adaptation. It's thus easy to quickly gain results using these exercises or movements, whereas it's much more difficult to use your increased strength in other contexts.

The gender variation mainly consists of the gap in upper body strength between men and women. Women's strength in their legs may be the same as that of men when making a comparison based of body weight that doesn't include fat. However, women are significantly weaker in their upper body. This explains why many female swimmers are just as good as men when swimming with leg kicks whereas only a few get the same effect when swimming with paddles and a pull buoy mainly using their arms.

YOUR SWIMMING: THE OPTIMUM TRAINING PROGRAM

Designing the ultimate training program takes a bit of hard work. The point of departure needs to be the athlete's present situation, and the program needs to accommodate the quest for the perfect technique, attempting to optimize the effects on heart and lungs as well as including the best type of strength training. The program then needs to be adapted according to age and gender. And we haven't even mentioned the dimension concerning the athlete's mentality.

What further complicates this process is that what works for one swimmer may not work for another. To a large extent, the way athletes respond to a training program depends on genetics. A training program that creates a champion might make other athletes in the same group sick, overtrained, or—less dramatically—not even close to reaching the same potential. Evaluating training programs is also tricky: is the program faulty or is the athlete lacking the potential to improve?

When conducting chemical experiments, you test with different conditions by removing an ingredient. Using this analogy on a training program, the ingredient could be "strength training for the legs," "training with paddles," or removing something in the athlete's diet, which we may refer to as "Vitamin X." However, in training theory, this methodology doesn't work, as the conditions present at the start of the experiment have changed. Not only has the swimmer become older, but the previous training has also accumulated, which results in a new set of ingredients that make exact comparisons impossible. So, while it's possible to make continuous training-related changes, it's difficult and scientifically unsound to claim that a single change is the entire or partial reason behind the result.

When Swedish canoeist Gert Fredriksson (who won six Olympic golds between 1948 and 1960) was still active, it was still possible to become the best by simply training more than your competitors. Fredriksson worked as a fire fighter for a coastal rescue service station in Sweden. Fredriksson would rig a device that enabled him to canoe in the place where the hoses were washed, allowing him to complete an intense training session whenever possible. Today, longer training is not automatically seen as better—that much we know. We also know that while it's possible to find the "perfect" training program, the variables are so numerous and complex that it's unlikely you'll be the one discovering the perfect combination.

It's easy to figure out that the maximum performance level of athletes occurs somewhere between the ages of 25 and 35. All you need to do is to study result lists from world championships, Olympics, and world record series. There have been studies on 100m runners suggesting that the maximum performance level occurs for men at the age of 25.4, and at the age of 26.1 for women. However, using a quantitative method is precarious. Looking at quantitative data on swimmers between 1960 and 1980, it looks like the best age for swimmers is between 17 and 23. In reality, this result has very little to do with exactly when the human body is the most capable of swimming fast—at that time, most swimmers ended their careers by the age of 23. Many swimmers still choose to quit at that age even though more and more swimmers are now offered both a training environment and a decent income for swimming after they turn 23.

The oldest Olympic gold medalist in track and field is Irishman Patrick McDonald, who was 42 years old when he won the hammer throw in Antwerp in 1920. However, McDonald's gold medal says very little about how long athletes may perform at top levels. Not only did this take place nearly a century ago, but the hammer throw was not a particularly developed sport at the time. Only a very small number of people participated in this event. It is likely that the number of licensed hammer throwers in a country like Lithuania today exceeds the total number in the world at that time.

More relevant is perhaps the 31-year-old Kenyan Albert Hill, who won the 1,500m race in Seoul in 1988. But his achievement also failed to upset the science of sport, as Hill's time was far from the world record (and 31 isn't that old). Jeannie Longo is a more inspiring example for everyone who didn't have an elite career when they were young. In Beijing in 2008, the Frenchwoman was no more than two tenths of a second from winning an Olympic medal in cycling, two days before she turned 50.

Tips: Plan your own training by using The Mystic Square (see page 348).

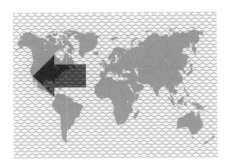

■ LOS ANGELES, CALIFORNIA, 1967. There are certainly extremes in swimming. When Dara Torres won the 4 x 100m freestyle for the United States in Los Angeles in 1984, she was an extremely promising 17-year-old.

Torres had grown up in Beverly Hills in a house with 10 bathrooms. Her father, Ed, was a property magnate and would end up buying several hotels in Las Vegas, including the Aladdin Hotel, where Elvis and Priscilla Presley got married the week before Dara was born. Naturally, the house with all the bathrooms came with a swimming pool, in which Dara bathed, swam, and sprayed water on her six siblings whenever possible.

Dara Torres was only 14 years old when she broke the world record in the new distance of 50m freestyle. She was then attending the most prestigious boarding school in California, the West Lake School for Girls, whose alumni include astronaut Sally Ride, child star Shirley Temple, and actress Maggie Gyllenhaal. The path to the prestigious schools of Harvard, Stanford, and Yale was wide open because her father could have "bought" her a spot at these esteemed universities. But this wasn't the route Dara wanted to go down, as she wanted to focus entirely on her swimming. Stanford certainly had a good team, but she didn't want to attend a school that focused too much on studying. She instead decided to go to Gainesville to swim at the University of Florida.

Dara Torres arrived in Florida as an Olympic medalist and she had definitely come to a place for winners. Because even if Tracey Caulkins (who'd won three Olympic golds) had stopped competing, Theresa Andrews (who'd won two gold medals in backstroke in Los Angeles) was still active. At Gainsville Dara also found Canadian swimmer Sandy Goss and Mark Stockwell from Australia, who both laid the foundation for a long tradition of strong foreign swimmers at the University of Florida. Anthony Nesty became the first black swimmer to win an Olympic gold when he won the 100m butterfly race for his native Suriname in 1988. Martin Lopez-Zubero would win the 200m backstroke at home in Barcelona four years later. Dana Vollmer, who had the 100m butterfly world record before it was broken by Sarah Sjöström, was also there for four years.

Everything looked good on the surface. Dara Torres wanted her training to be tough, but the step from playful training sessions doing 3,000 to 4,000m with Coach Terry back home in California to sessions lasting twice as long and held twice as often led by Coach Randy came close to breaking her. He'd throw chairs at the pool and chastise the female swimmers as if they'd betrayed their country. The best way to avoid getting yelled at was to swim for the entire duration of the session. When they weren't in the pool, they were doing so much strength training that their hands started bleeding, or pulling themselves across the football field using only their arms so that their knees got all chafed.

Each Monday, the swimmers had to step into Coach Randy's office to get weighed. If you weighed too much, you had to do eleven swimming sessions instead of nine that week. On Sundays, when they had a day off from training, Dara would run and eat next to nothing out of fear of stepping up on the scale the next day.

The time he found a large stack of hidden snacks in the women's locker room could have served as a wake-up call for Coach Randy to reconsider his cruel weight routine. Instead, he started weighing the female swimmers twice a week. Dara learned how to put her fingers down her throat from an athlete on another team, and just like that, the fastest female swimmer in the world had become bulimic. Her eating disorders put the brakes on her career and meant the most fun she had in Gainesville was with her pet, Melvin the lizard.

In spite of everything, she competed at the Seoul Olympics in 1988, where she won two relay medals and came in seventh in the 100m freestyle. By the time she won a new relay medal at the Barcelona Olympics, she'd also managed to get rid of her bulimia. In addition, she competed in volleyball for the University of Florida team. So far, Dara Torres's career was definitely interesting, but what happened in 1999 was what made it truly incredible.

By June 1999, the now 32-year-old Dara Torres was working as a model in New York. After a Meat Loaf concert, her date pointed out how excited she got when she talked about swimming. That night, she didn't dream about her date, but about swimming. She hadn't swum for six and a half years, but her date had clearly planted a seed.

The following morning, she called the coach she liked at Stanford, then quickly disassembled her life in New York and moved to California. Coach Richard Quick analyzed Dara's situation and had her take it easy for the first six weeks. She never swam with a heart rate higher than 150 beats per minute to prepare herself for proper training.

YOUR SWIMMING: FIVE SIGNS OF EATING DISORDERS

(1) Postponing meals, eating slowly, or wanting to eat alone

(2) Being critical of your body

(3) Feeling sad or experiencing anxiety

(4) Losing energy

(5) Exercising in order to maintain your weight

She then gradually increased her time in the strength training room while being coached by British discus thrower Robert Weir. Instead of crawling over football fields like she did in Florida, she kept doing basic exercises over and over again in order to upgrade the slim body of a model to that of a physical beast. Indeed, she gained 20 pounds (9 kilograms) from bench pressing weights of 110 to 210 pounds (50 to 95 kilograms). Her six meals a day were miles away from her Sundays of fasting in Gainesville. She got her energy from a diet consisting of 30 percent fat, 30 percent protein, and 40 percent carbohydrates. She also downed 25 pills a day of different food supplements.

Dara became obsessed. She stopped drinking alcohol and coffee, made sure that she slept well, and was always on time for her training in order to analyze Coach Richard's objective with each particular session. For her and her training buddy, Jenny Thompson, each session was now just as important as an Olympic final. When in Florida, Torres was too tired to reach race pace in her workouts.

This setup was new to her. Now, these two athletes trained completely differently: 20 hard 50m lengths at an average speed below 28 seconds, with only one minute of rest in between.

In Sydney in 2000, Dara Torres, 33 years old and with only one year of hard training behind her, won a whopping five medals. After this impressive performance, she retired once again. However, the process would repeat itself. After having been tempted back via a masters race in 2006, she initiated a two-year program with her eyes set on the 2008 Beijing Olympics. There, she became the first person over the age of 40 to win an Olympic medal in swimming; as a matter of fact, she was only one hundredth of a second away from beating German Britta Steffen in the 50m freestyle.

Her last performance came in 2012 at 45 years old when she was only a few hundredths of a second from getting a spot on the U.S. Olympic team. Dara Torres has become perhaps the world's greatest symbol of what women, mothers, and people are capable of doing.

SUPER HUMANS OR ORDINARY PEOPLE?

Scientists these days are not sure why performance levels tend to go down past the age of 35. The fact is that the lion's share of studies have not looked at top athletes, but "regular" people, who, due to natural reasons, tend to alter their physiological behavior around the age of 35. The person who at age 25 used to train four or five times a week and also go out clubbing for a few hours on Friday night is probably watching their children training from the sidelines at age 35.

Finances also play a role. The older we get, the more money tends to flow into the household. You trade in your bike for a car, and your college barebones shopping list is replaced by full shopping carts at the supermarket.

So, with knowledge-based training and an otherwise healthy life, it is possible to perform well until we're quite old. Even if absolute top performances require that the swimmer has been physically active for many years, it is nevertheless possible to develop technique, strength, flexibility, and endurance at more advanced ages than previously thought possible. The table with the best times for different ages (see pages 199–200) gives us an indication that performance doesn't necessarily need to drop drastically until the age of 60.

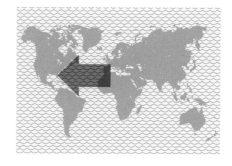

■ **ORLANDO, FLORIDA, OCTOBER 2014.** The men in the picture at right are quite old. They are Tiger Holmes, William Adams, Edwin Graves, and John Corse, and they are about to compete in the 4 x 200m freestyle in the age class of 360. In order to compete in this class, the combined age of the team members must be exactly 360. This means that a swimmer's average age is 90.

So, they're about to swim the 4 × 200m freestyle and this is the first time that a team in this age class is attempting to do this. The old men have brought lawn chairs, thermoses with coffee, and their heart medicine. They joke that the risk of false starts during changeovers is smaller than the risk of one of them keeling over during the race. They plan the relay so that the one who's in the worst shape goes first—so that he may complete his swimming before he starts feeling bad.

The old men reach the finish line and set a world record after having achieved an average time of a little over two minutes per 100m. Tiger Holmes mostly does the backstroke since he has a stiff neck and a hard time breathing. After the record, Edwin Graves reflects on the fact that it took so long before he was able to break a world record. It took a whole 25 years, since he started swimming when he was 65. The old men want to break new records, and their biggest challenge is keeping the team alive—literally.

The old guys in Florida Aquatics getting ready for a world-record race

BEST TIMES AT DIFFERENT AGES—50M FREESTYLE

Age	Men — Country/Year	Women — Country/Year
11–12	25.09 Michael Andrew, USA (2012)	26.21 Missy Franklin, USA (2008)
13–14	23.19 Michael Andrew, USA (2014)*	25.23 Missy Franklin, USA (2009)
15–16	22.34 Michael Andrew, USA (2015)	24.80 Simone Manuel, USA (2013)
17–18	21.53 Caleb Dressel, USA (2015)	23.99 Cate Campbell, AUS (2009)
19–24	20.91 Cesar Cielo, BRA (2009)	23.67 Sarah Sjöström, SWE (2009)
25–29	20.94 Frédérick Bousquet, FRA (2009)	23.73 Britta Steffen, GER (2009)
30–34	21.29 Ashley Callus, AUS (2009)	23.88 Therese Alshammar, SWE (2009)
35–39	22.28 Roland Schoemann, RSA (2015)	24.99 Therese Alshammar, SWE (2014)
40–44	23.31 Brian Jacobson, USA (2014)	24.07 Dara Torres, USA (2008)
45–49	23.98 Vladimir Predkin, RUS (2014)	24.80 Dara Torres, USA (2012)
50–54	24.08 Brent Barnes, JPN (2009)	27.09 Marie Fuzzati, FRA (2015)
55–59	24.45 Brent Barnes, JPN (2005)	28.69 Laura Val, USA (2018)
60–64	25.23 Richard Abrahams, USA (2006)	28.90 Jenny Whiteley, AUS (2018)
65–69	26.33 Richard Abrahams, USA (2010)	29.92 Laura Val, USA (2016)
70–74	27.71 Richard Abrahams, USA (2015)	33.02 Diann Uustall, USA (2017)
75–79	30.26 Ian Smith, CAN (2016)	34.85 Jane Asher, GBR (2006)
80–84	31.96 Roberto Albriche, ESP (2012)	37.61 Jane Asher, GBR (2012)
85–89	33.94 Keijiro Nakamura, JPN (2008)	38.98 Jane Asher, GBR (2016)
90–94	40.72 Woody Bowersock, USA (2003)	49.68 Olga Kokorina, RUS 49.68 (2013)
95–99	45.71 Willard Lamb, USA (2017)	1:04.02 Maurine Kornfeld, USA (2016)
100–104	56.12 George Corones, USA (2018)	1:41.88 Mieko Nagakoa, JPN (2014)

*Bold times = Within 10 percent of the world record. Times recorded until June 2018.

BEST TIMES AT DIFFERENT AGES—800M FREESTYLE

Age	Men Country/Year	Women Country/Year
11–12	8:48.59 Matthew Hirschberger, USA (2011)	8:55.44 Isabella Rongione, USA (2012)
13–14	8:08.75 Evan Pinion, USA (2009)*	8:28.54 Becca Mann, USA (2012)
15–16	7:52.05 Larsen Jensen, USA (2002)	8:13.86 Katie Ledecky, USA (2013)
17–18	7:39.16 Ian Thorpe, AUS (2001)	8:07.39 Katie Ledecky, USA (2013)
19–24	7:32.12 Lin Zhang, CHN (2009)	8:15.92 Lotte Friis, DEN (2009)
25–29	7:35.27 Ousama Mellouli, TUN (2009)	8:16.70 Camelia Potec, ROM (2009)
30–34	7:56.00 Ousama Mellouli, TUN (2015)	8:46.47 Dawn Heckman, USA (2011)
35–39	8:18.44 Petar Stoychev, BUL (2012)	9:08.47 Kirsten Cameron, AUS (2012)
40–44	8:37.81 Alex Kostich, USA (2010)	8:59.06 Janet Evans, USA (2011)
45–49	8:40.79 Fabio Calmasini, ITA (2015)	9:24.11 K. Pipes-Nielsen, USA (2007)
50–54	8:55.05 Marcus Mattioli, BRA (2010)	9:38.04 Lynn Marshall, CAN (2011)
55–59	9:00.09 Michael Mann, USA (2009)	9:46.56 Jill Hernandez, USA (2015)
60–64	9:35.50 Jim McConica, USA (2012)	10:27.71 Laura Val, USA (2011)
65–69	10:11.30 Jim McConica, USA (2015)	11:31.53 Charlotte Davis, USA (2015)
70–74	10:45.92 Graham Johnston, USA (2002)	12:13.07 Yoshiko Osaki, JPN (2009)
75–79	11:07.90 David Radcliff, USA (2009)	12:58.94 Jane Asher, GBR (2006)
80–84	11:49.29 David Radcliff, USA (2014)	13:51.21 Jane Asher, GBR (2011)
85–89	14:36.90 Willard Lamb, USA (2008)	16:45.59 Dorothy Dickey, AUS (2015)
90–94	16:28.37 Willard Lamb, USA (2013)	18:53.58 Rita Simonton, USA (2008)
95–99	22:28.28 Gus Langner, USA (1998)	21:53.69 Rita Simonton, USA (2013)
100–104		38:04.30 Mieko Nagakoa, JPN (2014)

*Bold times = Within 10 percent of the world record. Times recorded until June 2016.

AVERAGE AGE OF GOLD MEDALISTS IN OLYMPIC SWIMMING EVENTS

Year	Men	Women	Examples of Swimmers/Country/Swimming
1948	21.4	22	**Age 17** Jimmy McLane, United States, 1,500m freestyle
1956	19.3	20.6	**Age 22** Greta Andersen, Denmark, 100m freestyle
			Age 17 Murray Rose, Australia, 400m & 1,500m freestyle
			Age 30 Ursula Happe, Germany, 200m breaststroke
1964	18.6	17.0	**Age 19** Don Schollander, United States, 100m & 400m freestyle
			Age 22 Dawn Fraser, Australia, 100m freestyle
1972	21.2	16.4	**Age 21** Gunnar Larsson, Sweden, 200m & 400m medley
			Age 22 Mark Spitz, United States, 100m & 200m freestyle, 100m & 200m butterfly
1980	19.4	17.2	**Age 15** Shane Gould, Australia, 100m & 200m freestyle, 200m medley
			Age 18 Bengt Baron, Sweden, 100m backstroke
			Age 20 Per Arvidsson, Sweden, 100m butterfly
1988	21.8	21.5	**Age 18** Michelle Ford, Australia, 800m freestyle
			Age 28 Vladimir Salnikov, Soviet Union, 1,500m freestyle
1996	24.2	21.8	**Age 14** Kristina Egerszegi, Hungary, 200m backstroke
2004	22.4	22.0	No male teen gold medalist
2012	21.8	19.7	**Age 21** Alexander Popov, Russia, 50m & 100m freestyle
			Age 21 Penny Haynes, South Africa, 100m & 200m breaststroke

EIGHT SWIMMERS WHO'VE PUSHED THE AGE LIMITS

JANE ASHER has broken over 100 age class world records.
At the age of 81, she did 6:39 in the 400m freestyle.

KRIS HUMPHRIES did 27.71 in the 50m freestyle in 1995 at the age
of 10. This age class record would last for 19 years. Humphries stopped
swimming and focused on a career in basketball; he's
played in the NBA since 2004.

KYOKO IWASAKI won the gold medal in the 200m breaststroke at the
1992 Olympics in Barcelona, only six days after her fourteenth birthday.
At the age of 17, the 5'3" Iwasaki also competed in the next Olympics
without coming anywhere near her old times.

MICHAEL PHELPS is the youngest male world record holder. He
was 15 years and nine months old in March 2001 when he broke
the 200m butterfly world record with 1:54.92.

JANE CEDERQVIST won an Olympic silver medal in Rome in 1960 when
she'd just turned 15. She was the first woman to be awarded the Swedish
award Svenska Dagbladet Gold Medal. She would go on to get a PhD in
history and became the head of the Swedish National Historical Museum
and the Swedish Fortifications Agency.

JARING TIMMERMAN started competing in swimming at the age of
78. At the age of 104, he broke the world records in the 50m and 100m
freestyle in the age class of 100–104 with the times of 1:16.92 and
3:02.22. He also managed to break records in the age class of 105–109
before passing away in 2014.

DARA TORRES was 41 years old when she was a measly one hundredth of a second away from winning the Olympic gold in the 50m freestyle in 2008.

MARCUS MATTEOLI has an Olympic bronze medal in the 4 × 200m freestyle from Moscow in 1980. But what sets him apart are his times in recent years. At the age of 55, he performed a nice 2:16.78 in the 200m butterfly, and at the age of 50, he did 8:55 in the 800m freestyle.

CHAPTER 6

JACKS OF ALL TRADES

You see, if you make believe hard enough that something is true, then it is true for you.

– Ned Merrill

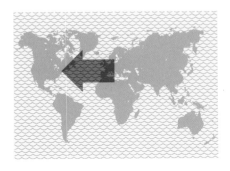

■ CONNECTICUT, JUNE 1964. It's a stunning Sunday in the middle of summer. A man in his 50s is walking through the woods, barefoot and wearing swim trunks. He's got a good spring in his step and he's whistling a tune. The sun's rays find their way through the canopy above and illuminate his tanned, muscular body. Even though Ned Merrill is handsome, his face reveals that he's older than one would first guess based on his fit body. Every once in a while, he leaps from one stone to the next with the steps of an elite athlete. Ned is strong, beautiful, and happy. Everything about him looks like a tribute to life on this perfect day.

Then he suddenly leaps out of the woods and into a suburban paradise: a lush garden, a house painted white. A newly constructed swimming pool. The garden of Don and Helen Westerhazy is a symphony of colors. Helen is lying on a sunbed and takes in the sun's warm rays. Don is sipping a drink. They're both wearing swimwear. Ned calls out to them as he passes a naked marble nymph and then disappears into the couple's 40-foot (12-meter) pool. Don and Helen wave. Ned swims a couple of laps with a powerful crawl. His eyes look through the blue water. Just like a Greek god, he then emerges from the pool to receive a drink served by Don.

Ned: Thanks.

Don: Where have you been keeping yourself?

Ned: Oh. Here and there. Here and there.

Don: So it's not because our service is bad, uh?

Ned: What a day! Did you ever see such a glorious day? Come have a swim. It puts oxygen in your blood. It's good for your hangover.

They continue to exchange pleasantries that further emphasize

Ned's physical prowess. Finally, he thinks of something and triumphantly blurts out:

Ned: I could do it. I could really do it.

Helen: Do what, Neddy?

Ned starts listing 10 swimming pools in the valley.

Ned: I'm gonna swim all the way home. Run and swim. The pools form a path of running water between your house and mine. I'm gonna call it the Lucinda River after my wife.

Helen: What a romantic tribute.

Ned: This is the day that Ned Merrill swims across the country!

Once again, he dives into the pool and swims a length before gracefully pulling himself up, only to disappear into the shrubbery on his way to the next light blue swimming pool.

However, the day doesn't end as energy-filled as it began for our 1960s gladiator. At every pool he stops at, more and more is revealed about him by the people there. One by one, meetings with people from the past break down Ned Merrill until nothing remains of the cheerful character from the beginning scenes of the movie *(The Swimmer)*.

Even though the day of fictitious Ned Merrill didn't turn out the way he'd imagined, he could very well have been the first to complete a swimrun—and with the most barebones equipment imaginable. Today's swimrun contestants are buoyed by nutrient solutions and energy bars; scotch and soda was the key to Merrill's pool-to-pool race.

Until Merrill's pool-to-pool race, swimming was rarely included in competitions combining various endurance sports. There are exceptions, as when the world's "most athletic man" was crowned in Great Britain in the nineteenth century by competing in rowing, running, cycling, walking, and swimming. The world's most athletic man is no longer crowned. Today, however, we see a number of competitions where swimming skills play a key role.

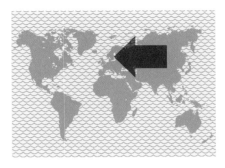

■ UTÖ INN, STOCKHOLM, SWEDEN, JULY 2003. A group of four people are sitting on an idyllic outdoor terrace in the Stockholm archipelago: two men in their 30s with their own businesses on the island and two younger lads, brothers who work extra in their free time. No one in the group has any real experience in practicing sports. Well, that's not entirely accurate. The youngest lad used to play baseball. If there was ever any muscle memory from the athletic performances of this group, it's now in a state of amnesia.

The conversation rhythmically moves between the latest gaffes of politicians, the opening hours of the island's grocery store, what's going on in the soccer league, what boats are new in the guest harbor, and who should order the next beer.

Then one of the young lads unfolds one of the restaurant napkins to show its printed map over the archipelago. He grabs a pen and starts drawing a few lines. "Look, guys. I'll be damned if it isn't possible to get all the way to Sandhamn."

"How? By boat? It's 50 miles, you goof."

"No, you swim and run. We'll do it in pairs. The last to get to Sandhamn picks up the check."

The final goal, the Sail Hotel in Sandhamn, had a bar that closed late and there were three more restaurants along the way. That insight motivated the older men. They decided to compete as a pair and to show the cocky young lads who's the boss. This rite of passage was to take place one month later.

Since none of them had ever done anything like this before, the four men had no idea what type of equipment was needed, or how long this feat would take, for that matter. Some islands were unexplored. After some guesstimation, they agreed that it would take between one and three days. As far as clothes were concerned, they settled on old spider web–covered windsurfing suits with uncomfortable zippers. Other things they brought along included vacuum-packed food, a camping stove, cellphones, and towels. All were packed in watertight sailor bags weighing approximately 20 pounds (9 kilograms) per adventurer.

A loud bang from an old shotgun and off they went, a tradition that lives on in the ÖTILLÖ (island to island race). The unfit men strolled away on Utö, down toward the small islets located between Utö and Ornö. Soon, the young lads started to feel as if victory was theirs, since one of the older men was far too slow when swimming.

The feat took more than 24 hours, which included a few hours of rest at night in sleeping bags under a spruce tree. Once they made it to Sandhamn, they were allowed to walk to the front of the line at the Diving Bar (and that's how their hangover came to last longer than the ache in their muscles). They'd reached their goal without realizing that they'd started something that

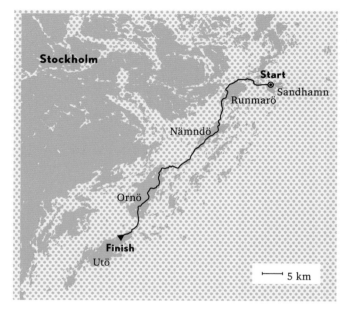

The original feat went from Utö to Sandhamn. Now it goes in the other direction.

is now the fastest-growing form of competition in the world.

The experienced adventurers Michael Lemmel and Mats Skott heard about the achievement of these four men. Michael had been one of the organizers of the multi-sport world championships, where Mats had competed. They both saw this as more than just a bar bet, and by 2006 they had organized it into a race. Nine teams signed up to get from Sandhamn to Utö. This time, the two brothers stood at the starting line together with multisport competitors, triathletes, and military personnel. Unlike the original race, resting at night was no longer allowed.

The organizers wanted the whole field to finish before nightfall. Only two teams managed to complete the race and the winning time was 12 hours. Several Swedish endurance personalities thought the race went one step too far. Physiology doctor and Ultraman Filip Larsen ("Doctor Phil") referred to it as "the most miserable race in Sweden" and said that it was impossible to prepare yourself for the unprecedented suffering facing the participants.

When Filip Larsen, teamed up with Antti Antonov to participate in the 2008 ÖTILLÖ race, they packed significantly lighter than any previous team: wetsuit, hood, water sack, and a four-gallon (15-liter) backpack for energy bars, emergency radio, and shoes and fins. The backpack created some nice sores on their shoulder blades and the wet suit burned their groins and the backs of their knees. After the race, Filip and Antti concluded

that switching between shoes and fins had taken far too long and that they should have worn their shoes while swimming. More people arrived at the same conclusion and the equipment soon became minimalistic.

Jesper Mars, Mats Andersson, Anders Malm, and Jan Lindeberg

Slowly but surely, the two brothers had become better prepared over the years. In 2008, they were well on their way to reaching the finish line when the youngest brother threw up everything he'd eaten at the last food station. But they didn't quit. After the older brother egged him on with the words, "My God, you're disgusting," they did what they had to do and finished the race.

(1) Determine your level

Swimruns may be more or less about competing. If you're not looking to shave off seconds, there is plenty to see and a competition can be an extraordinary adventure. Many competitions offer tracks in a location that's divinely beautiful and offer experiences that can change your life.

(2) Be in sync with your partner

You and your partner should have the same expectations concerning the race. Choose someone you enjoy spending time with—both during the race and when you prepare. If the two of you have differing skill levels (especially in the water), you might want to consider tying a rope between the two of you so that the faster swimmer can pull the slower one. This is a part of the sport. The equation for a swimrun is challenging but cordial as your running and swimming are added to that of your partner. A good swimrun experience is all about how you cooperate and merge your combined abilities.

(3) Do your homework on the race

Read the race website and create an idea of the course and what you need to know to finish it. How much is running and how much is swimming? Is the course hilly? What kind of water temperature should you expect? How many energy stations are there? Be prepared for the fact that in spite of your preparations, your bodies will offer surprises.

(4) Test the equipment

In order to finish the race, you need to test running and swimming in a wetsuit and shoes. And if you want to perform well, you need to test out all the equipment, including small details such as socks, carabiners, and the map case.

(5) Train

To get the most out of the race, you need to be well-trained. Design your training in accordance with your challenge: swim in water that's similar to that in the competition in terms of waves and temperature, and run in a similar terrain (i.e., forested or rocky). You also want to know how your body will function after a long period of intense activity. For many people, a marathon may go on for up to four hours. Swimrun races may last much longer than that, with expected race times of up to 14 hours. If possible, practice the expected race time at least once.

The History Behind Hand Paddles

The rules of most swimrun races allow hand paddles. At a presentation for swimmers, Michael Lemmel was asked why hand paddles were allowed at the ÖTILLÖ race. His answer: "Why not? I don't see it as a reason to restrict the competition."

Jan Swammerdam was a Belgian with many talents: biologist, anatomist, chemist, doctor, and explorer. Back in 1658, he showed the Duke of Tuscany how to stimulate a nerve using a pair of scissors. This was 129 years before Galvani claimed this discovery. In the nineteenth century, we have Duchenne de Boulogne, another jack of all trades, who was a doctor, engineer, physiologist, and therapist, and the first to use electrical muscle stimulation.

Inspired by Swammerdam and de Boulogne, the Belgian Léon Lewillie started exploring human movement. Lewillie referred to himself as a kinesiologist, inventor, ergonomist, biomechanist, physiologist, and historian. In addition, he was also a philosopher, humanist, and—by the standards of that time—an elite athlete. Lewillie's special distance was the 200m freestyle, in which he was the Belgian champion. But he liked everything that had to do with water sports. In 1941, he became a Belgian champion in water polo at the age of 16. Sure, this was remarkably young, but he was to become truly unique 40 years later, when he was once again on the winning team—now 56 years old. Ten years later, he found that he lacked the power to compete against younger men and instead started participating in masters swimming.

Lewillie's approach to sucess as a swimmer and in other water sports was all-around training. In the 1960s, he studied the effect of hand paddles. He concluded that paddles deliver a higher rate of efficiency; in other words, using paddles enables you to swim faster. Even if a set of paddles makes your shoulder and wing muscles sore, the increased speed is the result of a better technique rather than more power.

The single largest variable in terms of energy consumption is stroke frequency. A lower stroke frequency means lower energy consumption. Given that your shoulders can handle the load and that your swimming is not affected negatively, hand paddles represent the best tool for swimming fast and saving energy.

Later studies have confirmed Lewillie's results. There have even been studies that have attempted to find out whether training with paddles can help even when swimming without paddles. Research shows that the time of the anchoring phase of the arm stroke increases when using paddles whereas the time of the pull remains more or less the same. This results in you being able to keep a more even instantaneous speed when using paddles compared to when you're not, which means that you need to use less force for accelerating your body between arm strokes. There is also a correlation between both speed and efficiency and the size of the paddles. The larger the paddles, the faster the swimming and the less energy consumed. Of course, there's an upper limit, but given that the swimmer has a good technique, larger paddles will generally be beneficial.

GADGETS FOR A WELL-ROUNDED WORKOUT

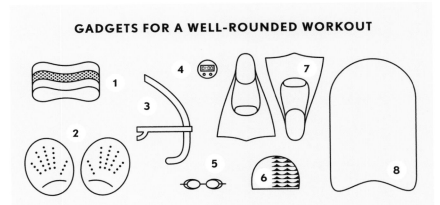

1: A PULL-BUOY is used either to increase speed through elevating the water position or to focus on how the body position is affected by the arm cycle.

2: HAND PADDLES can improve the feeling for the pull and to some extent improve strength.

3: The FRONT SNORKEL makes it easy to work on symmetry and alignment. Taping its mouth gives an incentive for more efficient swimming.

4: A TEMPO-TRAINER inside your swim cap gives a predestined stroke rate through beeping; for example, once every second.

5: The fit of SWIM GOGGLES is individual. When you find a good pair, make sure you have at least one spare.

6: A SWIM CAP is mandatory in many countries due to hygienic reasons.

7: SWIM FINS are shorter than the ones for diving. They are good for beginners and make new drills easier.

8: KICKBOARDS often isolate the kick, but can be used for more (see Shark Attack on page 317).

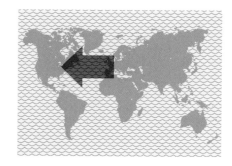

■ **LIVONIA, MICHIGAN, 1975.** As the youngest of eight siblings, Sheila Taormina and her twin brother began swimming at the Livonia YMCA at the age of six. Both enjoyed swimming so much that they switched to Clarenceville (a more competitive team) at the age of nine. The aim was a college scholarship.

After she met a coach from the University of Georgia at the U.S. championships, Sheila Taormina packed her bags to go to Athens, Georgia. Athens is a college town with 100,000 inhabitants located a little bit east of Atlanta. There were about 30,000 students and 2,500 teachers and other staff at the college. Taormina would go on to swim with the university team for four years under head coach Jack Bauerle, who was well on his way to becoming a legend.

For someone like Sheila, who was eager to train, the University of Georgia was a very good environment. The team consisted of 20 young men and 20 young women who worked hard to defend the school colors. There was always someone to compete against during training and to kid around with afterward. Everything was close, and it was possible to walk or bike between dorms, class-rooms, and the swimming pool. And the training sessions weren't crowded, even though Sheila had already left Athens before the new Gabrielsen Natatorium was inaugu-rated in 1995. The Natatorium was a swimming and diving facility named after a Norwegian who coached at UGA between 1948 and 1966.

Sheila became a college champion in the 400m medley and won the Southeastern Champion-ships during her last year. Unlike the majority of college swimmers, Sheila had not had enough of swimming, and decided to continue after graduation. Her goal was to represent the United States at the Atlanta Olympics in 1996, when she would be 27 years old—at that time, an almost fossil-like age for female swimmers.

She'd hoped to be able to live closer to her family, but was denied the opportunity to train with the University of Michigan's talented college team. Nor did she receive a spot at the permanent training camp of the U.S. national team in Colorado Springs. Sheila was simply not good enough. Instead, she would have to work out of her old club of Clarenceville based out of her old room in her parents' house. She walked to her training before dawn and ended her evening session after the sun was down. She did this day in and day out, week after week. Between her training sessions, she worked on the manufacturing floor in Detroit's automotive industry to finance traveling to competitions.

In the trials for the Olympics, her favorite event, the 400m medley was not an option, as there was only room for two female swimmers. When it came to the 200m freestyle, however, there were to be six female swimmers in the American relay team, which was predicted to win the gold. Four of these were to swim in the final while an additional two were to become part of the team as trial swimmers.

Sheila knew after the trial that taking one of the six positions in the team would be more difficult than she'd imagined. Sure, she'd broken her personal record with 2:01.36 and was in fifth place. But she was annoyed that the two 16-year-olds Ashley Whitney and Christina Teuscher had appeared out of nowhere and had been even faster in the morning. Among those behind her was the NCAA champion Jenny Thompson, who seemed to have lost some of her edge. The competitive Taormina let go of her doubts and focused on what she would have to do later in lane two in the lavish indoor pool in Indianapolis.

This is what Sheila's schedule looked like between the trial race and the final race: cool down by swimming for 20–30 minutes at various speeds to enable the body to recover better ahead of a new performance. A meal relatively soon after the race followed by a nap. Careful warm-up in the competition pool consisting of 15 minutes of slow swimming followed by 10 minutes of medley to soften the body. Finally, a few lengths to find the intensity and technique she was looking for that night. Then waiting with her warm-up clothes on and with the right music in her ears. Presentation. Up on the starting block.

Sheila looked at the scoreboard after the race: 2:02.08. She'd done worse than in the morning. This wasn't according to the plan. But her position was a relief as she had ended up in sixth place: 19 hundredths of a second before Jenny Thompson. Sheila was now an Olympic athlete despite not having the best financial, anatomical, or training conditions.

Once she had made the Olympic team, managing her everyday life became easier. No more working in the automotive industry, but a complete focus on preparing for Atlanta.

Once in Atlanta, however, it seemed as if the American gold in the 200m freestyle relay was under threat. The German swimmers Franziska van Almsick and Dagmar Hasse had won the silver and bronze medals in the 200m freestyle four days prior. The best American was Trina Jackson, who came in fourth, whereas the American favorite, Cristina Teuscher, seemed to have missed the taper and ended up sixth.

Sheila performed well in the relay trial race and was to join Teuscher, Jackson, and Jenny Thompson in the final. Once in the final, the Americans were able to win the gold after four lengths of hard work. As the national anthem faded out in Atlanta, Sheila's swimming career had also received the best possible goodbye ceremony. Back at the assembly line, her colleagues found her and her story so inspiring that a few months later she bought a used RV and traveled around the country telling her story to others. These inspirational lectures were completed in a few hours and paid significantly more than her job at the automotive company in the Motor City. She didn't stop training; she kept herself busy running, spinning, lifting weights, and swimming.

After having tried a charity triathlon, she was invited to a competition in South Africa. In the 1990s, the triathlon was an even more obscure part of the sporting world than today, even though it was possible to win an Olympic gold in the triathlon back in 1904. Back then, however, the events were long jump, shot put, and running 100 meters. The participant who placed the highest in all three events won the gold medal.

Seventy years after the 1904 Olympics, the athletes in the San Diego Track Club organized a competition in running, cycling, and swimming and called it a "triathlon." This was the first time in modern times that this word was used. In September 1994, it was decided that the triathlon was to be a test event at the Olympic Games in Sydney six years later. The distances were to be 1,500 meters of open water swimming, 24.8 miles (40 kilometers) of cycling and 6.2 miles (10 kilometers) of running.

In an eary triathlon, Sheila swam fast and still was in the lead after the bike. Unexpectedly, she was only passed by two professionals during the final running distance and ended up third. That race gave her cravings for more. Sheila now was a triathlete.

Even though swimming represents a relatively small part of triathlon races, Sheila enjoyed a big advantage in the initial discipline. Michigan-based coach Lew Kidder had coached triathletes ever since 1983 and taught Sheila how to save energy in the peloton, as well as how to find the right running speeds.

Generously enough, there were two qualifying competitions to get one of the three triathlon spots on the U.S. team that was going to the Sydney Olympics in 2000. The best American woman would get a spot on the Olympic team at the first qualifying competition which was held at the Olympic course in Sydney in April. At the transition following the swimming, Sheila was in the lead. Since she wanted to be in the lead ahead of the running distance, she cycled like crazy, but crashed badly. The remaining two spots were to be allocated six weeks later at the U.S. Olympic trials in Dallas.

An oppressive spring heat wave, lots of humidity, and hungry competitors made the Dallas competition a tough challenge for Sheila Taormina, who was ranked 48th. Together with the other strong swimmer in the race, Barb Lindquist, she drafted a plan that gave them a one-minute lead following the swimming in Lake Carolyn. Sheila and Barb then took turns breaking the wind when cycling and drove faster than was actually reasonable while the main field consisting of 13 strong triathletes had a hard time structuring their chase after the two in the lead.

When Sheila and Barb started running, the gap to the main field had been extended to as much as four minutes. They had foreseen that the running would be hot, but not as god-awfully hot as it actually was. The air trembled. Barb, who was ordinarily a strong runner, got dizzy and lost her stamina, which prompted her husband, Loren Lindquist, to take her off the course, crying. He immediately filed a complaint that there was no ice or water-filled sponges along the track. It was rejected. As a result, Sheila Taormina's second ticket to the Olympics—in a new sport—was confirmed.

At the Sydney Olympics, Sheila was obviously in the lead following the swimming. She fought hard, but was eventually passed by five cycling and running women. Nevertheless, she was the sixth best in the world in yet another sport in which she competed against the odds.

As a result of her enjoying her life as a triathlete, she now worked even harder on her cycling and running. As a famous swimming queen in a country where the triathlon had become the new hot item, she found it easy to finance her career by selling exercise plans by email and having well-paid one-on-one sessions with middle-aged men who'd traded their golf clubs for a bicycle and a wetsuit. They just needed to learn how to do the crawl properly and in a relaxed manner to not be completely exhausted in their legs once they had to get up on their bicycle.

In the end, Sheila Taormina never won an Olympic gold medal in the triathlon. Her swimming was strong as usual, but by the end she had to make do with coming in 23rd in the much stronger field at the Athens Olympics in 2004. Just like eight years before, she had her eyes set on a new Olympic event: the modern pentathlon.

As implied by the name, the modern pentathlon contains four events in addition to the 200 meters of swimming where she would collect points. And she was not accustomed to the 3,000m cross-country run. Shooting, fencing, and show jumping, on the other hand, represented quite a challenge. Yet, through her usual dedication to training, she managed to get a spot on the team to her fourth Olympic Games in her third Olympic sport.

Beijing was both good and bad for Sheila Taormina. Not surprisingly in the minus column was one of the events that was new to her. After a decent shooting event where she got 172 out of 200 points, she came in last in fencing. Here, all fencers meet one another, and after only 4 wins and 31 losses, her hopes of winning a medal were over. This was a major disappointment, as she believed that her fencing was finally up to par, after having gotten good results at a competition in Germany earlier that same year.

In her disappointment, she wanted to leave the competition, but with the support of her sister Sudee, she got up to swim.

Although she didn't have the same speed in her body as she did 12 years prior, the 39-year-old was still able to deliver the best swimming performance ever in an Olympic pentathlon competition. In addition, her 2:08.56 was better than any other female swimmer over the age of 35 that had performed that year. Just to compare: Kirsten Cameron won the masters world championships that year with 2:09.46.

In the next event, she hit the bullseye. As one of only three jumpers in the entire field, Sheila and the horse she'd been assigned through lottery were able to complete the course without any faults. Once the five events were finally added up, she came in at a decent 19th place.

Drafting

Swimming came free for Sheila Taormina when she started participating in the triathlon and modern pentathlon. The 20 hours a week she'd spent in the pool as a swimmer turned into 6 as a triathlete and 4 as a pentathlete. Everyone who's not capable of winning an Olympic gold in swimming before becoming a triathlete needs to pay attention to the details.

There was one factor benefitting Sheila Taormina's competitors during the swimming part: the starting procedure. When she competed in a pool, she was given her own lane, but in a triathlon competition, everyone starts together. Other swimmers colliding with her and sometimes trying to pull her feet was one thing, but learning to position herself behind someone who's faster was something completely different.

Already in 1991, American researchers studied the effect of so-called drafting on 600 meters of tough swimming. Among other things, they noted that the level of lactic acid dropped by more than 30 percent for swimmers positioned behind someone else, compared to a swimmer alone at the same speed. Furthermore, oxygen consumption dropped by 10 percent and the heart rate went down from 147 beats per minute to 138. In spite of this knowledge, using the wrong tactics has been disastrous for many swimmers—just ask American swimmer Chad Hundeby.

Hundeby was the favorite to win the 25km race at the 1995 world championships in Italy. At the time, you weren't allowed to swim less than three meters behind another competitor, and Chad Hundeby, who'd broken the record for crossing the English Channel, felt confident. His tactic was to swim energetically for the first two hours and then guard the big lead he expected to achieve. Unfortunately, the judges didn't follow the rules as hard as they should have, which led to a whole shoal of swimmers positioning themselves behind the soles of his feet.

With 1980s Hollywood films like *Karate Kid* and *Rocky IV* playing in his head, Hundeby fought hard to reach the happy ending. After 20 kilometers, he'd completely run out of energy and fell apart, after which the entire field passed the exhausted American. Hundeby's epic failure was a triggering factor when it came to amending the rules in order to allow drafting.

When positioning yourself in a field of swimmers, choose a position that doesn't put too much stress on you. Some like crowds and others don't. Then there are two ways to use drafting. One is to position yourself just behind a reasonably good swimmer. The second is to be next to the hip of the other swimmer. Triathletes are advised to adopt the somewhat easier position of behind, to "swim on someone's feet." Genenerally speaking, it's better to be positioned closer, because if the water isn't clear, it may be hard to see the foot soles you want to follow.

Junior European open water champion Ivan Sitic is colorblind and finds it difficult to swim in brownish waters, far from the crystal clear sea in his homeland of Croatia. In those kinds of conditions, he needs to touch the sole of the foot of the swimmer ahead of him once every six arm strokes in order to maintain the most favorable position.

Top triathletes try to ensure that they are as rested as possible when they sit down on their bicycle, so they focus on not exerting themselves during swimming. For swimmers competing for positions, on the other hand, it might be difficult to move up from a position of two meters behind someone to being the first to cross the finishing line. That's why swimmers need to learn how to use drafting while swimming next to someone else.

WATER POLO

The largest aquatic team sport is water polo. It is the most popular and best-played in south and central Europe, with Hungary, Italy, Greece, and the nations that formerly made up Yugoslavia at the top. When Serbia and Croatia met in the 2015 world championship final, it was the biggest news item in Serbian and Croatian media. Not just the biggest sports news, but the biggest news—period—in all categories. World-class water polo players are impressive athletes who spend almost as much time in the water as swimmers. That's why it wouldn't be surprising if they weren't also decent swimmers, perhaps even good ones.

The male Hungarian team won the first three Olympic tournaments of the twenty-first century. The average height of a player in the starting lineup was about 6'5" (196 cm). When Croatia won the Olympic gold in London in 2012, the average height was a whopping 6'8" (203 cm) . Standing 6'9" (206 cm) and weighing 250 pounds (113 kilograms), Damir Buric was literally one of the pillars that helped Croatia illustrate that modern water polo had developed into a more physical sport.

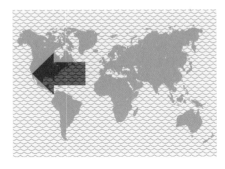

■ **LOS ANGELES, CALIFORNIA, MARCH 1972.** Kurt Krumpholz played water polo on the UCLA college team. Krumpholz, a so-called "country club swimmer" (as he picked up swimming in the pool at his parents' golf club), had picked water polo over swimming, even though he still tried to swim with the college team whenever he had time. And he was good when doing so, so good that he placed seventh in the 500 yard freestyle at the college championships.

Many Europeans find the 500 yard freestyle to be a particularly gruesome attraction at the amusement park of swimming. On the rest of the planet, the equivalent of this medium distance event is made up of 16 lengths and a total of 400 meters—but not in the United States. With a distance of 457 meters, this event includes an additional four painful lengths you need to prepare for mentally.

For quite some time, Krumpholz's goal had nothing to do with swimming, but concerned joining the national water polo team. But when his name was missing from the 1972 Olympic team, he gave himself a new goal: joining the national team in swimming. So once he was done with his exams at the end of May, he went to Santa Clara, a town outside of San Francisco, to train with Coach George Haines.

Kurt Krumpholz wasn't qualified for the Olympic qualifiers and only had two months to get his swimming up to par. Thanks to the explosive energy he'd acquired from chasing the ball in water polo, he didn't have any problems qualifying for the Olympic qualifying races in 100m and 200m freestyle.

However, Coach Haines also wanted him to swim the 400m freestyle, something Krumpholz wasn't all that thrilled about. He wanted to give everything he had to qualify for the Olympic team in 100m and 200m freestyle, where being among the top six competitors sufficed to get a spot. In the 400m freestyle, however, you had to be among the top three. The people around him were also skeptical whether a water polo player could manage 400m freestyle in a 50-meter swimming pool. A large pool means less explosive turns and needing to rely more on your swimming.

The difference between training with the water polo team and submitting himself to the training regime of George Haines was massive. Haines had already coached the U.S. Olympic team three times: Rome 1960, Tokyo 1964, and Mexico City 1968. In Tokyo, his swimmer Don Schollander became the first Olympic athlete to return home with four gold medals from the same games. All in all, 55 swimmers from the Santa Clara Swim Club went to the Olympics when he served as coach. They won a total of 33 Olympic gold medals, 11 silver medals, and 7 bronze medals. So Haines was an established guru within the world of swimming.

Swimmers from all over the country applied to join his training program and up to 60 swimmers could fill the pool in Santa Clara.

Basically all swimmers carried out the same training program, from young teens to returning college swimmers. Haines's philosophy was based on long distances. Even the 10-year-olds were made to swim long distances, as Haines argued that without a hefty base, it was impossible to develop them into swimmers of international level. This was a philosophy he defended throughout his entire coaching career by referring to swimmers such as Matt Biondi, Tom Jager, and Mark Spitz, who all started out swimming long distances and later, as adults, specialized in shorter races.

The playful ease and explosive speed in Krumpholz's body disappeared during the first week of training. As somewhat of a rough diamond from the golf club pool, he completely lacked what Haines saw as the ideal background.

Krumpholz only had two chances to qualify for the Olympic qualifying races for the 400m freestyle. His first chance was a competition in his home pool of Santa Clara. However, George Haines's tough training hadn't made him fast, just worn out. He felt like a geriatric patient when standing behind the starting block. And, as it turned out, he was nowhere close to making the qualifying time of 4:08. When he whined about this to Coach Haines, he received a brief answer: "You got to trust the master plan, son!"

A part of George Haines's clever plan was that the swimmers would develop an ability to adapt to muscular fatigue and oxygen debt without losing good technique. Most people are able to maintain their technique when fresh and rested, but swimming symmetrically and efficiently when your muscles are rebelling is more difficult. Haines argued that achieving this requires continuous and persistent training. When their bodies rebelled, his swimmers would be able to access the powers hidden deeply in muscle aches and psychological barriers.

The second and last chance to qualify for the Olympics was a competition in Los Angeles. This time, Krumpholz turned to veteran Swedish swimmer Gunnar Larsson, three-time European champion and a favorite in the Munich Olympics, both in medley and freestyle. The generous Swede asked, "What do you need to do to qualify?" The water polo player gratefully replied, "Under 4:10 and I'm there," whereupon the large and friendly Swede replied, "Alrighty then. Keep up with me and you'll make the qualifying time." And this time, Krumpholz did better. With his legs shaved, he got a time of 4:09.08, which meant that for the first time, he too began to fully believe in the monster training program he'd subjected himself to.

Once in Portage Park in Chicago for the thrilling Olympic qualifying races, things didn't turn out as planned at all when it came to the 100m race. The 200m freestyle race was better; after having finished the trials, he felt as if he had enough energy left in him to increase his pace in the final race. Nevertheless, it turned out that he didn't have the margins on his side. His trial time of 1:55.9, which had been sufficient for a third place at the previous Olympic qualifiers, meant that he came in ninth, only five hundredths of a second from being able to swim in the final race.

In the trials for the abhorrent 400m, Krumpholz swam in lane six in the same heat as Olympic champion Mike Burton, who was of course swimming in the middle lane. Haines had no hopes for the final except that Krumpholz would beat his personal record—perhaps a time under 4:04? But the race turned out better than that. Krumpholz was charging ahead and his swimming looked relaxed and powerful at the same time. When the speaker announced that the split times were at world record speeds, the surprised swimmers in the stands started cheering. The 400m freestyle world record was one of only a few not held by an American. In February that same year, Brad Cooper from Australia had reduced the world record of American Tom McBreen to 4:01.7 at the early Australian Olympic qualifiers.

The advantage of having early qualifiers, like in Australia, is that they give the swimmers who've qualified plenty of time to prepare for the Olympics. An argument against early qualifiers is that there is a risk of missing out on swimmers with steep development curves, such as Kurt Krumpholz. The water polo player heard the noise from the stands, but it wasn't until he glanced inwards after the 300m turn that he realized that the crowd was cheering for him. The favorite Mike Burton was a far 7–8 meters behind. This gave Krumpholz enough energy to give everything he had in the two final lengths. Once he touched the plate, he could cheer alongside the crowd over his sensational swimming: 4:00.11, a new world record—by a water polo player!

Kurt Krumpholz recovered and continued swimming and playing water polo. He won the silver medal in 200m freestyle at the world championships in Belgrade 1973 where he also won the gold medal in the relay race over the same distance. He won the U.S. Nationals twice with UCLA, where he coached both swimming and water polo after he finished his athletic career. His son

J.W. won the Olympic silver medal in water polo in Beijing 2008.

However, Krumpholz wasn't the fastest water polo player. That title instead goes to fellow American

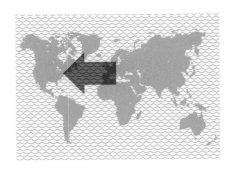

■ **ABU DHABI, FEBRUARY, 2015.** The 130 swimmers are on their way up from the water after the world cup race. Despite the fact that they've swum for 10 kilometers, most of the men come out of the water more or less at the same time. One of them looks as if he belongs in the movie *Pirates of the Caribbean*. A long, tangled beard hangs down like a blackout curtain over his Adam's apple. He answers to the nickname of "Hoots" and is an Australian living in the city of Perth. His real name is Simon Huitenga, and he's

Brad Schumacher, who was a sprinter and won two Olympic relay golds in Atlanta in 1996, then came in sixth with his water polo team four years later in Athens.

Australia's greatest Olympic hope in this event.

Since Australia didn't have anyone among the top 10 at the world championships in Kazan in the summer of 2015, its swimmers have no choice but to deliver in a qualifying event in the Portuguese city of Setubal in June. In the Olympics, 25 swimmers compete in both the men's and the women's events, and each country may only be represented by a maximum of two swimmers, but only if the two of them have qualified in the first of two competitions. The road to the Olympics in open water swimming is winding even though it's almost dead straight compared to the background of Hoots. In order to understand his background, we need to understand the swimming situation in Australia as compared to other countries.

Sweden has the second highest energy tax rates in Europe; only Denmark has a higher tax on energy that heats service facilities. The Netherlands, the United Kingdom and Switzerland have no tax at all. Nor does the United States. The lack of indoor pools in Sweden is due in large part to this energy tax. However, the national curriculum says that all students before seventh grade should be able to swim 200 meters (50 meters on their back) and be able to cope with water emergency situations.

Just like other children, major Swedish swimmers have generally earned the swimming badges of Baddaren (the Ripper), Fisken (Fish) and perhaps Kandidaten (the Candidate). In recent years, new badges like Bläckfisken (the Octopus), Sköldpaddan (Turtle) and Hajen (Jaws) have helped swimmers set new goals to fill up their displays before they enter junior high school. There has been an exponential growth in interest in all levels of swimming during the past 10 years. A new indoor pool opened in Tyresö in 2013. Already after a year or two, there were more than 500 children and adults on waiting lists due to insufficient capacity. The shower rooms are so crowded that privacy and personal space is something you can only dream about. Large cities like Stockholm, Gothenburg, Malmö, and Norrköping have experienced crowded conditions in their facilities for a long time, and the situation is starting to border on being unacceptable.

"Hoots"—Ironman and open water swimmer

In Australia, on the other hand, the situation is the complete opposite—swimming pools are rarely crowded. The ocean outside of Perth is around 65–75°F (18–24°C) all year round, but Hoots is still able to reach more than twenty 50-meter pools within a radius of 50 minutes of driving. Australia has 10,000 beaches and 85 percent of the population is able to get to the sea in less than one hour. Having the ability to swim is taken very seriously and is recommended by the age of six.

Hoots's dad competed in swimming and he learned how to swim at an early age. Still, Hoots didn't want to be a swimmer, but an Ironman. Not the kind of Ironman triathletes compete in—we're talking about a different type of Ironman.

Surfing at Australian beaches is lovely, but dangerous. Powerful currents can quickly pull down even the strongest surfers. In response to the large number of drowning accidents, Surf Lifesaving clubs began appearing at the end of the nineteenth century. The first two were formed in Sydney shortly after 1900. The organization concerning lifesaving and knowing how to swim has a long and strong tradition in Australia.

The lifeguards competed in running, swimming, surfski (lifesaving competitions with a long, narrow kayak), and paddleboard. The different parts were then combined to crown the most well-rounded athlete. Running on the beach was combined with a section each of: swimming (400m), paddleboarding (600m) and surfskiing (800m), where the competitors were to round floating buoys.

The first Ironman Championship was held in 1966 and the competition has only become more popular ever since. Ky Hurst won the Australian Ironman Championship four years in a row in 1999–2002. Hurst was also a solid pool swimmer. He trained together with world record–holder Grant Hackett and tried to qualify for the Olympics in 1,500m freestyle in both 2000 and 2004. His best time on this distance was 15:17. Following this, Hurst decided to instead focus on open water swimming. He participated in both the 2008 and 2012 Olympics in Beijing and London respectively where his best result was coming in eleventh. Hurst is still famous and can be seen in sports programs as well as pop culture shows like *Dancing with the Stars*.

Simon "Hoots" Huitenga wanted to follow in the footsteps of Ky Hurst and started to train with great intensity at the age of 15. He swam five mornings a week, and worked on various components in the afternoon, adding up to more than 20 hours of training a week, month after month. Even though he won the Western Australia championships, he was still unable to challenge the absolute top swimmers due to his small frame. Being 5'9" (175 cm) and weighing 160 pounds (73 kilograms) was a disadvantage when it came to handling the water vessels as well as his role model Ky Hurst did, who was 6'6" (198 cm) and weighed 200 pounds (90 kilograms).

Inspired by Hurst's path to the Olympics, Hoots decided at the age of 22 to change his track to open water swimming. There was only one problem: Hoots wasn't a particularly strong swimmer. In order to fix this, he turned to Matt Magee in the Perth City Swimming Club, whom he considered the best coach in the area. However, the grizzled Magee found Hoots about as welcome as a tapeworm—he just couldn't see how Hoots would fit into the training team: too old, too mediocre, too inquisitive. Nothing but trouble for a group running like clockwork. Disappointed, Hoots went down to the ocean where, during a long swimming session, he formulated his plan for persuading Magee. Back at the Perth City Swimming Club, he finally managed to persuade the coach.

Training for Magee was tough— at least seven two-hour training sessions a week at a significantly higher speed than what Hoots was accustomed to. The first months were repetitive—exercise-food-sleep-exercise-food-sleep—but it led to results. Hoots was finally able to keep up with the adolescents in the training group. The initially reluctant Magee saw his potential and understood that in spite of everything, Hoots had the right stuff.

After one year of training for Magee, Hoots became the third-best Australian in his first major international 10 kilometer open water race. At the world championships in Kazan in 2015 some years later, he became the best Australian by placing 15th, and his never-ending quest for a ticket to the Olympics was supported by an entire country obsessed with swimming.

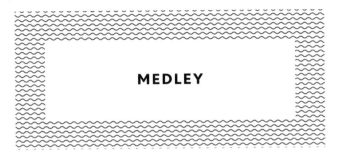

MEDLEY

The 400m medley is said to be the most demanding athletic event there is. During a race, the swimmer completes 100 meters each of butterfly, backstroke, breaststroke, and freestyle. The profile of requirements is very detailed, and these days swimmers need to perform at fantasy levels in order to do well internationally. Just look at Katinka Hosszu and Michael Phelps, world record holders on this distance, both of whom have stamina, are fast and strong, and possess an almost flawless technique.

Swimmers have different talents in the different swimming styles, so the development of a medley race usually varies more compared to a 400m freestyle race. Some swimmers use up too much energy when doing the demanding butterfly whereas others are strong breaststroke swimmers who are able to settle the race in that segment. It's crucial in this event to plan how to use your energy in the best way possible.

The history lesson with a capital H when it comes to planning a medley race has one Swede and two Americans playing the leading roles. Mark Spitz crushed his opponents in the Munich "Swimming Hall," but as a single race it was the 400m medley that would echo through history.

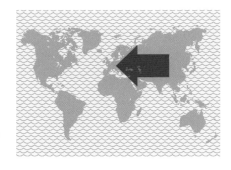

■ MUNICH, WEST GERMANY, AUGUST 30, 1972. As in so many races, there was a favorite in the Munich Olympic pool. In this race, it was American swimmer Gary Hall, who'd broken the 400m medley world record with 4:30.81 earlier that summer.

The 200m butterfly event had been settled two days before, and what Hall wanted to do in the 400m medley was to put an end to the Olympic gold medal dreams of his teammate Mark Spitz.

Spitz and Hall weren't only competing for the same country, but also for the same university in Indiana, being coached by James "Doc" Counsilman. In the 200m butterfly event, where the mustachioed Spitz had been the favorite, Hall had performed beautifully, beaten his

personal record by two seconds, and won the silver medal behind the outstanding Spitz.

The time had now come for Gary Hall to win his first Olympic gold and be the first to go below 4:30. The catch with this plan was that he was the favorite. It's easier to chase than to be chased. During the 200m butterfly race, he was able to complete his own race in the shadow of the giant Spitz. But today Hall was in the spotlight. He was the big topic of discussion in not only the U.S., but in the Olympic village as a whole. Being the favorite made Hall so nervous that he couldn't eat a single bite the entire day.

Even though the differences were significant in the qualifying races, several good swimmers had made it to the final. Europe fielded the 16-year-old Hungarian Andreas Hargitay and the 1970 European champion, Swede Gunnar Larsson from the city of Malmö. Larsson had won the European championship gold medal in 4:36 and had trained hard ever since. In California, he'd trained with and competed against swimmers who were better than the ones back home in the sparsely populated northern end of Europe.

Hall, Hargitay, and Larsson were all athletes with the bodies of modern swimmers: broad shoulders and standing between 6'1" (185 cm) and 6'2" (188 cm) in height. The one outlier was Florida swimmer Tim McKee, who was only 5'8" (173 cm) and was ranked number two in the world after Hall, after he'd achieved a time of 4:32 earlier that summer.

After suffering from being so nervous, Gary Hall decided to go all in and his strong butterfly swim gave him a spectacular lead. He was almost two seconds ahead of the swimmer in second place, Hargitay, at 58.38 when he turned. McKee was almost four seconds behind Hall, and Larsson appeared completely lost, as he was five seconds behind. Hall fought on and he was 1.5 seconds below his own world record pace after the backstroke. Hargitay and McKee turned alongside each other four seconds behind, whereas Gunnar Larsson was only sixth and not even the best Swede, as Hasse Ljungberg

was fourth. Larsson was 8.5 seconds behind Hall. This almost corresponds to 15 meters and at this point, only 200 meters remained in the race.

Breaststroke is the slowest swimming style, and it's also the part of a medley race where you can gain (or lose) the most time. Breaststroke was also Gary Hall's weakest style and probably the main reason why he was so nervous. At the same time, breaststroke was Gunnar Larsson's strongest style, along with freestyle, for which he'd broken the 400m world record with 4:02.6 two years before.

When Hall came up after his underwater pull, he experienced a very unpleasant oxygen debt. He'd hit the wall. He knew that he had a big lead, but he also knew that he had almost 200 meters left to go outside his comfort zone and that he was being followed by a pack of hungry wolves. Hall had made a beginner's mistake. After a catastrophic breast-stroke time of 1:25.72, he'd lost his lead to McKee, who managed to do 1:19.25. Larsson was still outside the podium after the breaststroke, but his

RESULTS LIST—400M MEDLEY AT 1972 OLYMPICS

	Butterfly	Backstroke	Breaststroke	Freestyle
1) Gunnar Larsson, SWE	1:03.41	2:14.67 (1:10.66)	3:32.17 (1:17.50)	**4:31.981 (59.81)**
2) Tim McKee, USA	1:02.06	2:10.66 (1:08.60)	**3:29.91 (1:19.25)**	**4:31.983 (1:02.07)**
3) Andreas Hargitay, HUN	1:00.22	2:10.80 (1:10.58)	3:31.62 (1:20.82)	4:32.70 (1:00.45)
4) Steve Furniss, USA	1:00.78	2:10.09 (1:09.31)	3:32.88 (1:22.79)	4:35.44 (1:02.56)
5) Gary Hall, USA	**58.38**	**2:06.32 (1:07.94)**	3:31.04 (1:25.72)	4:37.38 (1:06.v34)
6) Hans Ljungberg, SWE	1:01.05	2:11.15 (1:10.10)	3:36.11 (1:24.96)	4:37.96 (1:01.85)

WORLD RECORDS 2016

	Butterfly	Backstroke	Breaststroke	Freestyle
Women: Ye Shinen, CHI	1:02.19	2:11.73 (1:09.54)	3:29.75 (1:18.02)	4:28.43 (59.67)
Men: Michael Phelps, USA	54.92	1:56.49 (1:01.57)	3:07.05 (1:10.56)	4:03.84 (56.77)

1:17.50 wasn't just the fastest breast-stroke distance ever, it also put him in a position to fight for a medal.

While Hall and his devastated arms fell down to an abhorrent fifth place, McKee in the lead tried to defend himself against Hargitay and Larsson, who were getting closer. Larsson fought the hardest and approached McKee with an unrealistic speed. With 25 meters to go it looked as if McKee was about to win. With 10 meters to go, it was impossible to say who'd be first. And after they'd reached the finish? Both Larsson and McKee were registered at 4:31.98. Gunnar Larsson had swum the last 100 meters in under a minute. But who'd won?

Did the organizers perhaps have two gold medals engraved for the 400m medley?

The judges conferred for eight uncertain minutes before delivering their result. For the first and last time in world history, thousandths of a second were used for settling who won a race. It was ruled that Gunnar Larsson won the race with the tiny—and for McKee, grim—margin of two thousandths of a second. The Swedish national anthem was played over the loudspeakers as the blonde 21-year-old from Malmö received Sweden's first Olympic gold medal in swimming in 44 years, following an ice-cold and masterfully planned race.

SWIMRUN

From Bar Bet to World Championships

By its tenth anniversary in 2015, the ÖTILLÖ race had received not only a certain degree of status but also a cult following throughout the world. From the origins of the bet at Utö Inn, there are now hundreds of swimrun races organized in Sweden, Norway, Finland, Denmark, Belgium, the UK, the U.S., Germany, Australia, Spain, and France. And there will most likely be more, as the sport has proved to be a popular way of combining exploring nature with competing together with others.

Finding the optimal equipment requires rigorous testing. It's far from certain that the equipment that's seemingly the best fit is what really and

Björn Rosenthal and Jonatan Torshall Svensson advance up a cliff during the 2015 ÖTILLÖ race.

ultimately works out best for you and your partner. An easily navigated track and a watch give you an indication as to what is the fastest and most comfortable.

First, you need to pick out the right wetsuit and shoes. The wetsuit needs to be a tad larger than one used for swimming only as you'll be running in it. The shoes need to have a good grip and a low weight when wet. In races with longer runs, having a zipper on the chest of the wetsuit will offer relief, especially if the weather is hot.

After you've selected your shoes and wetsuit, there are additional equipment choices that aren't as critical. A rope can be used in two ways. If two people on a team don't have the same capacity for swimming, it's usually beneficial to be tied together with a rope so the stronger swimmer may pull the weaker one. In this configuration, the team only has half as much frontal resistance, versus if the two swimmers are positioned side by side. This configuration could save some energy that may be used later in the race. The rope is also useful when running; if the two teammates are tied together, the stronger runner doesn't need to look back to keep track of his or her teammate.

Pull buoys are commonly used in races with long swimming distances. Weak and heavier swimmers in particular benefit from using pull buoys, as they get a higher position in the water and thus experience less resistance Strong swimmers, on the other hand, swim almost as fast without this accessory.

The swimming sections in swimrun competitions are not as easily navigated as swimming sections during a triathlon. Swimmers with impaired vision may benefit greatly by getting prescription lenses in their swimming goggles. Even if the strongest swimmer in the team has good eyesight and is able to navigate faultlessly, prescription lenses may offer the teammate an opportunity to experience the often beautiful courses in the best way possible. Triathletes are well-acquainted with the time lost transitioning between swimming/cycling and cycling/running. Triathletes only transition twice whereas swimrun participants may need to enter and leave the water up to 40 times. Successful transitions are based on talent and expertise where the goal is for you and your partner to maintain movement without compromising your control.

In just a few years, swimrun has gone from a gathering of individual goofballs to a larger subculture on the cusp of becoming a wider movement. Swimrun became the fastest growing sport on the planet and offers people who appreciate nature and all-round endurance sports a new favorite adventure.

YOUR SWIMMING: FROM WATER TO LAND

The process of transitioning from water to land may be divided into four parts for the lead swimmer:

1. Aim carefully. Find the best place to get up on land. Aim to get close to the track markings, but not on an area that's too steep.

2. Safe steps. Make sure that you get a good grip with your feet to enable you to stand up without any problems.

3. Help your teammate. Once you're steady on the ground, make sure that your partner gets up in the best way possible.

4. Quick steps. A skillful swimrunner flies onward in his or her first steps on the cliffs.

YOUR SWIMMING: SWIMRUN RULES

Team: Each team consists of two participants.

Course: The team must follow the marked course.

Mandatory equipment: Wetsuit that fits the conditions. During hot days in temperate water, wearing a wetsuit may be hazardous.

Compass

First aid kit

Whistle

Safety: The team must stick together and members may be no farther than approximately 39 feet (12 meters) from each other. The team must assist others in emergency situations if asked to do so by competition officials.

EIGHT ALL-AROUND SWIMMERS

BRAD SCHUMACHER made history when he came in sixth with the U.S. water polo team in Sydney in 2000. Four years earlier, he'd won two gold medals in relay races at the Atlanta Olympics. These days, he coaches youths in water polo. After he lost a 9-year-old player to a rare disease, he decided to donate some of his bone marrow to save other children.

SHEILA TAORMINA is the only swimmer to have used her skills to participate in an additional two Olympic events: the triathlon and modern pentathlon. In Atlanta in 1996, she won the 4 × 200m freestyle.In Sydney in 2000 and in Athens in 2004, she participated in the triathlon, and in Beijing in 2008, she competed in the modern pentathlon.

ARNE BORG was the most well-rounded aquatic athlete of his time. At the European championships in Bologna in 1927, he first took Sweden to the 4 × 200m freestyle final, after which he lost four teeth in a water polo game against France. When he was to swim the 1,500m freestyle that same evening, he was so provoked by the sight of Italian flags on the podium that he abandoned his plan for the race. He started the race at a furious pace and during the race, he broke the world records in 400m, 500m, 800m, and 1,000m races. He won the race with a time of 19:07.2—almost three minutes ahead of the best Italian. Borg's world record was to last for 11 years.

RACHEL KOMISARZ started swimming at an age when most women had already stopped competing. She was training to be a gymnast, but damaged two vertebrae in her back and had to quit. Her doctor recommended that she start swimming to build up the muscles surrounding her spine. Eight years later, at the age of 26, she won a world championships medal in 400m freestyle. The following year, she won an Olympic gold in the 4 × 200m freestyle at the 2004 Olympics in Athens.

RYK NEETHLING had his breakthrough as a long-distance swimmer. In the Sydney Olympics in 2000, he came in fifth in 1,500m freestyle. He was hard to stop during training and used to do routines such as 15 × 100m with a start every 1:05. After that, his vast all-around abilities became even more noticeable. Four years later, he won an Olympic gold in 4 × 100m freestyle, and before he finished his career, he had also broken the 100m medley world record.

SHANE GOULD held every single world record in freestyle swimming by the age of 15—from 100m to 1,500m—something that's never happened before or since. In addition, she won a gold medal in the 200m medley at the 1972 Olympics in Munich.

RYAN LOCHTE has swum in the shadow of Michael Phelps his entire career. However, he is the swimmer who's won international championship medals in the largest number of different events (11): 100m, 200m, and 400m medley; 100m and 200m backstroke; 200m freestyle; 4 × 50m freestyle; 4 × 100m freestyle; 4 × 200m freestyle; 4 × 100m medley; and 4 × 100m freestyle mix.

KATINKA HOSSZU has tirelessly produced a wide spectrum of world-class results for many years. She's won international championship medals in 10 different events: 200m freestyle, 400m freestyle, 100m medley, 200m medley, 400m medley, 50m backstroke, 100m backstroke, 200m backstroke, 200m butterfly, and 4 × 200m freestyle.

CHAPTER 7

MAN AND
THE SEA

Nothing great comes easy.

– Okänd

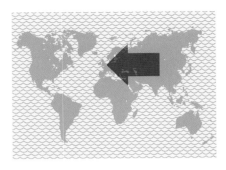

■ CALAIS, FRANCE, AUGUST 25, 1875.

The crew of the ship belonging to the British Royal Mail was hanging over the rails singing "Rule Britannia." Well, singing may not be an entirely accurate description. Resembling the soccer hooligans of our own time, they were cheering as loud as they could:

Rule, Britannia!
Britannia, rule the waves:
Britons never, never, never
will be slaves.

The object of their song, a man with a large mustache wearing a red-and-white-striped torso-covering swimsuit in knitted wool, now tried to stand up at the edge of the water. Matthew Webb had just finished swimming across the English Channel in 21 hours and 45 minutes. His swim would have been 21 miles if he'd followed a straight line. Instead, the 27-year-old captain in the Royal Navy had swum over 39 miles according to the notes of the boats accompanying him. Webb missed the goal by a half mile and was too tired to stand up. Still, victory was assured. Supported by a cousin and two Frenchmen, he was able to walk the last few meters to the beach of Calais.

Captain Webb, who had a hard time staying awake, got a comfortable room at the Hôtel de Paris. Before he went to sleep, he was

Matthew Webb, Channel swimmer

given hot wine. A doctor examined him and registered jellyfish burns on

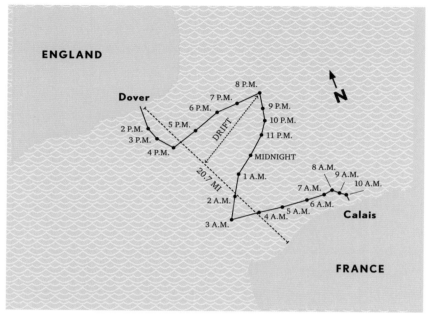

Captain Webb's Channel Crossing

his arms. He also noted that Webb had a normal body temperature, but that his heart rate was very low. When Webb woke up five hours later with a high fever, he drank a little bit more of the hot wine and was able to go back to sleep. When he woke up in the morning, he was in good shape, albeit a little bit sore.

Swimming across the English Channel launched a celebrity status larger than what was common at the time. Everybody wanted to meet Captain Webb: mayors, royalty, and fans. People wrote songs about him, he became a cartoon character, and he was offered money to perform exhibition swims.

Current swimming stars are seen on cereal boxes, in TV ads, and on the front pages of newspapers. The best means of exposure in the nineteenth century, however, was matchboxes, which is how the text "Captain Webb Matches—British Made—First Channel Swimmer" came to adorn the boxes of match manufacturer

Bryant & May's. Comedian Peter Sellers would later come across this box and use the stern face of Captain Webb as a model for his character Inspector Clouseau in the *Pink Panther* movies.

Paradoxically, Captain Webb's successful channel crossing caused a swim safety crisis. His achievement resulted in a drastic increase in drowning accidents as cocky men throughout England tried to swim across bodies of water in order to win bets or win the hearts of young women.

DEATH BY DROWNING

These days, about 370,000 people drown each year. According to the World Health Organization (WHO), this represents 7 percent of all injury-related deaths. West Africa, an area where many people have poor swimming skills, has the highest proportion of drowning accidents relative to population.

There is a clear correlation between the number of drowning accidents and the resources spent on teaching swimming. In the USA, around 5,000 people die by drowning annually; three fourths are men. A worrying development is that an increasing number of children still haven't learned to swim according to standards. In order to look upon this as something more than mere statistics, try to imagine what someone drowning goes through during the last moments of life. Drowning occurs in five phases:

SURPRISE You become terrified as you realize that you've ended up in an undesirable predicament. You try to stand up in the water and use your hands to pull yourself above the water surface as if it were made out of ice. You bend your neck backward and try to get your mouth as close to the surface as possible. You make no sound whatsoever—no cry for help. You're just trying to breathe.

INVOLUNTARY HOLDING OF YOUR BREATH You're now completely submerged in the water, even your hands. You realize that you're no longer visible above the surface. You understand that the chances of someone noticing and helping you have decreased significantly. You have water in your mouth and throat. Your body makes sure that you stop breathing through a reflex that folds down your epiglottis. Even if you get even more panicked, you can't emit a single sound. Without any oxygen, you'll lose consciousness within a minute.

UNCONSCIOUSNESS The lack of oxygen makes your body go into sleep mode. All non-crucial bodily functions are switched off. You float around in the water like seaweed. This sleep mode extends the time you have left to live. If someone strong and skillful saw you disappear, they could rescue you and you could still be revived at this point.

If no one finds you, you sink toward the bottom. Whether you sink slowly or quickly depends on the amount of air trapped in your lungs, how much you and your clothes weigh, and the amount of muscle in your body (as muscles weigh more than water). If you don't start breathing soon, you'll soon be gone. If the epiglottis detaches, water will rush into your lungs and you'll die faster.

You'll die faster in freshwater (two to three minutes) than salt water (eight to ten minutes). Freshwater is closer in composition to the blood in your body than salt water; it more easily crosses the membrane of the capillary walls and is absorbed into the bloodstream, quickly causing blood vessel damage.

CRAMPS As the ratio of carbon dioxide to oxygen in your blood increases, you'll get cramps. Your skin turns blue, especially your lips and nail beds. Your body gets stiff. You may start to shake violently and foam may come out of your mouth.

CLINICALLY DEAD You're not breathing. Your heart is no longer pumping, and has stopped for the first time since you were born. Vital organs such as your brain, liver, kidneys, and thyroid receive no blood and no oxygen. This lack of oxygen turns your skin blue. You're now dead.

THE CENTURY OF FEATS

The feat of Matthew Webb put open water swimming in the global spotlight. Previously, news concerning swimming adventures (or other news for that matter) had not spread all that quickly.

Ten thousand years ago, someone painted what archeologists believe to be swimmers on rocks in southern Egypt. Their style of swimming looks a bit like the dog paddle or possibly a primitive form of the breaststroke. The oldest known image of a crawler is also found in Egypt, this time on an artifact made out of dried mud. Archeologists have determined that the crawler image originates anywhere between 9,000 and 4,000 years ago.

That means that this year, we may celebrate the 6,500-year anniversary of freestyle swimming, plus or minus 2,500 years.

As the temperature in Egypt frequently exceeds 100°F (38°C), one could easily imagine that there would be loads of beaches along the Nile as a way of keeping the ancient swimming traditions alive. Paradoxically, however, people today rarely swim in the blue ribbon stretching over 4,000 miles (6,437 kilometers) because of problems related to the Aswan Dam installation.

Egypt needed more electricity in the 1950s, so the dam was built on the Nile. In addition to providing electricity, the dam solved another problem: regulating the amount of water available for farming. Before the dam, the river had previously flooded every year and thus distributed nutrition and minerals to the riverbed. Unfortunately the amount of rain varies each year, so the harvest was flooded some years and dried up in others.

When Soviet leader Nikita Khrushchev visited the Aswan Dam in 1964, he was thoroughly impressed and referred to it as "the eighth wonder of the world." But building the dam wasn't all good news. It turned out that freshwater snails carrying parasitic flatworms called schistosomes liked to live in the standing 70°F (21°C) water in the dam, and they multiplied at an alarming rate. These worms have the nasty ability to penetrate human skin where the parasite causes the fever disease known as schistosomiasis (bilharzia). This disease may cause liver damage, kidney failure and infertility. In children, it may cause stunted growth and learning difficulties.

Even though Egyptians don't swim in the Nile, they're not completely dry in terms of successes in competitive swimming. In the 1990s, the Egyptian swimming association hired Russian Aleksandr Seleznyov to serve as head coach. Shortly thereafter, the completely unknown Tamer Zenhum was able to perform the world's second-best time in the 50m freestyle: 22:25.

Soon after, Rania Elwani presented herself to the world. Not only was she a pioneer among Muslim women in swimsuits, she was also a very fast swimmer. After having participated in three Olympics (1992, 1996, and 2000), she studied to become an obstetrician and sat on the International Olympic Committee in 2004 through 2012. Since then, she has worked with doping issues within the World Anti-Doping Agency (WADA). Rania Elwani is still the most popular sports personality in Egypt, at least on days when the soccer team has been beaten by Mali or Burkina Faso. She has also served as a member of the Egyptian parliament since 2016.

AFRICAN SWIMMING STARS

Penelope Heyns, South Africa
When she won a gold in Atlanta in 1996, she became the first South African to win an Olympic gold after the country was once again allowed to compete in 1992 following 24 years of boycott. She won both the 100m and 200m breaststroke and became the first woman to win both events in the same year.

Chad Ho, South Africa
In 2015, Ho became the world champion in 5km open water. He trains in Durban where he's still the least known "swimming Chad," as the Olympic champion Chad le Clos also lives there.

Rania Elwani, Egypt
She participated in the Olympics three times (1992, 1996, 2000), was elected into the IOC in 2004 and is now serving as a member of parliament in her native Egypt.

Ousama Mellouli, Tunisia
When he won the 1,500m freestyle in Beijing in 2008, he became the first African male swimmer to win an individual event at the Olympics. Four years later, he won the 10km open water event in London and won the bronze medal in the 1,500m freestyle.

Kirsty Coventry, Zimbabwe

She became an Olympic champion in the 200m backstroke in 2004 and 2008, when she was training in the United States. In 2000, at the age of 16, she became the first female swimmer from Zimbabwe to reach the semifinals in the Olympics, when she still lived and trained in Harare.

Jason Dunford, Kenya

He's a butterfly swimmer who broke the 100m Olympic record with 51.14 at the semifinal in Beijing 2008. In the final (won by Michael Phelps), he came in fifth with 51:47.

Natalie du Toit, South Africa

After being hit by a car when she was 17, she was forced to amputate one of her legs below the knee. As one of two Paralympians participating in the 2008 Olympics, she came in sixteenth in the 10km open water event.

Malick Fall, Senegal

Breaststroke swimmer with a personal best of 1:01 and the Senegalese flagbearer at the Athens Olympics in 2004. Served at the 2016 Olympics in Rio de Janeiro and officiates at swimming competitions.

The most famous Egyptian swimmer is still Abdellatief Abouheif. He went to the exclusive boarding school Eton together with British barons and counts, but instead of becoming a prominent business leader like his classmates, he became a professional marathon swimmer. In 1952 at the age of 22, he won a race in the Seine where the finish line was located in the center of Paris. He gave the prize money to his French swimming buddy, who'd recently become paralyzed and was no longer able to support himself.

Three years later, in 1955, Abdellatief Abouheif participated in the first race across the English Channel. He won this race while also setting a new record for crossing the channel. This time too, he chose to donate his prize money—this time to the family of the first channel swimmer Matthew Webb. A few years later, he swam an unfathomable 85 miles (137 kilometers) across Lake Michigan, which took him 3s6 hours. He almost doubled this time the following year when he swam for 60 hours in Argentina, from Rosario to Buenos Aires.

At the end of Abouheif's career, a relay race of world champions was arranged where his partner was Italian Julio Travello. The race crossed a large open lake close to Montreal. After two hours, Travello started to feel bad, went to the hospital, and didn't return to the race. It's not possible to find any newspaper reports as to why he was forced to forfeit the race, if he was suffering from a bad stomach or any other type of disease. With no partner, Abouheif had to complete the race alone. Abouheif had 75 miles left to go when a storm broke out so that waves were splashing in all directions. Imagine a coffee cup ride at an amusement park, but in addition to spinning around and around, you're also thrown up and down. The sun was covered by dark clouds and it was pouring down rain, making it difficult to navigate even for the accompanying boats. The water was so rough the men in the boats got seasick and threw up. After the race, the reporter from *La Gazetta dello Sport* ended up in the same hospital room as Travello, a fellow Italian. One by one, the competitors were forced to quit the race from fatigue. Abouheif just kept swimming. After more than 30 hours of solo swimming, he reached the finish line and was crowned the best swimmer in the world. As a result, and in a spectacular fashion, Abdellatief Abouheif was able to carry on the 10,000-year-old tradition from the cradle of swimming.

YOUR SWIMMING: CHECKLIST FOR EXTREME
LONG-DISTANCE SWIMMING

Accompanying Boat

Safety should always come first. Having an accompanying boat is recommended for all forms of long-distance swimming. Sudden changes in the weather or the health of the swimmer could make seemingly simple swimming dangerous.

Swimwear

Swim briefs or swimsuits are standard. Wetsuits containing rubber are forbidden. British South African Lewis Pugh swam half a mile across the North Pole wearing swim briefs and Lynne Cox swam across the Bering Strait wearing a swimsuit. Diana Nyad wore a long-sleeved suit made out of fabric to protect her from aggressive marine life.

Floodlights

Once it gets dark, the swimmer must be able to see where he or she is going, and the accompanying boat must be able to see the swimmer. Wearing a bright swimming cap is not sufficient in the dark—you need a flashing light on your cap to ensure that the accompanying boat doesn't lose track of you or that you're not hit by some other vessel.

Food

Fluid is recommended for all forms of swimming lasting for more than an hour: hot fluids if the water is cold and cold fluids if the water is warm. Bringing along liquids containing the right electrolytes (salts) is important. Whether it's Maxim, flat Coca-Cola, or any other beverage is for you to decide. Energy bars and pieces of candy are common forms of solid food. Whatever food and drink suits you is up to you; the most important thing is that you've previously tried swimming with them.

Pharmacy

The swimmer may suffer from muscle aches, skin irritation, or diarrhea. Furthermore, both the swimmer and the crew onboard the accompanying boat may get seasick.

Warm and Dry Clothes

During or after a long race, the swimmer may get cooled down and need some heat. Even if the weather is sunny, it's recommended to bring along warm and spacious pants and a long-sleeved shirt, a windproof blanket, socks, and a hat.

The Egyptian wall paintings are the oldest known images of swimmers, but there is other proof that people swam at an early date. Paintings and mosaics have been found in Libya, Pompeii, and Latin America. The Indian palace of Mohenjo-Daro, which was built in approximately 2800 BC, contains a 100 × 200 foot (30 by 61 meters) pool presumed to have been used for swimming and bathing. The Minoan palace in Knossos on Crete also had pools. What these findings have in common is that they may be associated with prosperity.

Here we leave archeological swimming to move up to the Renaissance period (approximately AD 1400 to 1600). The word "renaissance" comes from French and means "rebirth." The Renaissance marked the end of the "dark" Middle Ages and constituted somewhat of a rebirth of the cultural heritage of antiquity through a renewed interest in culture and science. Leonardo da Vinci, one of the leading geniuses of the time, was fascinated with the ability to move smoothly in water. Among his many inventions we find a diving suit made out of pig skin and a floating device made out of a cow stomach.

Apart from that, this time was also characterized by a lack of knowledge on how to swim. In Europe, Nikolaus Wynmann and Everard Digby wrote books on how to swim in order to reduce the number of drowning accidents. Digby, who taught at Cambridge, even claimed that humans could learn how to swim faster than fish. His book published in 1587 depicts breaststroke, backstroke, and freestyle, and Digby highlights breaststroke in particular, as it gives the swimmer the best overview. At about the same time, Japanese emperor Go-Yozei decided that all school children should learn how to swim and face each other in competitions. On the U.S. East Coast in the eighteen century, Benjamin Franklin designed and used prototypes of hand paddles while swimming.

The number of humans who could swim increased gradually, and as a result the focus shifted from swimming for survival to increasing swimming performance. The hero status assigned to Matthew Webb after he crossed the English Channel resulted in a boom for extreme swimming.

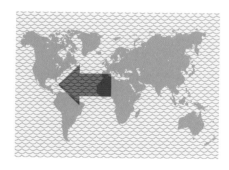

■ DOWNTOWN HAVANA, CUBA, MAY 12, 1997. A blonde young woman was standing on the beach, overlooking the ocean. She was set for the challenge of her young life.

Her body was covered in petroleum jelly from head to toe as she climbed into a strange cage attached to a boat. This was to protect her during the next two days of swimming, all the way until she reached American soil at the Florida Keys.

When swimming long distances in Swedish waters, the challenge is coping with the cold water—swimmers rarely have to worry about aggressive marine life. This, however, was exactly what Susie Maroney had to worry about as she climbed into the cage. Sharks may be quite intimidating at home in front of the TV, but imagine swimming next to one.

The database Shark Attack Data has collected data for more than 100 years of incidents of people being attacked and injured by sharks. A search in the database shows that people have been attacked by sharks more than 1,600 times around Cuba and along the East Coast of the United States. Out of these attacks, 158 had a fatal outcome.

Data show that 96 percent of these shark attacks consist of a single bite leaving open wounds, but without removing any muscle tissue. This is contrary to the previous view that sharks attack people in order to get something to eat. People have also discussed whether it's possible that a shark's vision is poor, and they mistake people for sea lions. However, this theory is also faulty, as sharks attack sea lions with powerful bites in the abdomen, but people almost always receive a bite in an arm or leg. So, the shark attacks must be the result of something other than us being a part of their menu. Regardless of the cause behind these attacks, it's understandable that you'd want to use a shark cage when swimming between Cuba and the United States.

So, Susie Maroney was about to swim from Havana to Florida. Australian Maroney was born with weakened muscles from cerebral palsy. Her parents had her take swimming lessons to combat it, but she showed a love for it. In 1995, she had swum in a pool for 24 hours during which she completed 93 kilometers (58 miles), which gives an average time of 23 minutes and 12 seconds per 1,500 meters. When she got up on the beach in Key West after swimming from Havana, she had swum the 180 kilometers (112 miles) in 24.5 hours. She had swum almost twice the distance during the same amount of time as in the pool, resulting in an astounding average time of 13:18 per 1,500 meters. Compare this with her fellow American Kieren Perkins, who then had the world record in a swimming pool at 14:41.

Portuguese man o'war

So, had 22-year-old Susie Maroney exponentially improved from two years before? Did the winds and currents bring her from communist Cuba to the capitalist U.S. at an incredible speed? Was there anything wrong with the stopwatch?

No, the answer was found in the shark cage. Not only did it offer protection from all kinds of aggressive marine life-forms, but it also provided her with an unnatural advantage by simultaneously pushing the water forward. Maroney had benefitted from drafting inside her protective cage.

In order to explain this phenomenon, let's imagine that we throw two oranges into the water from the accompanying boat. Oranges float, are round, and move predictably in the water. One orange lands just inside the cage, at the front, while the other lands outside. Let's say that the orange in the cage moves to the back of the cage after 25 seconds and that the orange outside of the cage has traveled the same distance (relative to the movement of the boat) after 20 seconds. Dividing 25 by 20 gives us 1.25. This means that the cage gave the first orange a 25 percent advantage in speed.

This drafting had given Susie Maroney a tremendous advantage and her record swim time was rejected by most observers. Nevertheless, the drafting principle is still very much alive in open water races, where swimmers try to save energy by swimming behind other swimmers and thus letting them be the ones wasting energy pushing the water forward.

SWIMMING IN OPEN WATER

Swimming in open water both resembles and differs from pool swimming. The movement pattern and the choice of four different swimming styles is roughly the same. A pool swimmer's skill will more or less correspond to his or her skill in open water. A swimmer who does 16 minutes when swimming 1,500 meters in a pool will always beat a swimmer who does 19 minutes over the same distance when they compete in open water. If, however, the difference between the two swimmers was to be less than one minute, then it would be more difficult to predict who would be the fastest in open water.

To understand why this may be the case, we need to take a closer look at the six different components of open water swimming. Many experienced personalities, such as the Greek demon coach Nikos Gemelli and the Croatian open water oracle Slave Sitic, describe the specific challenges of open water swimming similarly. The account below is based on how this is described by open water guru Steven Munatones.

Type of swimming: Competition or feat?
Distance: Longer or shorter swimming?
Type of water: Salt water or sweet water?
Direction of the water: Currents or still water?
Weather: Choppy or smooth water?
Temperature: Warm or cold water?

Type of Swimming: Feat

The desire to show that something is possible has inspired and fueled all kinds of crazy ventures. From asking whether it's possible to climb the tallest tree in the village to competing in an Ironman competition—each day for one month. Even if the ones carrying out these feats want to show what the "little man" is actually capable of, it's not hard to imagine an inner driving force to portray themselves as the "great man." "Temperantia" (moderation) is one of the four cardinal virtues and may be found in the term of temperance movements. Many feats ending in death or other types of misfortune could have been avoided with just a little bit of common sense—something the people participating in these adventures clearly lack.

Solo swimming frequently differs quite a bit from race swimming. It may involve doing something no one has ever done before, like when Jon Eriksson swam across the English Channel three times, one after the other. Or when Lynne Cox swam across the Bering Strait, a 2.7-mile (4.3-kilometer) swim in 39°F (4°C) water. Slovenian Martin Strel has also completed a number of endurance swims, including swimming the length of the Amazon River. However, since Strel wears a wetsuit, he doesn't receive all that much attention in open water circles. Not because they don't acknowledge his accomplishments, but because they focus on what they refer to as "real swimming without assistance."

Feats are frequently carried out as part of charity work to highlight various important issues. When Lewis Pugh swam across the North Pole in 2007, he did so in order to raise awareness of climate change. It shouldn't be possible to swim in open water there, as the water should be covered with ice. In 2014, Swedish triathlete Jonas Colting swam from Stockholm to Gothenburg to draw attention to the fact that not all people have access to clean water.

Solo swims frequently require a massive logistical effort. They require permits and an accompanying boat. Relevant vaccinations are needed, as well as a survey of how powerful currents, temperature, or marine life may impede the swimming. It may therefore be a costly venture to do what no one else (or only a few) have done in the past. With the exception of swims in very cold water, where the focus must be on one's ability to handle the cold temperature, the number-one challenge is endurance. As a solo swimmer, you don't need to be particularly fast, but you do need to have an attitude counteracting the increasingly stronger "this-is-it" signals sent by your body.

Type of Swimming: Competition

Competitive swimming involves a completely different set of requirements compared to solo swimming. This is what's needed for a tough race in open water swimming at the Olympic distance of 10 kilometers:

- An ability to start close to your top speed to position yourself where you want to be at the first buoy or to keep track of the front part of the pack.
- A high aerobic threshold to be able to swim for about two hours. Research shows that open water swimmers are able to stay at 94 percent of their maximum oxygen uptake during the bulk of the race. As much as any runner or cross-country skier.
- During the race, the ambitious swimmer needs to keep track of his or her competitors and brace him- or herself for the physical contact offered by the competitors.
- The race ends as a sprint for 5 to 10 minutes where the swimmer needs to use everything he or she has left in the tank.

YOUR SWIMMING: CHECKLIST FOR

INSPECTING THE COURSE

How does the start work?

Starting in the water?

Diving from a pier?

Starting on land and running down into the water?

What does the course look like?

Is it a loop with the start and finish in the same spot, or is it a course where

you swim from point A to point B?

If it's a loop course, what shape is it? How many laps are to be completed,

and in what direction?

Does the course go under bridges? If so,

how far between each bridge?

Are there any other structures easily recognized by swimmers

that also reveal distances?

Are there buoys indicating direction?

Do you need to pass any of the buoys on any particular side?

How far is it between each buoy?

Are there any other objects that may help you keep going

in the right direction?

What does the finish of the race look like?

Is it possible to test swim in order to better time the final stage?

This is also useful advice in triathlon competitions as it may be a good idea

to do a test run getting out of the water and running the first few steps

toward the transition area.

Swimming in open water has been an Olympic event since 2008. The Olympic distance is 10 kilometers, which means that the race takes approximately two hours. This is similar to three other types of trials involving similar physical requirements: the marathon for runners, the 50 km for cross-country skiers, and the Olympic distance triathlon.

Distance: Longer or Shorter Swimming

Both short and long swims might end up longer than necessary due to faulty navigation. Each successful navigation effort begins with inspecting the course.

Type of Water: Salt Water or Freshwater

The first place where you'll notice that you're swimming in salt water is in your mouth. Very salty water causes the receptors for saltiness on your tongue to react. Scientists use the term "salinity" to describe just how salty water is. Salinity is measured in practical salinity units (PSU) and is measured in parts per thousand. If you, on the other hand, want to keep your distance from the scientists, then you may refer to salinity as salt level and convert PSU to percent.

The oceans have a salt level of around 3 to 4 percent. Salt levels vary due to amounts of rain and inflow from rivers. Water containing less than 3 percent salt is called brackish, and the largest bodies of brackish water are the Black Sea and the Baltic Sea, with salt levels of 1 to 2 percent, whereas the salt level of the Dead Sea is 33 percent, slightly more than the Great Salt Lake in Utah.

Obviously, the salt taste doesn't affect your speed, but it does affect the density of the water. Salt water has a higher density than freshwater, so the higher the salt level, the higher the position of the swimmer in the water. Furthermore, salt water exerts more pressure on the sides of your body, which makes it easier to maintain your posture. However, this effect is not so strong that you can neglect working on your position in the water or ignore doing sit-ups for the sake of a good posture, but we still need to mention it to explain the feeling of improved buoyancy experienced by many swimmers in salty oceans.

You get "fat" by swimming in salt water. It's not unusual that your body looks bloated after spending an hour in salt water. This phenomenon is called "third spacing" and is the result of water positioning itself in the space between the skin and the membrane surrounding the muscles. This area is normally more or less vacuum-sealed, but after a salty swim, water is able to penetrate it to form a type of extra padding. There is no explanation as to why this occurs, but the phenomenon is purely cosmetic and the body returns to its normal appearance after a day or two.

Direction of the Water: Currents or Still Water

Being familiar with the currents in the waters where you train or compete is important. Competition swimmers naturally know their stuff, but even strong swimmers may be deceived by strong currents when it comes to situations requiring a high level of precision. At the Swedish championships in Halmstad in 2013, the races were ten laps around bridge abutments in the river of Nissan. At the bottom of the river, the swimmers were to round the Slottsbron bridge and at the top, they were to round the six pillars of the Österbro bridge. The design of this course resulted in some exciting swimming. Each lap first went against the current until the current shifted to come in from the left, as the swimmers rounded the massive pillars, followed by swimming with the current to then having the current coming in from the right when the swimmers turned at the top of the river. One of the favorites, Tim Arnesen, was not afraid of adopting an offensive tactic and decided to swim tightly around the bends. His tough tactics turned costly when he swam upstream as he hit his hand against the bridge foundations on almost every single lap.

As an open water swimmer, you may encounter currents going in all directions, and sometimes it may be difficult to know which way the water takes you. The most important thing to do in those instances is to stay calm, have a good position in the water, and keep on swimming at the pace planned beforehand. When the water is flowing sideways, you need to make more frequent navigational adjustments in order to maintain a good direction.

Weather: Choppy or Smooth Water

Water in swimming pools is so predictable that a swimmer is in an ideal position to practice and repeat identical movement patterns. In terms of your arms, this means entering the hand, anchoring, pull, finish, and return. The hand enters the water the same way arm stroke after arm stroke, while the body is not influenced by lateral forces and remains relatively straight. In open and turbulent water, on the other hand, the conditions for entering your hand, maintaining your posture, and everything else changes from stroke to stroke. This means that you must constantly adapt your movements in accordance with the situation at hand.

Temperature: Warm or Cold Water

While pool competitions are held in water temperatures of about 80°F (27°C), open water races and solo swims take place at temperatures ranging from 60 to 85°F (16 to 29°C). Both unusually warm and unusually cold water makes it harder to change pace and may force the swimmer to change his or her tactics. A swimmer who's good at sprinting, for instance, may need to place him- or herself in a more leading position than he or she would have otherwise.

Most competitive swimmers have a favorite temperature at which they swim at their best. Some swimmers get stiff and lose speed when the water temperature drops below 65°F (18°C), whereas others overheat and get listless when the temperature goes above 80°F (27°C). However, Bulgarian Petar Stoychev, who became the first swimmer to cross the English Channel in under seven hours in 2007, could handle all temperatures. He won world cup competitions over 10 kilometers in both 60 and 85°F (16 and 29°C) water. These days, however, competitions are not held in water that warm. On October 23, 2010, FINA held a world cup competition over 10 kilometers of open water in Fujairah, in the United Arab Emirates. The thermometer showed almost 105°F (41°C) in the air—unusually hot for that time of year. Among the male favorites in the 48-strong field were the Americans Alex Meyer and Fran Crippen (who had won a big race in Mexico the weekend before). The race was tough. A water temperature in excess of 85°F (29°C) resulted in a lot of normally strong swimmers dropping out unusually early in the race. Brazilian Allan do Carmo was taken to the hospital after the race. Petar Stoychev, crowned open water swimmer of the year the previous year, lost all energy and came in six minutes after the winner, placing 35th—the worst result of his career.

When only the slowest swimmers remained in the race, Alex Meyer suddenly noticed that his teammate was missing. He knew something must be wrong. Meyer called out to the other participants to swim the course backward and look for Crippen. Though exhausted after a race close to two hours long, nearly the entire field participated in the search. This time, they swam as a matter of life and death. After two hours of searching, Crippen's body was found on the sea floor some 500 yards (457 meters) from the finish line.

YOUR SWIMMING: TIPS FOR COLD TEMPERATURES

A number of factors influence the way the body reacts to extreme temperatures, which in turn makes it difficult for competition organizers to define the rules and make recommendations concerning temperatures that will suit everyone.

THE FOLLOWING VARIABLES AFFECT THE WAY
YOU EXPERIENCE THE TEMPERATURE WHEN SWIMMING:

Water Temperature

Every swimmer has their own ideal performance window when it comes to temperatures. Training outside your thermal comfort zone improves your ability to master extreme conditions.

Body Composition

Swimmers exposing themselves to long and cold swims frequently gain weight. The layer of body fat acts as an insulator.

Equipment

Wetsuits are standard in cold water competitions. A bandana or neoprene hat will warm your head. When training, it might feel good to wear a wool shirt underneath your wetsuit.

Training Level

An experienced swimmer is able to maintain a higher pace for a longer period and thus maintain a higher body temperature.

Weather

Bright sunlight will keep your body warm for a longer period.

Nutrition
Salt binds water in your body. Salt deficiency accelerates
the cooling of your body.

Swimming Duration
When swimming for more than half an hour, it's important to be
prepared and to have done your homework.

Experience
An experienced swimmer knows his or her limits.
Train in conditions similar to those of your challenge.

The report released later came to the conclusion that the cause of death was complicated. The extremely hot conditions could have triggered an asthma attack as a result of exertion and/or caused a defect in Crippen's heart. Regardless, it was determined that heat is a safety concern for swim races. The upper temperature limit in competitions is set at 88°F (31°C), but as a result of this tragic event, competitions in warm countries are now held during cooler times of the year.

Despite cold water in Sweden, interest in open water swimming started to grow in the middle of the 2000s, and came into full bloom just a few years later. Competitions such as Ironman in Kalmar, the Vansbrosimmingen, and ÖTILLÖ were steadily seeing increases in the number of participants to the tune of around 20 percent annually. Triathletes were good ambassadors for swimming when they showed that it's possible even for a stiff banker or an overweight carpenter to learn how to swim the crawl as an adult. There were only a handful of open water races in Sweden in the 1990s. Twenty years later, they have increased to almost 100.

Matthew Webb didn't stop swimming after he defeated the channel dragon in 1875. His further achievements include staying afloat in a tank at the Horticultural Hall in Boston for a staggering 128 hours in the summer of 1879. The following year he performed a similar feat at the Royal Aquarium in Westminster.

Even though he made his living swimming, he was still not guaranteed any income. Like in competitions against his rival Beckwith, where they were to swim ten-hour sessions in a 65-foot (20-meter) pool for six consecutive days, and where the entire prize sum of $420 was awarded to the swimmer who completed the most laps, Webb lost.

The next major challenge was swimming across the border between the United States and Canada below Niagara Falls. Webb was no longer the fit young man he'd been when he'd crossed the English Channel eight years earlier, but he needed the money to support his growing family. The immensely rich railway companies of the time had offered a $10,000 reward to the swimmer able to defy the currents and sharp cliffs at Whirlpool Rapids. In today's money, the reward was a bit over $200,000.

On the afternoon of July 24, 1883, Matthew Webb was ready to transform his life and the life of his family. The stream he was going to cross was a little over 100 yards. Initially, everything appeared to be going according to plan, but after 10 minutes, the large audience could no longer see any mustache or red-and-white-striped swimsuit.

Matthew Webb's body was found four days later, face down in exactly the same position he had been swimming in. His teeth were clenched and his eyes were staring wide open with an expression of anxiety. One of his toes was missing a nail and a four-inch deep wound in his head led the doctors performing the autopsy to conclude that he'd hit his head on an underwater rock and most likely lost consciousness. Below the water surface, the great weight of the water had knocked out his neural system and prevented him from breathing and using his arms and legs. According to the definition of the time, the great canal swimmer had not drowned, but suffocated. On Matthew Webb's tombstone, it says, "Nothing Great Is Easy."

EIGHT OPEN WATER COMPETITIONS

MIDMAR MILE, Durban, South Africa
Length: 1.6 km
Type of water: Ocean
Time of Year (usually): February

SWIM MIAMI, Miami, United States
Length: 1.6 km and 5 km
Type of water: Bay
Time of Year (usually): April

GREAT NORTH SWIM, Lake Windermere, United Kingdom
Length: 1.6 km, 3.2 km, and 10 km
Type of water: Cold lake with beautiful surroundings
Time of Year (usually): June

VANSBROSIMNINGEN, Vansbro, Sweden
Length: 3 km
Type of water: Smooth, running water, usually 57 to 66°F (14 to 19°C), two kilometers with the current, one kilometer against. 15,000 swimmers.
Time of Year (usually): July

BOSPHORUS INTERNATIONAL SWIM, Istanbul, Turkey

Length: 7.1 km

Type of water: Strait, partially currents, temperate

Time of Year (usually): July

MARATONA DEL GOLFO CAPRI-NAPOLI, Capri-Napoli, Italy

Length: 36 km

Type of water: Ocean, 82°F (28°C) open water that can be quite choppy

Time of Year (usually): July

VOULIAGMENI SWIM CHALLENGE, Athens, Greece

Length: 1 km, 2.5 km, and 5 km

Type of water: Ocean, 70 to 75°F (21 to 24°C)

Time of Year (usually): October

MOROCCO SWIM TREK, Dakhla, Morocco

Length: 30 km in four days. 6.5, 8.5, 10.0, and 5.0 km per swim

Type of water: lagoon in desert

Temperatures: Around 70 to 72°F (21 to 22°C)

Time of Year (usually): December

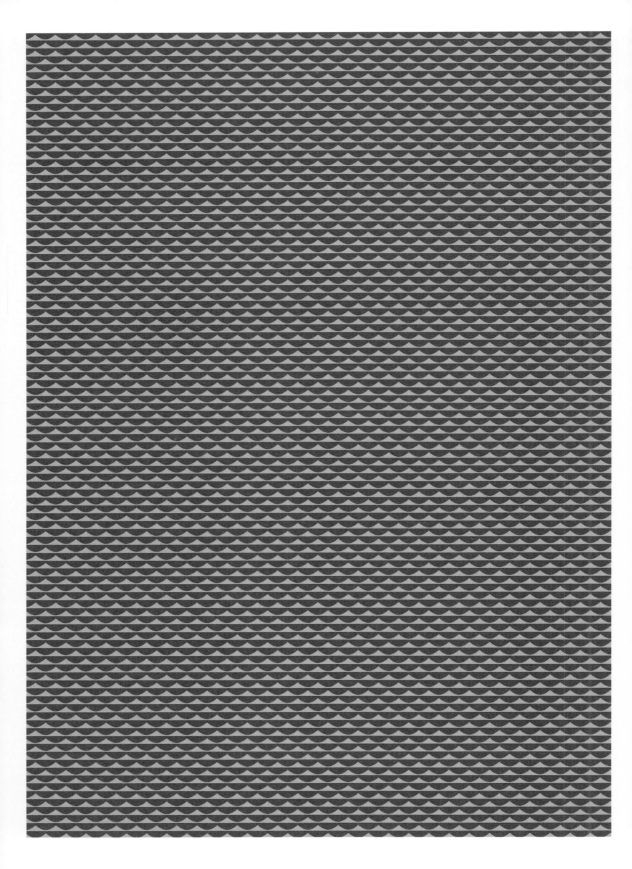

CHAPTER 8

THE PERFECT
BODY

With swimming, I burn a lot of calories. I'm able to eat pretty much anything and it won't affect me. But I don't.

– Ryan Lochte

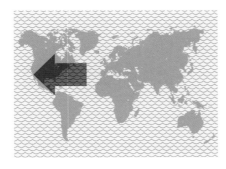

■ **LOS ANGELES, FEBRUARY 13, 2014.** Fredrik Wikingsson: I saw a picture of Michael Phelps the other day.

Filip Hammar: The American swimmer who won eight Olympic golds in Beijing.

FW: Was that Michael Phelps? Wasn't that Ian Thorpe?

FH: Phelps was the one who finally did it.

FW: OK. He won a crazy amount. And now he—you know he would have been in 9/11, at the World Trade Center, the day that 9/11 exploded. He was standing outside.

FH: Just like Seth MacFarlane was supposed to be in one of the airplanes.

FW: Really?

FH: He rebooked at the last minute.

FW: Phelps has had a lot of problems and the like, suffered from abuse and so on. Manic depressive.

FH: Well. Mostly Thorpe.

FW: Yeah, I mean Thorpe. Yes. No. Was it?

FH: The Australian who was so successful at the Sydney Olympics in 2000.

FW: That's it. And he had exceptionally large feet.

FH: Yes.

FW: And hands. I suppose that's what . . . also very sexy . . .

FW: . . . I saw a picture of him . . . [jumping] up out of the water while still sort of wearing his swimming goggles and one hand making a fist toward the sky when he'd won yet another gold at the Sydney Olympics in 2000. That's a typical image of these swimmers. That's what you often see, when their mouth is sort of open and chlorine water is coming out. It's simply triumph. It's simply . . . and SEX! He's so . . . swimmer bodies might be the most perfect.

FH: Yes, I suppose. I'd agree to that. Out of everyone. I believe orienteers have good bodies too.

FW: Eh. Orienteers don't have the same definition at all. They have no need for an upper body in the same way.

FH: But they're also so lean.

FW: Sure, but there are muscles in a completely different way. Swimmers are just as much animals as they are people. They're just as much shrimp. They're magnificent specimens. They're also very immodest concerning their "almost nakedness" wearing these minimal speedos.

This lively discussion is available on their podcast *Filip & Fredrik*, episode 181: "Filip's Return to the Nightlife." In this podcast, in addition to praising the bodies of swimmers, they bring up the interesting phenomenon of people who are experts in one area, like cooking (Leif Mannerström), and adopt the role of expert in other contexts (like marine biology).

THE HUMAN BODY AND SWIMMING

Filip Hammar and Fredrik Wikingsson are not the only ones to highlight the aesthetic excellence of the swimmer's body. Leonardo da Vinci had noted that different body shapes were suited for different activities.

The average NBA player is 6'7" (201 cm) and weighs 220 pounds (100 kg). The Chinese player Yao Ming was 7'6" (229 cm) and weighed 310 pounds (141 kg) when he was still playing, whereas Shaquille O'Neal was 7'1" (216 cm) and weighed 350 pounds (159 kg). The first 10 women to finish the marathon race at the 2012 London Olympics all weighed 115 pounds (52 kg) or less. Kenyan long-distance runner Tegla Loroupe weighed less than 90 pounds (41 kg), far less than a third of Yao Ming's 310 pounds. Both Yao Ming and Tegla Loroupe would have been less successful had they switched sports.

Size is a factor when it comes to classifying athletes, but the proportions of their body parts (i.e., anthropometrics) also play a part. The first real compilation of such data was carried out at the Mexico City Olympics in 1968, where information was collected on 1,265 out of more than 5,000 participants. All sports except equestrian sports were represented in the study. A variety of measurements were registered even though no one at the time knew what they might be used for.

After six years, the data collected on the athletes in the Mexico City Olympics was compiled into a 256-page book. The book sends a clear message: the measurements of the athletes' bodies provide us with clear clues as to which event they're competing in. Within track and field, for instance, hurdling had the majority of tall runners. A hurdler benefits greatly from having a high center of gravity, as jumping over hurdles without having to shift your center of gravity vertically is energy efficient.

So what about swimmers? It was noted already in the 1960s that their legs were disproportionately short. Although swimmers were on average 0.5 inch (1.3 centimeters) taller than sprint runners, their legs were a full 1.5 inches (3.8 centimeters) shorter. Having a longer torso and shorter legs gives swimmers a longer vessel with a larger body surface. Michael Phelps, who's 6'4" (193 cm), and Hicham El Guerrouj, the 5'9" (175 cm) world record holder for running a mile, wear jeans with the same inseam.

The long arms and upper body of swimming champion Phelps are weapons for winning. This body type, common among successful swimmers, together with hypermobile joints are signs of Marfan syndrome.

Marfan syndrome originates in a mutation of the FBN1 gene located in chromosome 15. This gene controls the creation of the protein fibrillin, which is a part of the body's connective tissue. Connective tissue is found throughout the entire body and consists of thin interlocking threads that hold organs in place, hold muscles, joints, blood vessels, and bones together, and attach heart valves and lenses in the eyes. The mutation behind the Marfan syndrome results in thinner connective tissues. In the case of Michael Phelps, if he had this mutation, it could have a positive effect on his swimming and offer an explanation for his unbelievably agile shoulder movements.

Hugh Jackman's X-Men character Wolverine is equipped with sharp senses, enhanced physical capacity, retractable claws between his knuckles, and a healing factor that helps him recover from injuries, diseases, and poison. This healing factor also slows down his aging process, giving him a much longer life span than a regular human. Even though he was born at the end of the nineteenth century, he doesn't look a day older than 35.

So, could you say that Michael Phelps is the X-Men character of the Olympic pool? To the extent that he almost always comes out of the toughest challenges with a new notch on his revolver, it's true. But unlike Wolverine, real mutations are frequently deadly. A worst-case scenario for someone with Marfan syndrome is aortic rupture, where the connective tissue surrounding the aorta becomes so thin that it breaks. This is so serious that if this occurs and you don't immediately get to a well-equipped hospital, you will die.

However, we have no idea if Michael Phelps in fact has Marfan syndrome. But the possibility raises a breathtaking perspective of a future with more and more extreme athletes.

ANATOMICAL CHARACTERISTICS THAT BENEFIT SWIMMERS

Long body

Wide shoulders

Narrow hips

Large hands and feet

Muscular arms

Long arms in relation to body height

Long forearms in relation to upper arms

Research also shows that young swimmers develop differently than their classmates. Swimmers have more muscle mass (especially in their arms) and they weigh more. They also have very good stamina, which can be explained by the repetitive strain and the relatively hard training. Swimmers also have a larger chest circumference and a greater lung volume. An explanation for this could be the breathing-related restrictions that swimmers are exposed to. The way that swimmers are forced to breathe resembles hyperventilation, which increases lung volume. Young swimmers also develop their chest circumference and lung volume more than other young athletes. Why this happens isn't entirely clear, but it's conceivable that it's because swimmers must hold their breath for large chunks of their training, and they breathe in more frequently than other athletes do.

Height Above All

Body height, which is a result of both genetics and environment, is defined as the distance from the soles of the feet to the top of the head of a standing person. The average height of humans has changed drastically throughout the ages. Archeological findings of skeletons have enabled an overview of how the human body has developed from prehistoric times to our present time. The prehistoric human species *Homo habilis*, who lived approximately two million years ago, was between 4 and 5 feet (122 and 152 centimeters) tall. Its successor, *Homo erectus*, was somewhat larger with body heights ranging from 5 to 6 feet (152 to 182 centimeters) in some instances. Five thousand years ago, the estimated average height of *Homo sapiens* was 5'3" (160 cm) (men) and 5'1" (155 cm) (women). By the Middle Ages, it had increased to 5'7" (170 cm) and 5'3" (160 cm), respectively.

Scientists agree that height is the single most important physical factor for swimmers. Everything else being equal, a taller swimmer is faster than a shorter swimmer. The larger scale of the body increases efficiency and lowers stroke frequency for the same mechanical work. During pool races with flip turns, tall swimmers swim a shorter distance than short swimmers, as they are able to turn with their center of gravity a little bit farther away from the side of the pool.

Yet another reason why tall swimmers are able to maintain a higher speed is something called (in nautical terms) displacement speed, or hull speed. This is the speed at which the wavelength of a boat's bow wave corresponds to the length of the boat at the waterline. The boat approaching or exceeding its displacement speed means that a higher forward-driving effect produces less and less of an increase in speed.

The speed of waves in water is proportional to the square root of the wavelength. When a swimmer increases his or her speed, the waves he or she creates will become longer so that the wavelength corresponds to the speed. Eventually, the distance between the bow wave (which occurs when the swimmer pushes water in front of him or her) and the stern wave (which occurs when the water returns to the location behind the feet when the swimmer has passed) will be exactly one wavelength. This means that the swimmer is located in the valley between the two waves. To increase his or her speed in excess of the displacement speed, the swimmer needs to climb up higher on the bow wave or place him- or herself farther into it, thus leaving the stern wave behind in a way that is not energy efficient. Displacement speed is not an absolute limiting factor as to how fast a swimmer may travel in the water. If we look at a larger boat traveling a longer distance, its speed (both for both cruising and top speed) is set at close to the displacement speed. Otherwise, the boat will consume an inordinate amount of fuel. When it comes to swimming, it's important to be energy efficient in all distances longer than 50 meters.

Height is also the easiest factor to account for. Michael Phelps was clearly the best American butterfly swimmer at the 2008 Olympics. The second-best American in the 200m butterfly was Gil Stovall. Phelps's swimming was more interesting than Stovall's in every regard, except for one: Memphis native Stovall's was only 5'8" (173 cm), a whopping eight inches shorter than Phelps. Sure, Stovall was soundly beaten by Phelps, but at the same time, he beat both the 6'4" (193 cm) Croatia-born Austrian Dinko Jukic and 6'5" (196 cm) Canadian Adam Sioui. Being tall is a definite advantage when swimming, but as illustrated by Stovall, it doesn't have to be a determining factor.

Open water swimming differs from pool swimming in that height doesn't seem to be an excluding factor for the former. However, this doesn't mean that there aren't any tall open water swimmers. Maarten van der Weijden, who won the 2008 Olympics open water swim, may be unable to fit into just any car at 6'9" (206 cm). Meanwhile, South African swimmer Chad Ho, who won the 2005 world championships, is 14 inches (36 centimeters) shorter. We see a similar distribution when it comes to women; there is a 5-inch (13-centimeter) difference between the two world champions Ana Marcela Cunha, Brazil (5'5" [165 cm]), and Keri-anne Payne, Great Britain (5'10" [178 cm]).

The height differences among world-class open water swimmers may seem strange, but this may be explained by the simple fact that there are no flip turns to benefit taller swimmers.

AVERAGE HEIGHT BY COUNTRY

Country (area)	Men	Women
Sudan (ethnic group: Dinka)	6'3" (191 cm)	5'11" (180 cm)
Dinaric Alps	6'1" (185 cm)	5'7" (170 cm)
The Netherlands	6' (183 cm)	5'7" (170 cm)
Sweden	6' (183 cm)	5'6" (168 cm)
United Kingdom	5'10" (178 cm)	5'5" (165 cm)
United States	5'10" (178 cm)	5'4" (163 cm)
Japan	5'8" (173 cm)	5'2" (157 cm)
Brazil	5'7" (170 cm)	5'2" (157 cm)
China	5'6" (168 cm)	5'2" (157 cm)
India	5'3" (160 cm)	5' (152 cm)
Guatemala (ethnic group: Maya)	5'2" (157 cm)	4'8" (142 cm)

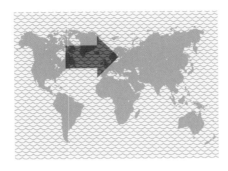

at 6'10" (208 cm).

When he was young, Ari-Pekka Liukkonen tried to play volleyball like his father, but he grew so quickly at such a young age that he was unable to retain his motor skills. When he tried orienteering, he suffered from allergic reactions to the bugs in the forest. In swimming, however, Ari-Pekka found a home. His tall body was positioned high in the water, which, in combination with his obviously high proportion of fast-twitch muscle fibers, meant that he was able to swim fast on the short distances. At the age of 16, he did 25 seconds in the 50m freestyle. Compared to Michael Phelps, who came in fifth at the Olympics when he was the same age, he was still an amateur. But Ari-Pekka slowly but surely developed so that in 2014, he put on his tuxedo and stepped into the elite circles after he won a bronze medal at the European championship in 50m freestyle with a time of 21:93.

Most of Ari-Pekka Liukkonen's competitors are also uncommonly tall: Brazilian Cesar Cielo is 6'5" (196 cm) and American Nathan

■ **ESPOO, FINLAND, FEBRUARY 2016.** It's a dark and snowy morning outside the Hagalund pool in Espoo, Finland. A tall man with pale skin walks along the large glass wall by the short side of the pool. He's carrying a black mesh bag containing swimming gear. The tall man drops his bag and starts to warm up. After a few minutes, he puts on a blue swimming cap and a pair of goggles with reflective lenses before breaking the blue water's surface, rendering the warmth of his bed a distant memory in his explosive body. The tall man is unique in a number of ways. He received worldwide praise when he came out as gay (one of the first Finnish athletes to do so) just before the Olympic flame was about to be lit in Sochi in Russia. He is also the tallest elite swimmer in the world

Adrian is 6'6" (198 cm), as is Frenchman Florent Manaudou and George Bovell from Trinidad. Cameron McEvoy, Australia, and Vladimir Morozov, Russia, are among the shortest in this event at 6' (183 cm) and 5'11" (180 cm) respectively.

These days, Swedes tend to be tall, but this wasn't always the case. At the beginning of the nineteenth century, the average height in Sweden dropped drastically as the result of a poor diet. But thanks to an increased material standard during the twentieth century, Swedes started soaring again. This development is demonstrated by an increase in average height of military recruits from 5'6" (168 cm) in 1850 to 5'11" (180 cm) in 2004.

Otherwise, you find some of the tallest people on the planet around the mountain range of the Dinaric Alps, an area located in southeastern Europe and extending from Slovenia in the northwest via Croatia, Bosnia and Herzegovina, Montenegro, and Kosovo to Albania in the southeast. There, the average height is 6'1" (185 cm) for men and 5'7" (170 cm) for women.

TALL SOUTH SLAVIC ATHLETES

Vlade Divac, SRB, basketball, NBA, Olympic silver	7'1" (216 cm)
Vladimir Miličić, SRB, basketball, NBA champion	7' (213 cm)
Ivo Karlovic, CRO, tennis, 6 ATP titles	6'11" (211 cm)
Predrag Stojaković, SRB, basketball, NBA, world championship gold	6'10" (208 cm)
Ivan Miljkovic, SRB, volleyball, Olympic gold	6'9" (206 cm)
Damir Buric, CRO, water polo, Olympic gold	6'9" (206 cm)
Andrija Geric, SRB, volleyball, Olympic gold	6'8" (203 cm)
Mladen "The Scorpion Sting" Brestovac, CRO, kickboxing, 33 KOs	6'6" (198 cm)

Luka Špik, SLO, rowing, Olympic gold	6'5" (196 cm)
Duje Draganja, CRO, freestyle swimming, Olympic silver	6'5" (196 cm)
Milorad Čavić, SRB, butterfly swimming, Olympic silver	6'5" (196 cm)
Emir Bekrić, SRB, track and field, 400 meter hurdles, world championship bronze	6'4" (193 cm)
Goran Ivanisevic, CRO, tennis, Wimbledon champion	6'4" (193 cm)
Blanka Vlasic, CRO, high jump, world championship gold	6'4" (193 cm)
Igor Tudor, CRO, soccer, world championship bronze	6'4"(193 cm)
Anze Kopitar, SLO, ice hockey, Stanley Cup champion	6'4" (193 cm)
Neven Subotic, SRB, soccer	6'3" (191 cm)
Ivan Stanić, CRO, muay thai, world champion	6'3" (191 cm)
Nemanja Vidic, SRB, soccer	6'3" (191cm)
Elis Guri, ALB, wrestling, world champion	6'3" (191 cm)
Novak Djokovic, SRB, tennis	6'2" (188 cm)
Mirko "Cro Cop" Filipović, CRO, MMA, world champion	6'2" (188 cm)
Ana Ivanović, SRB, tennis, French Open champion	6' (183 cm)
Sandra Perkovic, CRO, discus, Olympic gold	6' (183 cm)
Milica Mandić, SRB, taekwondo, Olympic gold	5'11" (180 cm)
Tatjana Jelača, SRB, javelin throw, Olympic silver	5'11" (180 cm)
Mirna Jukic, CRO/AUT, breaststroke swimming, Olympic bronze	5'10" (178 cm)
Petra Majdič, SLO, cross-country skiing, 24 world cup wins	5'10" (178 cm)
Ivana Španović, SRB, long jump, world championship bronze	5'10" (178 cm)
Jelena Janković, SRB, tennis, ranked number one	5'10" (178 cm)
Janica Kostelic, CRO, downhill skiing, Olympic gold	5'9" (175 cm)

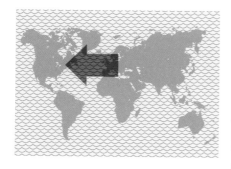

■ MONTREAL, AUGUST, 1976.

Twenty-one-year-old Enith Brigitha stood out in the starting field of the 100m freestyle race. As the only black participant in the final, it was impossible not to notice the Dutchwoman standing next to the brawny East German women in the middle lanes. Here, we also find the main character of the race, 17-year-old superstar Kornelia Ender, who'd won this distance at the 1973 and 1975 world championships. She was already the best in the world at age 14, and she'd developed further since. Her 165 pounds (75 kilograms) were distributed across her tall 5'11" (180 cm) frame. Ender had shoulders as broad as those of a heavyweight boxer and her arm muscles were clearly defined.

According to plan, Ender crushed all resistance. She won the double distance, 200m freestyle by a margin of two seconds, and the 100m butterfly by almost a second. On the 100m freestyle, she crossed the finish line eight tenths of a second before the next swimmer, 15-year-old East German Petra Priemer. However, Enith Brigitha managed to get the bronze medal with a margin of only the blink of an eye before the two best Americans and the third East German. Winning the bronze medal constituted a historical accomplishment as a black woman had never before won a medal in an Olympic swimming pool.

Enith Brigitha was born on the Caribbean island of Curaçao. It's located about 40 miles (64 kilometers) north of Venezuela and is one of the ABC islands, along with Aruba and Bonaire. The island was conquered by the Dutch in the seventeenth century as they needed salt for their herring industry since Spain and Portugal had strategically blocked the salt supply. Curaçao came to be a center for the slave trade for two centuries until slavery was abolished in 1863. It was during this time period that Enith's ancestors arrived from Africa on a slave ship.

Her parents divorced when she was young and she moved to Amsterdam, where she quickly became one of the best female swimmers in the country. In 1976, she was at the top of her career; a few days after her first bronze medal, she also won a second bronze medal in the 200m freestyle. In the two relay events, the Netherlands came in fourth and fifth. Enith Brigitha moved back to Curaçao at the age of 35, where she opened a school offering swimming lessons for children, which seemed to be a good business idea on an island where almost the entire population lives near the coast. Just like most other athletes, she remembers her career with joy. However, one thing is different.

The East German women trounced all other swimmers at the Montreal Olympics, winning 11 out of 13 gold medals. At the Munich Olympics four years prior, they had not won a single gold medal. Kornelia Ender, who'd won three individual gold medals with incredible world records, had to bear the brunt of the envy of the rest of the world. A West German newspaper rhetorically belittled her: "Ist das ein Mädchen?" ("Is this really a girl?")

The world of swimming tried to figure out what made the East German girls so superior, but East Germany had been a closed country since 1965. The regime saw athletic success as a way of demonstrating the superiority of the communist ideology, and the East German female swimmers won almost every available medal in the 1970s and 1980s.

When the archives of the East German secret police were opened in 1993, what many had already known deep down was confirmed: there had been systematic doping of East German athletes between 1971 and 1990. Sure, athletes from other nations also cheated, but nowhere else did doping constitute a part of the development plan for all athletes to the same extent as in East Germany. Swimmers Andrea Pollack and Daniela Hunger, both

Olympic gold medalists, accused their coaches of having doped them, and a German court subsequently ruled that there had been systematic doping. This led to the U.S. Olympic Committee demanding that the result lists be changed, even though the International Olympic Committee eventually decided to let the names of the East German female swimmers remain in the history books. If Enith Brigitha hadn't swam against the two doped East German swimmers, she could have won the 100m freestyle event, instead of returning home with "just" a bronze medal.

The state-employed East German scientists did more than just force their promising children and teens to take anabolic steroids. They had also developed a talent identification program where the national athletic associations collaborated with the school system. The best children in each second grade class were picked out to train with the best students at school twice a week. The absolute best of these were then picked and moved to special schools with an athletic focus. There were nine such schools located in the largest cities in East Germany: Magdeburg, Leipzig, Potsdam, Halle, and Karl-Marx-Stadt.

The children could in most cases still live at home, but 20 percent of the promising swimmers came from rural areas, so many children were housed in the athletic factories when they were in primary school. Sometimes, the children's families moved to one of the major cities, provided that the regime was able to find jobs for the parents.

The selection was made after careful scientific testing in addition to analyzing the abilities displayed by the children at nine years old. The children's wrists were X-rayed in order to determine their biological age, which in younger years is an important factor behind differences in swimming speed. Once at the athletic schools, the children were first taught the four swimming styles. Then the coaches, all of whom were trained at the four-year coaching program at the university in Leipzig, started to build endurance in their swimmers.

Horst Röeder, the vice president of the DDR Gymnastik und Sport Union, explained East German success in the 1970s with these words: "The government and the Socialist Party have created a good environment for athletic youth. In addition to the training system, all youths are able to travel for free throughout the country to train and compete. Our youth train hard and they use intelligently designed training programs. There is no magic." The training was mostly carried out at school, but when the bell rang, it was perfectly fine to continue training. All East German children paid what corresponded to one cent in the 1980s to a fund that gave them free access to all sports facilities in the country.

DO YOU GET ASTHMA FROM SWIMMING OR DO ASTHMATICS START SWIMMING?

Even the most perfect swimmer may suffer from various problems related to swimming. With so many hours spent in the pool, chlorine sensitivity is a problem for many swimmers, such as Swedish Olympic gold medalist Lars Frölander, who won the 100m butterfly in 2000. But asthma is common among swimmers. Both asthma and diabetes may be tricky to combine with serious training, but there are examples of swimmers who've learned how to manage these unwelcome companions in life so well that they've gone all the way to becoming the best in the world.

There are figures suggesting that asthma may be considered a public health risk. Around 16 to 17 percent of the general population have asthma, but 37 percent of elite swimmers suffer from it—and there's data floating around that suggest that number could be as high as 70 percent.

Before we answer the question in the heading, we need to take a closer look at what this disease entails and how it affects swimmers and other athletes. Asthma means sensitive and easily irritated airways that are constantly inflamed. The disease is lifelong and there's no cure, even though it's possible to alleviate the symptoms. Most athletes are fortunately able to train and compete as usual in spite of the disease. There are even plenty of examples of asthmatics performing at a high level; a quarter of the British track and field team at the 2012 Olympics were asthmatics.

British runner Paula Radcliffe, who holds the world record in the marathon, was diagnosed with asthma at the age of 14. "I plan my training carefully and I'm extra careful when I feel as if I have a cold. I take my medicine before and after each training session."

Cyclists Jan Ullrich and Bradley Wiggins have also become the best in the world against tough competition while managing their asthma. It may seem crazy to take up such brutal endurance sports when you're suffering from a lung disease, but they have nonetheless shaken off all their doubts and figured out how best to continue doing what they love to do. Bradley Wiggins says, "Asthma is only an obstacle if you allow it to be. There are now so many good drugs and so much knowledge on how to train that it's just a matter of adapting. I understand if you break down when you get the diagnosis, but after a while you're able to use it to your advantage."

Other exceptional athletes who've handled their asthma well include Jackie Joyner-Kersee, whose 1988 world record in heptathlon still holds. Jackie kept her asthma a secret from her coaches as she feared losing her track and field scholarship at UCLA. Unlike Radcliffe, Ullrich, and Wiggins, Jackie Joyner-Kersee didn't take the disease seriously. She frequently missed taking her medication, something that almost ended her life when she ended up in the emergency room, suffering from a severe asthma attack. The ER is where her coach found out about her disease.

Knowledge and increasingly better medication are the best weapons for fighting asthma. Those who develop asthma frequently have a family history of hay fever, eczema, and allergies. If the swimmer is careful about taking his or her medication and avoids triggers, it may be months between these troubling attacks.

Typical triggers include dust, animal fur, perfumes, cigarette smoke, and dry, cold air. Vacuum cleaners, aquarium fish, unperfumed soap, nicotine patches, and moving to Florida may deal with those triggers, but there's one trigger swimmers find difficult to avoid: swimming pools are cleaned using chemicals that may potentially trigger asthma attacks. Kerstin Romberg, a researcher in the Respiratory Medicine and Allergology department at Lund University in Sweden, states that, "When resting, we normally breathe in 1.5 gallons (5.7 liters) of air per minute. A hard-working swimmer may inhale 50 gallons (189 liters) per minute over short periods." Swimmers are highly exposed to the harmful chemicals found at the water surface and are swimming in the area with the highest concentration of harmful substances. Furthermore, a swimmer frequently trains twice a day, which may lead to the body not having enough time to recover from exposure to harmful chemicals between training sessions.

SWIMMERS WITH ASTHMA

Mark Spitz won seven Olympic golds in Munich in 1972.

Peter Vanderkaay won an Olympic gold in relay in 2008.

Allison Streeter has swum across the English Channel more than 40 times.

Nancy Hogshead won three Olympic golds in 1984.

Amy van Dyken won six Olympic golds in 1996 and 2000.

YOUR SWIMMING: TRAINING WITH ASTHMA

Be Careful About Your Medication

Long-acting medicines help the mucus membranes react less when irritated. Quick-acting medicines open up the airways in the lung bronchi and make it easier to breathe. Taking too much, however, may lead to positive results in doping tests.

Warm Up Slowly

Begin sessions with swimming at an easy pace and perform technique exercises without rapid increases in speed that might increase the ventilation rate.

Feel Free to Do Interval Training

Swim training is perfect for planning suitable natural breaks. For a runner, 60 minutes is almost always continuous. For a swimmer, on the other hand, it works out very well to swim a distance that takes five minutes, rest for a minute, and then repeat 10 times.

Don't Train if You're Sick

The consequences of training with an infection in your body almost always results in difficulties for asthmatics. Keep an eye on your resting heart rate, body temperature, and look out for other signs of infection.

Avoid Cold Air

By "cold," we're talking winter air—freezing temperatures. Most people who only do swim training don't normally encounter cold air, unless they're training in Utah and Colorado, where outdoor pools are used all year round. If you're training in the winter for multisport events (e.g., triathlons or

ÖTILLÖ), you might want to consider alternatives to running, cycling, and skiing in cold temperatures. Is it possible to replace cold-weather outdoor training with water running, leg-kick swimming, or other forms of indoor training? A radical proposal for the asthmatic is to go to a training camp or even move south when the winter is at its coldest.

Swim in Good Pools
In outdoor pools, there's good ventilation to dissipate substances that may trigger attacks. Indoors, conditions are improved if swimmers take a shower before jumping in the water.

The question of whether you get asthma from swimming or whether asthmatics start swimming is best answered with, "a little bit of both." Indoor pools that don't work that well may be a factor behind asthma. Then there are obviously also people with asthma who are attracted to swimming because it's a form of exercise that is well suited for their condition.

STRENGTH TRAINING AND SWIMMING

Strength training has been a frequent and sometimes hotly debated topic in the swimming world since the 1950s, when it started to become fashionable as a complementary form of training for a number of sports. In 1942, during the middle of a destructive world war, coach David Armbruster pointed out the benefits of training on land in his book

Swimming and Diving. Armbruster recommended that the swimmer run in place and stretch his or her groin. Swimmers were advised not to lift weights as it was believed that weight training would build muscles that would limit flexibility and make the swimmer heavier. However, the perspective on strength training was about to change. In the 1970s, even chess players engaged in strength training—Bobby Fischer was seen both lifting dumbbells and pulling a chest expander.

The first wave of heavier strength training may without a doubt be attributed to James "Doc" Counsilman. Prior to Counsilman, American coaches hadn't been all that interested in research. Doc Counsilman was born in December 1920 and as a young boy developed an interest in fish and other water animals. In his hometown of St. Louis, Missouri, he'd capture snakes, which he then dropped into the bathtub at home to see how they swam. After he fell into the water when he was 13 years old, he decided to learn how to swim. But swimming at the YMCA cost money, so he had to work extra at several places to be able to afford it.

Counsilman was a college swimmer in his 20s when David Armbruster, who served as the head coach at the University of Iowa, published *Swimming and Diving.* After the Japanese humiliated the American men's team at the 1932 Olympics in Los Angeles, the Americans realized that they had to do something. The large universities had had swimming teams competing against each other since 1924, but the biggest stars, such as Johnny Weissmuller, preferred swimming for money in hotel pools rather than toiling night and day at swim training and university studies. Nor was there any American swimming association until 1980. The Olympic sports were instead grouped together under the umbrella of AAU, the Amateur Athletic Union. Its chairman, Avery Brundage, arranged the first national college championships in swimming in 1937, where the University of Michigan beat Ohio State University.

The University of Michigan had the charismatic coach Matthew Mann, who had a deep passion for teaching others how to swim. Mann was born in the English town of Leeds and came from a poor home. As a kid, he could only afford to go swimming once a week—on the so-called "dirty days"; it only cost a penny to swim the day before the pool was cleaned. Mann became a British junior champion at the age of 9 and a senior champion at the age of 14. At the age of 20, he emigrated to New York without a nickel in his pocket.

On Ellis Island, where every immigrant was received, he was stopped as he didn't have enough money, and was subsequently sent to Toronto in a locked railway car with two dollars in his wallet. There he managed to find a room for one dollar a week and bought meal vouchers with the other dollar. "I was on top of the world. I had no money but my needs were taken care of and I had a whole week to look for a job." After working on various physical jobs, he eventually started to be involved in swimming again and started to build his life working with the young swimmers at the University of Michigan. His maize and blue from the Detroit suburb of Ann Arbor won the first three college championships.

The United States of the 1930s was still recovering from the Great Depression and Southern universities had little money for swimming programs when Ottilia Counsilman had to put her two intelligent boys in college. Since Doc Counsilman wanted to swim with the best coaches and the greatest swimmers, he dreamed of going north to Michigan. But studying at a college outside your own state was expensive, so he looked further down in the result lists of the college championships for other possibilities. He found that Ohio State University had come in second, but Ohio was also too far away to be a realistic option.

Fortunately, however, the U.S. college championships were being held in St. Louis in 1941. Had these championships been arranged anywhere else, it would have been impossible for Doc Counsilman to afford the trip. During the championships, Mike Peppe, the coach of Ohio State, thought Counsilman performed so well on the 200m breaststroke that he talked to him after the race. When Peppe heard that the pious Mrs. Counsilman was stretched thin (being single with two boys), he made sure to reduce the expenses so the young breaststroke swimmer could come to Columbus, where Ohio State is located. Soon both the coach and the swimmer got what they wanted. Counsilman got to share a tiny apartment with a swimmer from Hawaii, and worked at a job in one of the tallest buildings in Ohio, where he made sure that men in gray suits in elevators got off at the right floor.

Also swimming for Ohio State was the very talented breaststroke swimmer Herbert Higgins. Higgins had placed fourth at the Berlin Olympics in 1936. His time in the semifinal would have been enough to win a medal, but he hit the wall in the final and lost the medal in the last length. For many athletes, a disappointing setback is the absolute best spark for new and better efforts, and this is what triggered Higgins to train hard to become the best.

The 1940 Olympics were set to take place in Tokyo, but were understandably canceled due to the war. Higgins, however, found new goals. Doc Counsilman became good friends with the older and successful Higgins, and Counsilman was also to become a prominent breaststroke swimmer. While Higgins became an American college champion, Counsilman also made great progress as a result of his diligence and a great curiosity about swimming. Both of them also tested new forms of strength training, which led to major improvements for Counsilman, whose results while training pointed

Present coach Ray Looze has headed Indiana University in their rise back to the powerhouse they were under Counsilman.

toward a world record. However, with only a week to go before the most important competition in 1943, Counsilman had to report for duty in the Army to fight in the war. His results on the military's intelligence tests were among the highest ever measured, and he was immediately sent to training.

The 1944 Olympics, which were supposed to be held in London, were also called off. On the night of June 6, 1944, forces consisting of British, American, and Canadian soldiers landed in Normandy under the codename Operation Overlord. More than 10,000 allied soldiers died in what is known as D-Day, an event considered the turning point in the Second World War. The German response was the V-1 rocket— short for "Vengeance Weapon 1," also referred to as "the buzz bomb." Just a week after D-Day, the first V-1 was launched at London and these rockets rained over the intended Olympic city for the entire summer. More than 6,000 people were killed in the attacks and three times as many people were injured.

The enormous tragedies brought on by the war cast a long shadow on the history of sports. More athletes than Doc Counsilman missed the opportunity to compete—and perhaps win—at the Olympics. American sprinter and long jumper Eulace Peacock defeated Jesse Owens in the United States several times in 1936, but pulled a muscle in his thigh and was unable to go to the Berlin Olympics. Swede Gunder Hägg was the best middle-distance runner in the world during the war and broke 16 world records. It's very likely that both Hägg and Peacock would have won medals at the 1940 and 1944 Olympics. Though many athlete's stories during this time were of missed opportunities, several of the greatest swimmers of the time were to suffer a crueler fate.

Two men, both born on December 12, 1913, did 57.6 in the 100m freestyle during the 1936 Olympics in Berlin. One of them, Yale student Peter Fick, the definite favorite after having beaten Johnny Weissmuller's record on the distance three times, came to Berlin with a personal record of 56.8. Fick also easily broke the Olympic record during the trials, but was clocked at a time more than two seconds slower in the final. The Americans found this incomprehensible, and they submitted a protest with photographic proof that Fick was in a position to win a medal—not sixth as claimed by the judges. The protest was rejected in front of the large home crowd, who saw Fick getting beaten by the German favorite Helmut Fischer.

Instead, the star of the Olympics became the Hungarian medical student Ferenc Csik, who was the same age as Fick. He won the 100m race and got the same time as Fick in the trials. Despite his slow teammates, Csik was able to win a bronze medal for Hungary in the 4 × 200m freestyle.

Peter Fick was the favorite ahead of the 1940 Olympics, but the outbreak of the war prevented him from getting a rematch with Csik. The

1936 Olympic star, a newly graduated doctor, was killed during World War II while tending to a wounded soldier.

The war claimed more victims among the swimmers. The German friends Hans Freese and Hermann Heibel both competed in freestyle swimming at the Berlin Olympics. Five years later, Freese had fallen in battle in Bremen and Heibel was dying in a tent outside of Leningrad, suffering from severe injuries from an explosion.

The silver medalist in the 100m freestyle in Los Angeles in 1932, Takuro Kawaishi, died from a bomb blast in Iwo Jima in 1945. The champion from the 1928 Olympics, New Zealander David Lindsay, was killed by friendly fire in Italy in 1943.

Doc Counsilman was also drafted into military service in January 1945 and sent to serve in Italy. Instead of exploring how good he could get in the pool, he was now serving as a pilot of a B-24 bomber, dropping gruesome amounts of explosives on German military and industrial facilities.

After the end of the war, Counsilman returned to the United States in August 1945, certain that having been drafted into the Air Force meant the end of his swimming career. But coach Peppe was of a different mind and a long escalation period was initiated so that Counsilman would finally be able to swim at the American college championships in March 1946, where he came in second. "Not bad for a war veteran," he thought.

Doc Counsilman started working as a coach while doing his PhD in physiology at the University of Iowa, and this is when he met David Armbruster. Swimming for Iowa was the best freestyle swimmer at the time, Wally Ris, who was also a pioneer of using weights for strength training.

Counsilman's first job as a head coach was at Cortland State in upstate New York. One of the student athletes he coached was George Breen. Breen had been a competitive rower who had only started swimming at the age of 17 when Counsilman had persuaded him to change sports. Counsilman felt as if Breen was in a position to experiment freely, due to his physiological background and the lack of pressure to produce good results for the athletically mediocre college. The reward came in 1956 when George Breen won three medals at the Melbourne Olympics, where he also broke the 1,500m freestyle world record.

The next wave of strength training came in the 1990s in the wake of the 50-meter distance being included in the international program. Fifty meters is so fast that the swimmers are not troubled by muscle weight or lack of oxygen.

Oleksander Dzaburia from Ukraine arrived at the 1994 Swedish Swim Games larger and seemingly stronger than what breaststroke swimmers looked like before the 50m distance was added to the program. Even before he made his amazing time of 27.3 in 50m breaststroke, Swedish swimmers had already given him the nickname "The Kiosk." Swimmers with a physique like that of Dzaburia have become more common; for instance, American swimmer Josh Schneider is 6'4" (193 cm) and weighs more than 220 pounds (100 kilograms). Schneider was ranked sixth in the world in 50m freestyle in 2015. On twice that distance, however, he was only ranked 31st.

It's now common knowledge that swimmers need some form of strength training to reach their full potential. But not everyone has the same build as Schneider and The Kiosk. Sean Ryan came in fourth at the open water world championships in 2015, and even though he's just as tall as Schneider, he only weighs 140 pounds (64 kilograms). His coaches at the University of Michigan often joked that it's cheap having him on the team, as they are able to fax him to competitions instead of buying airline tickets.

Which body shape is the best for swimmers to increase their top speed, or to maintain a high speed for a long period is still one of the most hotly debated topics in the world of swimming. Furthermore, there is no clear definition of the term "strength training," as it has different meanings in different training environments.

Strength training affects swimming performance by:

- Increasing your swimming speed as your arms and legs create more power. This power may translate into a higher speed or the ability to maintain your speed for more repetitions. A swimmer should primarily try to increase his or her strength without increasing his or her weight in the water.
- Preventing injuries, primarily as the swimmer builds up his or her muscles and increases flexibility around the joints that receive the most beatings. Above all, the swimmer needs tough shoulders and elbows. The knees of a breaststroke swimmer are also particularly vulnerable. Well-balanced muscles prevent unnecessary wear by making swimming more symmetrical.
- Improving the timing of swimming movements by strengthening and developing the upper body muscles to enable better control of the swimmer's strength. This is done in order to focus the power in the desired direction and thereby increase the swimmer's speed.
- Making the body more hydrodynamic.

To delve into this issue, we first need the right terms. The three terms we need to know are strength, power, and muscular endurance:

STRENGTH: The power a muscle is capable of producing for one single repetition of a movement.

POWER: Power is more specific and represents movement in the manner required in the relevant sport. The same range of motion and desired speed.

MUSCULAR ENDURANCE: This concerns the number of times the specific movement may be repeated without the muscle getting worn out to the point of less effectiveness or even injury. Different distances have different muscular endurance requirements. Requirements would differ for Florent Manaudou and Sarah Sjöström, who swim 50m or 100m, Michael Phelps, who swims 200m, or Katie Ledecky, who swims 800m or 1,500m.

EFFECTS OF HEAVY AND EXPLOSIVE STRENGTH TRAINING ON ENDURANCE SPORTS

Possible positive physiological and performance-related effect		Proven change	
Improved VO$_2$ maximum	No	Increased body weight	No
Improved movement economy	Yes	Reduced relative VO$_2$ maximum	No
Improved anaerobic capacity	Yes		
Improved lactose threshold	Yes	Increased diffusion distance	No
Less fatigue	Yes	Reduced capillarization	No
Improved maximum strength	Yes	Reduced enzyme activity	No
Improved generation of power	Yes		
Improved maximum speed	Yes		
Improved endurance	Yes		

A 2013 study on endurance athletes praised the effects of strength training. The athletes participating in the study lifted as much weight as they could possibly lift four to ten times per set. The idea was that by doing this, they would become stronger and be able to lift more the next session.

It's easy to think that the effect would be the same for swimmers, but this correlation has been harder to prove. In the 1980s, researcher Steven Shaw had a group of swimmers using a swimming bench perform one single maximum pull each. In his first study, he was able to show a correlation between how hard the swimmers were able to pull and how fast they could swim 25 yards. But when he repeated the study a year later, he was unable to find any correlation between power and speed. Based on this and subsequent studies with the same results, the acceptable assumption is that there is no linear correlation between strength on land and speed in water.

In his next study, Shaw tested swimmers in the water, where they were attached to a rubber band to swim with resistance. A sensor was attached to the band to enable a reading of the power generated by the swimmer. This time, Shaw found a strong correlation: the more power the swimmers were able to generate while attached to the rubber band, the faster they were able to swim 25 yards.

The conclusion of Shaw's experiment is that strength—and increasing your strength—is only beneficial if you're able to use it in your swimming. To do this, you first need to increase your forward-driving force. This is determined by the timing of your arm and leg movements, but also on the work of your hips, which create your body rotation. Second, a more muscular swimmer will have to meet the challenge of a higher weight in the water and the risk of having to deal with a deeper water position, which eventually leads to a higher resistance. That increased resistance would cause the speed to go down, perhaps even more if there hadn't been an increase in power. Swimmers with a good feeling for their swimming, such as Lars Frölander or Therese Alshammar, are able to use increased strength to swim faster. At the same time, strength training may be counterproductive for less talented swimmers.

Which Exercises Should Be Avoided?

The military press, dips, and push-ups have all turned out to be risky for swimmers. They may cause friction between the humerus and the shoulder joint—a form of friction that frequently leads to a drawn-out inflammation. Many swimmers are certainly capable of performing these exercises whereas others have a more fragile anatomy. Once inflammation occurs, it may be difficult to get rid of.

How Frequently Should a Swimmer Engage in Strength Training?

A swimmer should spend most of his or her training time engaged in various forms of swimming. For competitive swimmers, 3×45 minutes of strength training in combination with 8 to 9×120 minutes of swimming a week is usually adequate for both sprint and long-distance swimmers. It's also a good idea to begin swimming sessions with 15 minutes of warm-up for upper body and shoulders.

Strength Training Before or After a Swimming Session?

Here, opinions diverge: Doing strength training before a swimming session means that the muscles are rested when lifting heavy weights, but not when swimming. And the opposite holds true if swimming precedes strength training. What determines the placement of strength training sessions is how well the swimmer responds to his or her key sessions. The advantage of training your upper body before swimming is that it makes it easier for you to feel when you are using the correct upper body muscles when swimming.

Is It Possible to Swim Without Getting Wet?

For swimmers, the equivalent of the ski training machine used by cross-country skiers is the swimming bench (the innovation Stephen Shaw used for measuring strength). While positioned lying down on his or her stomach on a slightly tilted bench, the swimmer is able to target relevant muscles by pulling handles offering resistance.

Even though the swimming bench is the closest we get to swimming on land, it still doesn't match swimming in water. A Japanese study has shown that when training on the swimming bench, it's not even possible to get up to 80 percent of the oxygen consumption taking place when swimming in water. This is due to several reasons: First, there is no water resistance. Second, the swimmer is lying down flat on his or her stomach without using the upper body the same way as in real swimming. And finally, the swimmer doesn't have to use energy to return the arm to the original position the same way he or she would in water.

That's why exercising your heart and lungs on a swimming bench is not recommended as a primary method of training for the ambitious swimmer. Bench swimming is best used as a temporary or emergency solution if the swimmer is unable to be in the water for some time, perhaps as a result of some surgery.

Muscle Strength

Swimming is considered a relatively complete form of training. During hard swimming, the majority of muscles are used, even if certain muscles are used more or less in the different styles. Swimming causes many movement cycle repetitions, where muscular adaptation increases muscle volume and where the long duration of training periods burns a great deal of fat, which in turn contributes to a swimmer's small waist. The cobra-shaped body of swimmers, with broad shoulders and small waists, is carved out from mile after mile in the pool.

If we divide the crawl movement into three phases, it looks something like this: (1) During the return and when entering the hand, the freestyle swimmer uses the same primary muscles: trapezius (upper), rhomboideus major/minor, serratus anterior, supraspinatus, and the front and middle part of the deltoid muscle. (2) The actual pull starts with an activation of the large chest muscle, followed by the wing muscle doing a little bit more of the work later in the pull. (3) In cases where the swimmer uses a shallow elbow during the pull (just like Sarah Sjöström and Michael Phelps), then the biceps, brachioradialis, flexor carpi ulnaris, and triceps are used. The more effort the swimmer puts in, the more he or she uses the triceps.

Backstroke is not all that different from freestyle swimming. The deltoid muscle, rhomboideus, supraspinatus, upper trapezius, and serratus anterior are at work when entering the hand and at the finish, whereas the scapulothoracic joint muscles hold the shoulder in a good position in order to prevent nerves from getting pinched. Latissimus dorsi, subscapularis, and teres minor are at work during the pull.

The butterfly style seems to create swimmers with the broadest shoulders. The entire forward propulsion is done by both arms at the same time, so the swimmer has to generate more power compared to freestyle and butterfly swimming, where the forward-driving force shifts from arm to arm. The deltoid muscle, supraspinatus, infraspinatus, trapezius, and rhomboid muscles work together when entering the hand and at the finish of the pull. The large chest muscle and latissimus dorsi carry out the essential job of creating the force necessary to move the body forward, whereas teres minor and subscapularis rotate and stabilize the shoulder.

YOUR SWIMMING: WHICH EXERCISES AND HOW OFTEN?

Three ways of choosing strength exercises		Suitable for . . .
Whole body	You run through exercises for your whole body in the same strength training session. You teach your body to use more muscle fibers without them necessarily enlarging.	. . . someone who rarely engages in strength training—once or twice a week. . . . someone doing lighter strength training in order to prevent injuries.
Upper/ lower body	You alternate focusing on your legs and your upper body in each session.	. . . someone who loves heavy workouts.
Threefold	Three sessions mean (1) legs (2) chest, shoulders, and triceps (3) back, biceps, and abdomen.	. . . someone with more time and energy for strength training.

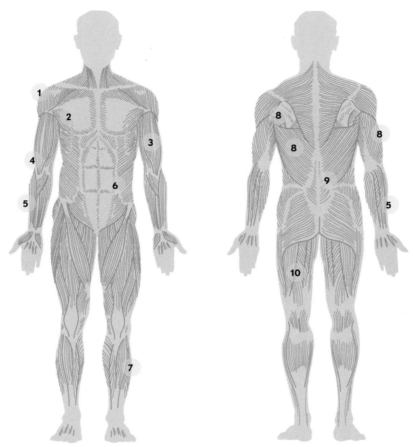

THE SWIMMER'S MUSCLES FROM THE FRONT

THE SWIMMER'S MUSCLES FROM THE REAR

*(1) **Deltoids:** When the butterfly swimmer is so tired that he or she can hardly move his or her arms forward, that's when the deltoids have given up.*

*(2) **Pectoralis major:** Just like for the penguin, the large chest muscle plays an important role when the swimmer creates his or her forward-driving force.*

*(3) **Biceps:** Although the triceps are the upper arm muscles that drive the swimmer the most forward, biceps are still needed for the anchoring and finish of the arm stroke, as well as for the strength balance of the arm.*

*(4) **Brachialis:** Key in the anchoring phase of the arm stroke.*

*(5) The muscles of the **hand and forearm** are used for stabilizing the hand when pulling the arm through the water.*

*(6) The straight and diagonal **abdominal muscles** are usually tense the whole time and help the swimmer link his or her arms and legs together.*

*(7) The muscles of the **ankle joint** are particularly important for starting and turning, as well as for the leg stroke when doing the breaststroke.*

*(8) **Latissimus dorsi, triceps, and teres major,** together with pectoralis major, are the muscles doing the most work during the pull of the arm. They provide the largest part of the forward-driving force in all styles, except for breaststroke.*

*(9) **Sacrospinalis:** A strong upper body provides a stable posture.*

*(10) **Gluteus maximus, hamstrings, and gastrocnemius** are important for starting and turning, as well as for the leg stroke when doing the breaststroke.*

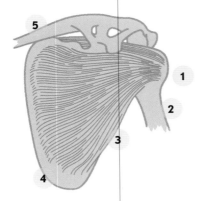

THE SHOULDER GIRDLE FROM THE FRONT

(1) The shoulder joint: It's important that your shoulder joint is working properly in order to swim long and hard without any problems. If the head of the humerus is not in the right position against the shoulder blade, harmful friction may easily occur. Training large and small muscles around the shoulder should balance the shoulder joint.

(2) Humerus

(3) Subscapularis: This triangular muscle underneath the shoulder blade keeps the head of the humerus pressed up against the shoulder blade's joint cavity. It's activated when the arm rotates inward.

(4) Shoulder blade

(5) Collarbone

YOUR SWIMMING: LOOK AFTER YOUR SHOULDERS

Swimming-related shoulder pain is so common that it's been given a name: "swimmer's shoulder." This means pain in the front and outer part of the shoulder, which is referred to as subacromial in medical contexts (i.e., below the acromion). The shoulder joint is the most flexible joint in the human body, and even though swimming isn't even close to the jerky movements of throwing sports, it's not uncommon that it suffers from strains experienced as both painful and annoying.

Swimmer's shoulder may lead to a deterioration of:

- *posture*
- *flexibility of the shoulder joint*
- *local neuromuscular control*
- *muscle strength*

When Rebecca Soni does the breaststroke, about 80 percent of her forward-driving force originates from her legs. This doesn't mean that she doesn't need to train her arms, but gives you an indication of the importance of having flexible, strong, and explosive leg muscles when doing the breaststroke.

Legs and Training on Land

These days, swimmers use fins when training their legs. Fins give you a higher speed (especially at a lower intensity), and while large enough to provide more water resistance, they're small enough not to alter your leg movements. Fins cause increased work for the muscles and increased possible power development.

Training on land has also progressed quite a bit, and there are now exercises with barbells and medicine balls developed for the physiologically explosive requirements of swimmers.

Common Causes Behind Shoulder Problems

The shoulders are the most important joints for a swimmer. An injured shoulder may heal very slowly and therefore it is critical to keep them functional. Increasing the workload too rapidly and swimming with an incorrect technique are the most common causes of shoulder problems. Most elite swimmers prevent further hassle by warming up their shoulders before entering each workout.

Situations that lead to shoulder problems:

- A rise in your training dose that is too steep or simply a dose that is too high.
- Working too hard too early in the session without warming up your shoulders may cause detrimental effects.
- Swimming with paddles increases the initial burden of the pull whereas swimming with a kickboard places the shoulder joint at a fully elevated position and rotates it inward. If you've felt pain or discomfort in your shoulder, then stay away from the drills and exercises causing it.
- An overly strenuous movement sequence or a so-called "ugly technique" may ruin your shoulders. Crossing the center line time and time again

not only wastes kinetic energy that you could otherwise have turned into speed, but also contributes to a jamming syndrome. An optimal body rotation enables you to retain a first-class breakwater function and allows other muscles, such as your abdominals and latissimus dorsi, to take care of a large part of the shoulder girdle's workload.

How to Prevent Shoulder Problems

Here are some tips:

- GET A BETTER POSTURE Defects in your posture are rarely anatomical but acquired physiologically after years of poor posture when standing up, sitting down, walking, and lying down. Your back is usually what suffers the most from poor posture, but your shoulder joints are also at risk.
- STABILIZE YOUR SHOULDER GIRDLE An unstable shoulder girdle alters the demands on the rotator cuff (a muscle group in the upper arm), which is why stabilizing exercises have been shown to have a very positive effect on shoulder health. You don't need to do such exercises with heavy weights. Initially, these exercises appear ridiculously simple to carry out, but once the muscles get tired, it becomes tough—just like any other form of strength training!

The rotator cuff may be strengthened using eccentric, concentric, isometric, and plyometric exercises. Research suggests doing functional exercises in current movement patterns using more resistance than usually encountered when swimming. One example for freestyle swimmers is swimming in a stationary position with the help of a rubber band or using a swimming bench.

If Your Shoulders Still Hurt

- SWIM LESS Fewer and/or shorter sessions may ease the strain enough to enable you to continue swimming.
- VARY YOUR TRAINING Varying swimming styles during your sessions may reduce strain and increase flexibility.

- AVOID HAND PADDLES A careless entering of the hand may put more strain on your shoulder than necessary.

YOUR SWIMMING: HOW TO EXERCISE YOUR UPPER BODY

The upper body is particularly important for swimmers. Of course, it's important for other athletes, but a swimmer is unable to use any form of solid surface for moving forward (except in turns), so you can't neglect the center part of your body.

Your arms are connected with your legs (and each other) through a strong upper body. The breakthrough of underwater kicks has made the lower abdominals and lumbar muscles even more important. Well-trained abdominals are a prerequisite for creating a competitive forward-driving movement. You also need endurance in your abdominals to maintain speed at the end of your training series or races.

It wasn't that long ago that swimmers did sit-ups for 20 minutes before each afternoon session. This is now seen as obsolete for several reasons: (1) A sit-up exercises one or more abdominal muscles depending on how it's carried out, whereas the upper body consists of many muscles in different layers. Some include all muscles all the way from the hips up to the shoulders as part of the upper body. Since swimmers use their shoulders more than other athletes, it makes sense to include the hips as part of the upper body, but not the shoulders. That is why upper body exercises should be more complex than sit-ups. (2) Doing a lot of repetitions may be good for upper body stability, but it doesn't build upper body strength. (3) Movements or static contractions involving arms and legs need to be linked together with upper body training to access upper body strength when swimming.

The Perfect Body in Practice

Swimming at a high level requires many muscles to work together harmoniously and powerfully, and as we have seen, there are several ways in which you may prepare them for this task.

Strength training using weights is one way. It's very important that you have an objective with your strength training, as its main purpose is to prevent injuries. Swimmers also need flexible and strong muscles around their shoulders in particular in order to be able to swim long, often, and hard. Swimmers may also improve their performance by getting stronger. But this is where things start to get complicated as the fact that a strong muscle doesn't necessarily mean that the swimmer is able to use it the right way. As recently as 10 to 15 years ago, swimmers did general strength training without any special adaptation to their particular sport. Today, swimmers increasingly try to make their exercises mimic the movements they use in the water.

At adult swimming competitions, it's obvious that technique is more important than how fit the swimmer is or which body shape he or she has. Preparing your body to swim as fast as possible is a complex task. Since a large body glides through the water with more resistance, the swimmer must be lean for optimal effect. At the same time, one's anthropometrics are hard to alter.

Swimmers start with naturally broad shoulders due to good bone structure—a large chest and long collarbones—and proper strength training and stubborn swim training will make the shoulders even broader. But without flexibility, broad shoulders won't take you very far and might be a burden.

If you weren't fortunate enough to be born with a body designed for swimming but still want to swim fast, then you need top-notch technical know-how. For example, if you have a smaller ratio between your forearm and hand in relation to the total length of your arm, then you need to put in more work to anchor your arm at an early stage to move your body more efficiently in the water.

EIGHT COMPONENTS OF YOUR STRENGTH TRAINING PROGRAM

Lunges

All leg muscles plus upper body. This exercise has infinite variations and swimmers should add arm movements.

Rowing

Rowing targets back muscles in general and the lumbar region in particular. Can be done using a bar, rubber band, or machines.

Chin-Ups or Pull-Ups

When well performed, they increase the strength of the latissimus dorsi and the complementary muscles that are active in the pulls of the swimmer. They are possible to carry out with a rubber band. Way too often swimmers have such strong arms that they lift more with their arms and shoulders than with the desired upper back muscles.

The Plank

Your upper body muscles are more or less constantly at work when you swim. The plank is a good way to strengthen these muscles. Vary your position so your arms and legs are not static.

Tricep Press

The tricep (located on the back side of the upper arm) is an important muscle for swimmers. You may use a dumbbell or fixed weights.

Chest Press

Use a bar (bench press) or various forms of push-ups.

Light Shoulder Exercises

For example, push-ups without bending your elbows and instead letting your shoulder girdle do the work.

Biceps

The bicep is the antagonist of the tricep and should be trained to balance your arms. Dumbbells and barbells work well.

APPENDIX

SWIMMING DRILLS What sometimes separates good from not-so-good swimmers is strength and endurance. It's more possible for any competitive swimmer to outswim Arnold Schwarzenegger or Serena Williams due to his or her superior technique than it is for a swimmer with a poor technique to beat one with a good technique.

A swimming drill focuses on one or several components in the swimmer's movement pattern: water position, coordination, flexibility, or alignment/direction. In addition, the swimmer also exercises his or her proprioception (i.e., the ability to determine the relative position of his or her own body parts). It turns out that the body uses a special type of receptor, proprioceptors, which detect the position of the joints by registering tension in muscles and tendons. Ordinarily, this gathering of information is not a conscious process; instead, the proprioceptors send the information to the cerebellum, where a decision to act is made. In this section, I present a number of technique exercises for freestyle swimming, but there are definitely more available.

Furthermore, it's possible to simplify or further refine many of the exercises with the help of a pull buoy, paddles, snorkel, fins, or ankle straps. Each exercise is described in terms of execution and objective. In addition, their effects are assessed on a scale from one to five, where five is the most beneficial. If it's unclear how you're supposed to execute a particular exercise, look for them at the Instagram account @human_ambition, the hashtag #swimdrillvids, or check out swimming technique guru Glenn Mills at @goswimtv.

CROCODILE

ALTERNATE NAME: The Gator

EXECUTION: When your hand enters the water, stretch it far out in front of your shoulder. Your hand is meant to bite like the jaws of a crocodile, smacking against the surface of the water when your thumb hits your fingers. Repeat, but this time aiming to reach even farther ahead of you.

FOCUS: On a long and stable body at the surface of the water with your head, hips, and heels all positioned at the same level.

PURPOSE: To extend your pull. A long vessel slides faster than a short vessel as long as it stays straight.

BACKGROUND: (1) If you stretch your arm so far that your elbow crease points up, this will make it hard to keep a high elbow in the catch phase and thereby use your entire forearm in the pull. (2) If you enter your hand in front of your head, then your hip is likely to sway in the opposite direction.

EXERCISE LEVEL:
Water position 4
Coordination 3
Flexibility 2
Direction 4

DEMONT

ALTERNATE NAME: Single-arm

EXECUTION: One arm completes full arm strokes, the other is passive and placed backward. Breathe toward the side of your passive arm, and don't start the pull until you've finished breathing and your head is once again positioned downward.

PURPOSE: A very good exercise for refining your position in the water. Executing it in such a way that you actually move forward may be difficult for beginner and experienced competitive swimmers alike. When a beginner tries to execute this exercise, they tend to feel like they're drowning. Even after ten attempts at this exercise, it may still feel uncomfortable, but hopefully things will improve with each repetition. An alternative way to perform this is to double the breathing movements, which make it easier to turn back the head before starting the pull. Swim fins are helpful for the rookie swimmer.

BACKGROUND: The 1970s Olympic star Rick DeMont, who was the first man to swim the 400m freestyle in under four minutes at the Montreal Olympics, was one of the earliest to master this exercise.

EXERCISE LEVEL:

Water position 5

Coordination 4

Flexibility 2

Direction 5

TRIPLE SWITCH

EXECUTION: Every third arm stroke, stop with one hand stretched out forward and the other hand backward. Count to three, let your legs propel you lightly forward, and then execute three new arm strokes. You may breathe both during the arm strokes and the extended gliding phase. Your breathing will differ depending on where you place the breath.

PURPOSE: The main objective is to preserve the speed you get from the three arm strokes and thus focus on both water position and direction. Your posture plays an important role here.

BACKGROUND: This exercise is an extension of the familiar Alabama, which only consists of sliding arm strokes.

EXERCISE LEVEL:

Water position 4

Coordination 3

Flexibility 2

Direction 4

REPLAY

ALTERNATE NAME: Rerun

EXECUTION: The recovery is repeated an additional time. When the hand enters the water, the swimmer "rewinds" the stroke to the exit point and repeats the recovery.

PURPOSE: Good for maintaining your position in the water despite experiencing a disruption to your rhythm.

BACKGROUND: You might find it difficult to maintain your position in the water. Most people do this exercise over short distances and at an easy pace without any stress. Fins help.

EXERCISE LEVEL:

Water position 4

Coordination 4

Flexibility 2

Direction 3

SHARK ATTACK

ALTERNATE NAME: Brazilian, Shark Fin

EXECUTION: While swimming, a kickboard is placed between your legs, resembling a shark fin. The goal is to prevent the fin from swaying side to side. This means that your hips need to stay completely flat while swimming.

PURPOSE: Exercises your core muscles and is good for your posture in the water. This drill also reveals the difference between shoulder rotation and hip rotation.

BACKGROUND: Brazilian Fernando Scherer (number one in 50m and 100m freestyle in 1999 with 22.1 and 48.6 respectively) carried out this exercise in Coral Springs that same year.

EXERCISE LEVEL:
Water position 3
Coordination 3
Flexibility 4
Direction 4

ZIPPER

ALTERNATE NAME: Unzip.

EXECUTION: At the return, your hand (your thumb or your thumb and forefinger) follows the side of your body from your thigh to your armpit, as if you are closing a zipper.

PURPOSE: Good for muscular relaxation and for exercising the range of motion of your shoulder joint. In addition, maintaining your alignment is more difficult. Since your recovery is somewhat slower, keeping your front hand in the sliding position slightly longer is also more challenging.

BACKGROUND: This exercise is one of the most common active stretching drills around.

EXERCISE LEVEL:
Water position 3
Coordination 2
Flexibility 5
Direction 4

SUBMARINES

ALTERNATE NAME: Underwater swims

EXECUTION: After a rather deep push off, swim freestyle submerged. Aim for a constant depth.

PURPOSE: Gives you a good feel for the resistance of the water, as well as information on how different levels of air in your lungs affect your water position.

EXERCISE LEVEL:
Water position 3
Coordination 3
Flexibility 2
Direction 5

TRIPLE TOUCH

EXECUTION: Pat your buttocks, shoulder, and head at each recovery. If you think this is way too easy, try clenching and opening your fist before and after each pat. This will increase the level of coordination needed.

PURPOSE: Helps a relaxed return and maintained direction, despite a different form of recovery.

BACKGROUND: This drill stresses the importance of keeping your arm outstretched to act as a wave breaker.

EXERCISE LEVEL:
Water position 4
Coordination 4
Flexibility 4
Direction 4

SINGLE-ARM

EXECUTION: The swimmer breathes under the active arm at every arm stroke. The passive arm is stretched forward in front of the shoulder, helping to avoid too much wobbling during the breathing motion. In order to further demonstrate the importance of keeping the head from deviating from the bow line, try successfully performing two arm strokes at once in each direction.

PURPOSE: Keeping the ship straight and reducing head wobbling when breathing.

BACKGROUND: This is a progression from the simple one arm exercise. Chad le Clos has been spotted warming up with this drill.

EXERCISE LEVEL:
Water position 3
Coordination 3
Flexibility 2
Direction 5

POLO CRAWL

EXECUTION: Keep your chin above the water's surface while breathing straight ahead.

PURPOSE: Good polo swimming requires you to catch the water at an early stage and keep your legs working. It also strengthens your shoulders.

BACKGROUND: A common technique exercise—not least among fast-swimming polo swimmers. Polo swimmer Brad Schumacher won two Olympic golds in swimming in 1996 and played on the U.S. polo team.

EXERCISE LEVEL:
Water position 4
Coordination 3
Flexibility 3
Direction 3

REVERSE CATCH-UP

ALTERNATE NAME: Thumb in the leg

EXECUTION: Allow each arm stroke to catch up to the other at the end of the pull so that you always have at least one thumb against the thigh.

PURPOSE: Good for the start of the pull. The fact that you become a little bit shorter as a vessel makes it difficult to keep both direction and water position. Mastering this exercise in terms of coordination may also prove difficult.

BACKGROUND: This is an exercise frequently used by elite swimmers for highlighting and mastering the catch phase of the pull.

EXERCISE LEVEL:
Water position 3
Coordination 4
Flexibility 2
Direction 4

THE DRYER

ALTERNATE NAME: One-count breathing

EXECUTION: Breath after EACH arm stroke.

PURPOSE: Good for stressing as few lateral forces as possible while breathing, as well as keeping the top of the head facing the same direction throughout the entire turn.

BACKGROUND: Tamas Darnyi, the king of medley in the 1990s, used one-count breathing when swimming the final lengths of his 400m medley.

EXERCISE LEVEL:
Water position 3
Coordination 4
Flexibility 2
Direction 5

POPOV

ALTERNATE NAME: Freestyle with butterfly kick

EXECUTION: Performed exactly as it sounds.

PURPOSE: Increases flexibility in the hips if you're stiff, while forcing you to use your abdominal and back muscles.

BACKGROUND: Michael Klim has achieved fast times when swimming this way in competitions. A great drill for warming up the hips.

EXERCISE LEVEL:
Water position 3
Coordination 3
Flexibility 4
Direction 2

THE OTHER SIDE

EXECUTION: During the return, move your arm over your back. Once your hand is in the water, allow it to splash on the opposite side behind your back.

PURPOSE: Good for maintaining your

position in the water in spite of a severely altered body position. The movement pattern on the outskirts of your range of motion allows for increased flexibility in the long run.

BACKGROUND: This exercise has frequently been used as a cooldown exercise for stretching after tough sets.

EXERCISE LEVEL:
Water position 4
Coordination 3
Flexibility 4
Direction 4

FIST

EXECUTION: The swimmer has clenched fists during the entire arm stroke cycle.

PURPOSE: When adding in this exercise for a few strokes, the swimmer is able to notice the difference between a good and a not-so-good grip with his or her forearm. Helps in catching the water at an early stage.

BACKGROUND: One of many successful swimming coaches who have used this drill to great success is Olympic Head Coach David Marsh.

EXERCISE LEVEL:
Water position 3
Coordination 2
Flexibility 2
Direction 4

ALABAMA

EXECUTION: The arms are outstretched for three seconds, one at the front position of the pull and the other at the very rear, as if Superman is getting ready to fly off. Appears in varieties where the swimmer performs various numbers of leg kicks before switching sides.

PURPOSE: Good for water position, posture, and alignment.

BACKGROUND: Don Gambril, college coach in Alabama in the early 1970s, is said to have invented this drill, which is why it is called "Alabama."

EXERCISE LEVEL:
Water position 3
Coordination 2
Flexibility 3
Direction 5

SCULLING

ALTERNATE NAME: Frontal Sculling

EXECUTION: The arms are stretched out in front of the body at shoulder width. The forearms and hands swing back and forth like the pendulum on a grandfather clock, providing a forward-driving force.

PURPOSE: Good for getting a sense of the catch phase. This may also provide some good work for your muscles if performed intensely or for a long time. Intense sculling is a great way for the traveling swimmer to get a decent workout in a small hotel pool.

BACKGROUND: Synchronized swimmers started sculling in order to move gracefully underwater.

EXERCISE LEVEL:
Water position 3
Coordination 3
Flexibility 3
Direction 4

ALTERNATE NAME: Squeeze

PURPOSE: During the return, the hand is made into a fist as if to squeeze the water out of a dish rag.

OBJECTIVE: This is meant to help the swimmer relax during the return, in addition to encouraging an energy efficient swimming technique.

BACKGROUND: Former world record holder Kieren Perkins swam the 800m freestyle in 8:07 while using this drill.

EXERCISE LEVEL:
Water position 2
Coordination 4
Flexibility 3
Direction 3

ALTERNATE NAME: The machine gun

EXECUTION: The hips are rotated in an exaggerated way so that the navel is pointing horizontally toward the side of the pool. Or another way: if the navel were a machine gun, then a bullet fired at the maximum rotation would hit the tiles of the pool right below the surface.

PURPOSE: Challenges the swimmer's direction and posture, and acts as a hip flexibility drill.

BACKGROUND: Working with your hips often benefits your stroke as long as you don't lose your alignment. In such a case, your hip rotation easily ends up being counterproductive.

EXERCISE LEVEL:
Water position 3
Coordination 3
Flexibility 4
Direction 5

FINGERTIPS

ALTERNATE NAME: Fingertip drill

EXECUTION: Your fingertips maintain a straight line on the surface of the water during the entire return.

PURPOSE: This relaxing exercise helps you maintain your direction as well as prevents you from "shot putting" during your return.

BACKGROUND: This drill belongs to the same category of antitetanic exercises as The Rag.

EXERCISE LEVEL:

Water position 2
Coordination 3
Flexibility 3
Direction 4

KLIM

ALTERNATE NAME: Windmill

EXECUTION: Keep arms straight during the return.

PURPOSE: Allows for a different feeling during the return. Good for motor skills, as an exercise buddy may easily compare a performed movement and an imagined movement.

BACKGROUND: In the early 90s, Australian world record holder Michael Klim was a pioneer in using this style.

EXERCISE LEVEL:

Water position 2
Coordination 3
Flexibility 2
Direction 3

BLOW-OUT

EXECUTION: Deflate your lungs as much as possible during each slow breathing cycle.

PURPOSE: Your body is given an opportunity to work on remaining in a beneficial position in the water.

BACKGROUND: A swimmer's body weighs 3 to 12 pounds in the water. The fact that this weight is so low means that you may significantly alter your position in the water by adjusting the amount of air in your lungs.

EXERCISE LEVEL:

Water position 5
Coordination 3
Flexibility 1
Direction 2

THE NORWEGIAN RADIATOR

ALTERNATE NAMES: The radiator, or the water chase

EXECUTION: During the underwater phase of the stroke, the forearm and hand are pulled in a slalom-like pattern six to eight times while the passive arm is stretched forward. The elbow of the active arm is right below the water's surface.

PURPOSE: A good opportunity to calibrate joint angles in the pull.

BACKGROUND: A stroke can always be better. Scratch your forearm a lot to get an even better feeling for how the water travels on your skin.

EXERCISE LEVEL:

Water position 4

Coordination 3

Flexibility 2

Direction 4

DRAW-A-PIG

EXECUTION: During the return phase of your stroke, your arm stops and points straight up in the sky. Then, draw a pig. The stretched-out arm stays stretched until you're done drawing the pig's tail.

PURPOSE: This is a good opportunity for working on "the long ship," and to practice keeping your water position when your weight is off center. This also tests the flexibility of the arm that's outstretched.

BACKGROUND: I have used this exercise since 2008. Any other use is unknown.

EXERCISE LEVEL:

Water position 4

Coordination 4

Flexibility 4

Direction 4

STUN GUN

ALTERNATE NAME: Freeze

EXECUTION: During the recovery phase of the stroke, stop your arm approximately eight inches before hitting the water. Hold this position for two to three seconds while your legs continue to move you forward. The passive arm is stationary in its extended position.

PURPOSE: Yet another exercise in the battery of technique exercises working on "the long ship."

BACKGROUND: A variation of catch-up.

EXERCISE LEVEL:

Water position 4

Coordination 4

Flexibility 2

Direction 4

FRONT LIFE

ALTERNATE NAME: Catch-drill 2.

EXECUTION: Your arm enters and catches the water as usual, but is then pulled up by your ear. This exercise only completes the first half of the pull.

PURPOSE: This exercise focuses on the "entry" and the "catch" in the stroke. A poor catch phase represents a limitation in technique for many swimmers and this exercise will help fix it.

BACKGROUND: Derived from bio-mechanical theories.

EXERCISE LEVEL:
Water position 4
Coordination 4
Flexibility 2
Direction 3

RELEASE PARTY

ALTERNATE NAME: Ear candy

EXECUTION: Your arm enters and catches the water by your ear, after which the pull is carried out as usual. This exercise only completes the second part of the pull.

PURPOSE: This exercise makes it easy for you to identify weaknesses in the last part of the pull. It also makes it easier to see whether the finish of the pull pushes you down in the water or makes you sway.

BACKGROUND: Derived from bio-mechanical theories.

EXERCISE LEVEL:
Water position 4
Coordination 4
Flexibility 2
Direction 3

CHICKEN WING SWIM

EXECUTION: The full stroke is carried out with your thumb in constant contact with your armpit.

PURPOSE: Imagine how swimming must feel for chickens. This exercise works on body position, becoming even more important with smooth breathing motions and joint angles.

BACKGROUND: This exercise has mostly been used while goofing around, but it still has quite a bit to offer for the ambitious swimmer.

EXERCISE LEVEL:
Water position 5
Coordination 4
Flexibility 4
Direction 4

FIRE EXTINGUISHER

ALTERNATE NAME: Splash!

EXECUTION: The entry phase is carried out with the palm of your hand so that water is splashed forward—forward and not to the side.

PURPOSE: This exercise promotes a good sense of direction and is also good for shoulder flexibility.

BACKGROUND: There are many reasons for splashing water on your friends, especially in water polo.

EXERCISE LEVEL:

Water position 3

Coordination 2

Flexibility 3

Direction 4

YANKO

EXECUTION: The base is a constant freestyle flutter kick. Two breaststrokes are followed by one freestyle stroke (right) while the passive arm is extended forward. This is followed by two breaststrokes plus a freestyle stroke (left) while the passive arm is extended forward. Breast-breast-left-free-breast breast-right-free while keeping the flutter kick.

PURPOSE: This exercise offers water position, posture exercise, flexibility, and control of your direction. Above all, your coordination gets a really good workout. The main objective is to keep your leg kicks running without interruption as you're breaking the rhythm of your arm strokes.

BACKGROUND: The first time I heard about it, it was being used by master swimmers in Wisconsin.

EXERCISE LEVEL:

Water position 3

Coordination 4

Flexibility 3

Direction 4

SKIPPER

ALTERNATE NAME: Penguin stroke

EXECUTION: Make your way through the water by keeping your elbows against the side of your body. The forward-driving force of your arms is limited to what your forearms and hands are able to muster. Your posture, starting with the position of your head, is important when trying to imitate the streamlined body of a penguin.

PURPOSE: To find the best possible body position and to optimally use your torso rotation.

BACKGROUND: Penguins are fast swimmers and this is a good attempt to try out their style.

EXERCISE LEVEL:

Water position 4

Coordination 4

Flexibility 2

Direction 4

OCTOPUS

EXECUTION: From a vertical position with your arms above your head, move backward by jet propulsion by folding the body so that your arms meet your legs. Your buttocks lead you horizontally underwater. This movement is similar to the old-fashioned abdominal exercise "the pocket knife."

PURPOSE: To achieve excellent control over how the muscles in your upper body operate and to use water resistance in the best possible way. The rapidly accelerating octopus gives us inspiration from the depths of the sea.

BACKGROUND: Israeli swimmer Guy Barnea became a viral phenomenon when he presented this exercise on social media in 2016.

EXERCISE LEVEL:
Water position 4
Coordination 4
Flexibility 2
Direction 4

SIAMESE TWIN

ALTERNATE NAME: Bonding buddy

EXECUTION: Two swimmers crawl at the same pace with both of them holding onto the same ring-shaped water toy between them. One swimmer holds it in his or her left hand and the other holds in his or her right hand.

PURPOSE: This exercise forces both swimmers to make small adjustments to turn the initially odd movement pattern into a well-oiled machine.

BACKGROUND: This is an exercise that's resulted in laughter in swimming pools all around the world. Swimming in the same rhythm as your partner can also be performed without a chaining device, and is then called "The Mirror." In this instance, swimmer B tries to mimic swimmer A with exactly the same pace and style.

EXERCISE LEVEL:
Water position 4
Coordination 5
Flexibility 3
Direction 4

PACE LIST

50m	100m	200m	400m	800m	1000m	1500m	3000m	1930m	3860m	5km	1h
0:30.0	1:00	2:00	4:00	8:00	10:00	15:00	30:00	19:19	38:37	50:00	6,000 m
0:32.5	1:05	2:10	4:20	8:40	10:50	16:15	32:30	20:55	41:50	54:10	5,535 m
0:35.0	1:10	2:20	4:40	9:20	11:40	17:30	35:00	22:32	45:03	58:20	5,140 m
0:37.5	1:15	2:30	5:00	10:00	12:30	18:45	37:30	24:09	48:17	1:00:50	4,800 m
0:40.0	1:20	2:40	5:20	10:40	13:20	20:00	40:00	25:45	51:30	1:02:30	4,500 m
0:42.5	1:25	2:50	5:40	11:20	14:10	21:15	42:30	27:20	54:40	1:06:40	4,235 m
0:45.0	1:30	3:00	6:00	12:00	15:00	22:30	45:00	28:58	57:56	1:15:00	4,000 m
0:47.5	1:35	3:10	6:20	12:40	15:50	23:45	47:30	30:35	1:01:09	1:19:10	3,765 m
0:50.0	1:40	3:20	6:40	13:20	16:40	25:00	50:00	32:11	1:04:22	1:23:20	3,600 m
0:52,5	1:45	3:30	7:00	14:00	17:30	26:15	52:50	33:48	1:07:35	1:27:30	3,425 m
0:55.0	1:50	3:40	7:20	14:40	18:20	27:30	55:00	35:24	1:10:48	1:31:40	3,270 m
0:57.5	1:55	3:50	7:40	15:20	19:10	28:45	57:30	36:56	1:13:51	1:35:50	3,130 m
1:00.0	2:00	4:00	8:00	16:00	20:00	30:00	60:00	38:39	1:17:17	1:40:00	3,000 m
1:02.5	2:05	4:10	8:20	16:40	20:50	31:15	62:30	40:13	1:20:26	1:44:10	2,880 m
1:05.0	2:10	4:20	8:40	17:20	21:40	32:30	65:00	41:51	1:23:41	1:48:20	2,765 m
1:07.5	2:15	4:30	9:00	18:00	22:30	33:45	67:30	43:28	1:26:55	1:52:30	2,665 m
1:10.0	2:20	4:40	9:20	18:40	23:20	35:00	70:00	45:04	1:30:07	1:56:40	2,570 m
1:12.5	2:25	4:50	9:40	19:20	24:10	36:15	72:30	46:40	1:33:20	2:00:50	2,400 m
1:15.0	2:30	5:00	10:00	20:00	25:00	37:30	75:00	48:17	1:36:33	2:05.00	2,250 m

ETIQUETTE AT THE SWIMMING POOL

Rules

Know and follow the rules of the pool. In Catholic countries, it's quite common that you must wear slippers to access the pool area or put on a swimming cap before you jump into the water. If you think that the rules don't make any sense, contact the manager with your suggestions for improvements. The more swimmers signing your proposals for improvement, the greater your leverage and the higher the chances of getting things changed.

Equipment

Don't scatter your stuff more than is necessary—other swimmers may trip over your things. Use a mesh bag, which allows the contents to dry without having to hang them up after each training session. Write your name on your equipment to avoid confusion or unnecessary conflicts about who owns what.

Positioning

Select your lane based on two criteria: one with only a few swimmers, and one with the most swimmers of your skill level. Doing so means that you avoid having to pass people unnecessarily, which may be a nuisance for you as well as the other swimmers.

Hygiene

Use a swimming cap, and wash off perfume, sweat, and dirt before you jump in the water.

Contact

Avoid touching other swimmers as much as possible. Plan your swimming so that you may pass slower swimmers without disturbing them. Also be prepared when faster swimmers pass you. Keep to the rope and let the passing occur in the middle of the lane.

Circle Swim

Keep to the right in the lane. Even if you're currently alone in the lane, you may get company in the blink of an eye. Make your turns at the middle of the short side of the lane. In Australia, the United Kingdom, and South Africa, people hold to the left of the lane.

Rest

If you are resting, be sure not to place yourself in the center of the ends of the lane. That area needs to be clear of people so that swimmers are able to turn without colliding with resting swimmers not paying attention.

Be Courteous and Diplomatic

An initial conversation with someone you don't know may offer surprises. Be courteous and diplomatic to ensure that the atmosphere in the pool remains good long-term.

Note: Lots of pools in Sweden generally don't have enough room for swimming. This is a quick reference guide to get the most out of your swimming without disturbing others.

PACKING

Going away to compete means that you have a lot to think about. The actual competition itself is stressful and there's no need for additional stress. Forgetting one or a number of important items at home doesn't necessarily mean that you won't make it to the start, but it does result in a few minutes of unnecessary misery that you could certainly put to better use.

A packing list is therefore priceless for your peace of mind. Sofia Demnert (swimrun), James Lenger (modern pentathlon), and Björn Rosenthal (triathlon) have offered their own lists below to help out. Let these lists be the starting point for your own list. You may always add or remove items.

Packing List: Swimming in a Pool

- ☐ Backpack
- ☐ 2 pairs of swimming goggles
- ☐ 2–3 swimming caps
- ☐ 3 pairs of training swim briefs
- ☐ 2–3 pairs of competition suits (depending on the number of races you compete in)
- ☐ 2 large towels
- ☐ Earplugs (if you use them)
- ☐ Body lotion
- ☐ T-shirt and shorts (in the club colors)
- ☐ Warm-up clothes (in the club colors)
- ☐ Shoes or slippers
- ☐ 2 pairs of socks
- ☐ Water bottle
- ☐ Snacks
- ☐ Toothbrush (some people experience a refreshing effect when competing with newly brushed teeth)
- ☐ Highlighter and pen (for finding your name on the starting list and for writing down your split times)
- ☐ Cash (for buying snacks or other items)
- ☐ Suncreen (when competing outdoors)
- ☐ Headphones, a deck of cards, a football, or other items to entertain yourself between races

Packing List: Triathlon

- [ ] Full competition suit or tank top and pants
- [ ] Holder (for displaying your number, including safety pins)
- [ ] Sunglasses
- [ ] Shoe powder
- [ ] Sunscreen
- [ ] Heart rate monitor with chest strap
- [ ] Water bottle
- [ ] Energy bars
- [ ] Energy gel
- [ ] Sports drinks
- [ ] Towel
- [ ] Warm warm-up clothes
- [ ] Extra running shoes
- [ ] Competition license
- [ ] Food and drink for after the competition
- [ ] 2 pairs of swimming goggles (if you use them)
- [ ] Wetsuit
- [ ] Earplugs (if you use them)
- [ ] Petroleum jelly (to avoid chafing)
- [ ] Extra swimming cap (for under the competition cap if the water is cold)
- [ ] Bicycle shoes
- [ ] Bicycle helmet
- [ ] Extra inner tube and extra tires
- [ ] Long-sleeved bicycle shirt (if the weather is cold)
- [ ] Socks
- [ ] Water bottles
- [ ] Bicycle pump
- [ ] CO_2 canisters (for quickly repairing a flat tire)
- [ ] Tools
- [ ] Running shoes
- [ ] Baseball hat
- [ ] Socks

Packing List: Modern Pentathlon

- [ ] Laser pistol and towel
- [ ] 2 competition suits for swimming
- [ ] 2 training swimming briefs
- [ ] 3 pairs of goggles
- [ ] 2–4 swimming caps
- [ ] 2–4 energy bars
- [ ] 2 apples
- [ ] 2 bags of energy candy containing caffeine
- [ ] Amino acids
- [ ] Pen
- [ ] 3 pairs of short socks
- [ ] 2 pairs of socks (for fencing)
- [ ] 2 pairs of compression shorts
- [ ] Shoes for fencing

- ☐ Running shoes or spike shoes (depending on the surface of the competition)
- ☐ Riding boots
- ☐ Riding pants
- ☐ Shirt and jacket for riding
- ☐ Riding helmet
- ☐ Fencing mask
- ☐ Fencing jacket
- ☐ Chest protector
- ☐ Fencing breeches
- ☐ Fencing glove
- ☐ 4–6 fencing weapons (3–4 French grip, 1–2 pistol grip)

- ☐ Wiring for fencing
- ☐ Repair kit for fencing

Warm weather:

- ☐ 2 pairs of running shorts
- ☐ 2 running tank tops
- ☐ Running hat
- ☐ Running glasses

Cold weather:

- ☐ Running tights
- ☐ Long-sleeved running shirt
- ☐ Running gloves

Packing List: Open Water Swimming

- ☐ Wetsuit (if allowed)
- ☐ Swim briefs/swimsuit
- ☐ 2 pairs of dark swimming goggles (for sunny days)
- ☐ 2 pairs of light swimming goggles (for dark days)
- ☐ 2 swimming caps. If the competition has its own swimming cap, it may be a good idea to wear an extra swimming cap underneath in cold water

- ☐ Neoprene hood or neoprene bandana (in cold water)
- ☐ 2 towels
- ☐ Sunscreen
- ☐ Petroleum jelly (to prevent chafing and for warming up your joints)
- ☐ Warm, dry clothes

Packing List: Swimrun

- ☐ Wetsuit. A swimrun suit has a zipper at the front and/or in the back so that you may easily open it when running
- ☐ Swimming cap, often supplied by race organizers—otherwise, you should use one that's colorful to make you visible
- ☐ Earplugs (may reduce dizziness when getting up from the water and offer help against seasickness in cases of high waves)
- ☐ Swimming goggles (There is a plethora of models, from under $10 and upward. Select a pair that satisfies you and your wallet.)
- ☐ Neoprene bandana (Nice to wear if the water is cold. Also small and easy to bring along. May be replaced by a neoprene hood, but you typically don't need anything more than the swimming cap.)
- ☐ Sports bra (a merino wool bra doesn't absorb too much water and stays warm even when wet)
- ☐ Merino wool tank top (to stay warm)
- ☐ Merino wool underwear (keeps your bottom warm)
- ☐ Merino wool compression socks (for warmth, and knee-high socks or "calf sleeves" also protect your shins from being cut by nature)
- ☐ Hand paddles (for a better grip in the water and for swimming faster)
- ☐ Snap-hook (for attaching hand paddles to your waist belt when not using them)
- ☐ Waist belt with room for energy bars or mandatory equipment (you may also attach your paddles or pull buoy to this belt)
- ☐ Pull buoy (improves your floating position in the water)
- ☐ Elastic rope (for keeping you and your teammate together)
- ☐ Cut-off legs from the wetsuit (for floating position and for staying warm)
- ☐ Shoes (choose a pair with a low weight when wet and a good grip on slippery rocks)

WALL OF FAME

SWIMMING WORLD: Swimmer of the Year

American magazine *Swimming World* has crowned the "Swimmer of the Year" since 1964. Michael Phelps has received this award eight times, more than any other swimmer. NOTE: Following the discovery of the systematic doping in East Germany, it was decided in December 2013 to remove all East German swimmers from this list who'd previously received this award.

Year	Women	Country	Men	Country
1964	Not awarded		Don Schollander	United States
1965	Not awarded		Dick Roth	United States
1966	Claudia Kolb	United States	Mike Burton	United States
1967	Debbie Meyer	United States	Mark Spitz	United States
1968	Debbie Meyer	United States	Charlie Hickcox	United States
1969	Debbie Meyer	United States	Gary Hall, Sr.	United States
1970	Alice Jones	Australia	Gary Hall, Sr.	United States
1971	Shane Gould	Australia	Mark Spitz	United States
1972	Shane Gould	Australia	Mark Spitz	United States
1973	~~Kornelia Ender~~	East Germany	Rick DeMont	United States
1974	~~Ulrike Tauber~~	East Germany	Tim Shaw	United States
1975	~~Kornelia Ender~~	East Germany	Tim Shaw	United States
1976	~~Kornelia Ender~~	East Germany	John Naber	United States
1977	~~Ulrike Tauber~~	East Germany	Brian Goodell	United States
1978	Tracy Caulkins	United States	Jesse Vassallo	United States
1979	Cynthia Woodhead	United States	Vladimir Salnikov	Soviet Union
1980	~~Petra Schneider~~	East Germany	Rowdy Gaines	United States

Year	Women	Country	Men	County
1981	Mary T. Meagher	United States	Alex Baumann	Canada
1982	~~Petra Schneider~~	East Germany	Vladimir Salnikov	Soviet Union
1983	~~Ute Geweniger~~	East Germany	Rick Carey	Soviet Union
1984	~~Kristin Otto~~	East Germany	Alex Baumann	Canada
1985	Mary T. Meagher	United States	Michael Gross	West Germany
1986	~~Kristin Otto~~	East Germany	Matt Biondi	United States
1987	Janet Evans	United States	Tamás Darnyi	Hungary
1988	~~Kristin Otto~~	East Germany	Matt Biondi	United States
1989	Janet Evans	United States	Mike Barrowman	United States
1990	Janet Evans	United States	Mike Barrowman	United States
1991	Krisztina Egerszegi	Hungary	Tamás Darnyi	Hungary
1992	Krisztina Egerszegi	Hungary	Yevgeny Sadovyi	CIS/Russia
1993	Franziska van Almsick	Germany	Károly Güttler	Hungary
1994	Samantha Riley	Australia	Kieren Perkins	Australia
1995	Krisztina Egerszegi	Hungary	Denis Pankratov	Russia
1996	Penny Heyns	South Africa	Denis Pankratov	Russia
1997	Claudia Poll	Costa Rica	Michael Klim	Australia
1998	Jenny Thompson	United States	Ian Thorpe	Australia
1999	Penny Heyns	South Africa	Ian Thorpe	Australia
2000	Inge de Bruijn	The Netherlands	Pieter van den Hoogenband	The Netherlands
2001	Inge de Bruijn	The Netherlands	Ian Thorpe	Australia
2002	Natalie Coughlin	United States	Ian Thorpe	Australia
2003	Hannah Stockbauer	Germany	Michael Phelps	United States
2004	Yana Klochkova	Ukraine	Michael Phelps	United States
2005	Leisel Jones	Australia	Grant Hackett	Australia
2006	Leisel Jones	Australia	Michael Phelps	United States
2007	Laure Manaudou	France	Michael Phelps	United States
2008	Stephanie Rice	Australia	Michael Phelps	United States

Year	Women	Country	Men	Country
2009	Federica Pellegrini	Italy	Michael Phelps	United States
2010	Rebecca Soni	United States	Ryan Lochte	United States
2011	Rebecca Soni	United States	Ryan Lochte	United States
2012	Missy Franklin	United States	Michael Phelps	United States
2013	Katie Ledecky	United States	Sun Yang	China
2014	Katie Ledecky	United States	Kosuke Hagino	Japan
2015	Katie Ledecky	United States	Adam Peaty	United Kingdom
2016	Katie Ledecky	United States	Michael Phelps	United States
2017	Sarah Sjöström	Sweden	Caeleb Dressel	United States

FINA WORLD: Swimmer of the Year

Delegates from the international swimming federation (FINA) have given out the "Swimmer of the Year" award since 2010.

Year	Women	Country	Men	Country
2010	Therese Alshammar	Sweden	Ryan Lochte	United States
2011	Missy Franklin	United States	Ryan Lochte	United States
2012	Missy Franklin	United States	Michael Phelps	United States
2013	Katie Ledecky	United States	Ryan Lochte	United States
2014	Katinka Hosszú	Hungary	Chad le Clos	South Africa
2015	Katinka Hosszú	Hungary	Mitch Larkin	Australia
2016	Katinka Hosszú	Hungary	Michael Phelps	United States
2017	Sarah Sjöström	Sweden	Caeleb Dressel	United States

SWIMMING WORLD: Open Water Swimmer of the Year

Swimming World has given an award to the best swimmer in open water since 2005. This award goes to swimmers who swim distances recognized by the international swimming federation (FINA): 5km, 10km, and 25km.

Year	Women	Country	Men	Country
2005	Edith van Dijk	The Netherlands	Thomas Lurz	Germany
			Chip Peterson	United States
2006	Larisa Ilchenko	Russia	Thomas Lurz	Germany
2007	Larisa Ilchenko	Russia	Vladimir Dyatchin	Russia
2008	Larisa Ilchenko	Russia	Maarten van der Weijden	The Netherlands
2009	Keri-Anne Payne	United Kingdom	Thomas Lurz	Germany
2010	Martina Grimaldi	Italy	Valerio Cleri	Italy
2011	Keri-Anne Payne	United Kingdom	Thomas Lurz	Germany
			Spyridon Gianniotis	Greece
2012	Éva Risztov	Hungary	Oussama Mellouli	Tunisia
2013	Poliana Okimoto	Brazil	Thomas Lurz	Germany
2014	Sharon van Rouwendaal	The Netherlands	Andrew Gemmell	United States
2015	Aurélie Muller	France	Jordan Wilimovsky	United States
2016	Sharon van Rouwendaal	The Netherlands	Ferry Weertman	The Netherlands
2017	Aurélie Muller	France	Ferry Weertman	The Netherlands

FINA: Open Water Swimmer of the Year

The international swimming federation has given an award to the "Open Water Swimmer of the Year" since 2010. Brazilian swimmers have won the most awards (six). Four of these have been won by Ana Marcela Cunha from São Paulo, who specializes in the 25km.

Year	Women	Country	Men	Country
2010	Ana Marcela Cunha	Brazil	Valerio Cleri	Italy
2011	Keri-Anne Payne	United Kingdom	Thomas Lurz	Germany
2012	Éva Risztov	Hungary	Oussama Mellouli	Tunisia
2013	Poliana Okimoto	Brazil	Thomas Lurz	Germany
2014	Ana Marcela Cunha	Brazil	Allan do Carmo	Brazil
2015	Ana Marcela Cunha	Brazil	Jordan Wilimovsky	United States
2016	Sharon van Rouwendaal	The Netherlands	Ferry Weertman	The Netherlands
2017	Ana Marcela Cunha	Brazil	Marc-Antoine Olivier	France

SWIMMING WORLD: Disabled Swimmer of the Year

Swimming World has given the "Disabled Swimmer of the Year" award since 2003. Among the winners is Natalie du Toit, who came in 16th in the 10km open water swim in Beijing in 2008.

Year	Women	Country	Men	Country
2003	Danielle Watts	United Kingdom	Sergei Punko	Belarus
2004				
2005	Erin Popovich	United States	Benoît Huot	Canada
2006	Jessica Long	United States	Wang Xiaofu	China
2007	Valérie Grand'Maison	Canada	Matthew Cowdrey	Australia
2008	Natalie du Toit	South Africa	Matthew Cowdrey	Australia
2009	Mallory Weggemann	United States	Daniel Dias	Brazil
2010	Mallory Weggemann	United States	Daniel Dias	Brazil
2011	Jessica Long	United States	Daniel Dias	Brazil
2012	Jacqueline Freney	Australia	Matthew Cowdrey	Australia
2013	Sophie Pascoe	New Zealand	Daniel Dias	Brazil
2014	Ingrid Thunem	Norway	Ian Silverman	United
2015	Rebecca Meyers	United States	Ihar Boki	States
2016	Rebecca Meyers	United States	Daniel Dias	Belarus
2017	Sophie Pascoe	New Zealand	Vincenzo Boni	Italy

Ironman World Championships

Ironman was the first major triathlon competition, first held on the Hawaiian island of Oahu in 1978. The distances were adapted according to three local endurance races. First, the competitors swam 2.4 miles (3.9 km) (Waikiki Rough Water Swim), followed by cycling for 112 miles (180 km) (Around Oahu Bike Race), and finally running 26.2 miles (42 km) (Honolulu Marathon). Paula Newby-Fraser has the most wins (eight).

Year	Men	Time	Women	Time
1978	Gordon Haller, USA	11:46:58		
1979	Tom Warren, USA	11:15:56	Lyn Lemaire, USA	12:55:38
1980	Dave Scott, USA	9:24:33	Robin Beck, USA	11:21:24
1981	John Howard, USA	9:38:29	Linda Sweeney, USA	12:02:32
1982 (Feb)	Scott Tinley, USA	9:19:41	Kathleen McCartney, USA	11:09:40
1982 (Oct)	Dave Scott, USA	9:08:23	Julie Leach, USA	10:54:08
1983	Dave Scott, USA	9:05:57	Sylviane Puntous, CAN	10:43:36
1984	Dave Scott, USA	8:54:20	Sylviane Puntous, CAN	10:25:13
1985	Scott Tinley, USA	8:50:54	Joanne Ernst, USA	10:25:22
1986	Dave Scott, USA	8:28:37	Paula Newby-Fraser, ZIM	9:49:14
1987	Dave Scott, USA	8:34:13	Erin Baker, NZL	9:35:25
1988	Scott Molina, USA	8:31:00	Paula Newby-Fraser, ZIM	9:01:01
1989	Mark Allen, USA	8:09:14	Paula Newby-Fraser, ZIM	9:00:56
1990	Mark Allen, USA	8:28:17	Erin Baker, NZL	9:13:42
1991	Mark Allen, USA	8:18:32	Paula Newby-Fraser, ZIM	9:07:52
1992	Mark Allen, USA	8:09:08	Paula Newby-Fraser, ZIM	8:55:28
1993	Mark Allen, USA	8:07:45	Paula Newby-Fraser, USA	8:58:23
1994	Greg Welch, AUS	8:20:27	Paula Newby-Fraser, USA	9:20:14
1995	Mark Allen, USA	8:20:34	Karen Smyers, USA	9:16:46
1996	Luc Van Lierde, BEL	8:04:08	Paula Newby-Fraser, USA	9:06:49
1997	Thomas Hellriegel, GER	8:33:01	Heather Fuhr, CAN	9:31:43
1998	Peter Reid, CAN	8:24:20	Natascha Badmann, SUI	9:24:16

Year	Men	Time	Women	Time
1999	Luc Van Lierde, BEL	8:17:17	Lori Bowden, CAN	9:13:02
2000	Peter Reid, CAN	8:21:01	Natascha Badmann, SUI	9:26:17
2001	Tim DeBoom, USA	8:31:18	Natascha Badmann, SUI	9:28:37
2002	Tim DeBoom, USA	8:29:56	Natascha Badmann, SUI	9:07:54
2003	Peter Reid, CAN	8:22:35	Lori Bowden, CAN	9:11:55
2004	Normann Stadler, GER	8:33:29	Natascha Badmann, SUI	9:50:04
2005	Faris Al-Sultan, GER	8:14:17	Natascha Badmann, SUI	9:09:30
2006	Normann Stadler, GER	8:11:58	Michellie Jones, AUS	9:18:31
2007	Chris McCormack, AUS	8:15:34	Chrissie Wellington, GBR	9:08:45
2008	Craig Alexander, AUS	8:17:45	Chrissie Wellington, GBR	9:06:23
2009	Craig Alexander, AUS	8:20:21	Chrissie Wellington, GBR	8:54:02
2010	Chris McCormack, AUS	8:10:37	Mirinda Carfrae, AUS	8:58:36
2011	Craig Alexander, AUS	8:03:56	Chrissie Wellington, GBR	8:55:08
2012	Pete Jacobs, AUS	8:18:37	Leanda Cave, GBR	9:15:54
2013	Frederik Van Lierde, BEL	8:12:29	Mirinda Carfrae, AUS	8:52:14
2014	Sebastian Kienle, GER	8:14:18	Mirinda Carfrae, AUS	9:00:55
2015	Jan Frodeno, GER	8:14:40	Daniela Ryf, SUI	8:57:57
2016	Jan Frodeno, GER	8:06:30	Daniela Ryf, SUI	8:46:46
2017	Patrick Lange, GER	8:01:40	Daniela Ryf, SUI	8:50:47

Triathlon, Olympics

The triathlon has been an Olympic event since 2000. The distances are 1,500m swimming, 40km cycling, and 10km running. German Jan Frodeno is the only one to win both the Ironman World Championship and an Olympic gold.

Year	Men	Time	Women	Time
Sydney 2000	Simon Whitfield, Canada	1:48:24	Brigitte McMahon, Switzerland	2:00:40
Athens 2004	Hamish Carter, New Zealand	1:51:07	Kate Allen, Austria	2:04:43
Beijing 2008	Jan Frodeno, Germany	1:48:53	Emma Snowsill, Australia	1:58:27
London 2012	Alistair Brownlee, Great Britain	1:46:25	Nicola Spirig, Switzerland	1:59:48
Rio de Janeiro 2016	Alistair Brownlee, Great Britain	1:45:01	Gwen Jorgensen, USA	1:56:16

ÖTILLÖ World Championships

In the still-young sport of swimrun, the ÖTILLÖ race has mostly been won by Swedish endurance athletes. However, Finland has also scored some wins through Petri Forsman, Ville Niemelä, Ingrid Stengård, and Mikko Kolehmainen. Canada has scored a couple wins through Gordo Byrn and Paul Krochak.

Year	Men	Women	Mixed
2006	Petri Forsman & Ville Niemilä (12:00)		
2007	Martin Flinta & Ted Ås		
2008	Pasi Salonen & Jonas Colting (10:14)		
2009	Martin Flinta & Jonas Colting (8:53)	Åsa Annerstedt & Annie Gustafsson (11:09)	Ingrid Stengård & Mikko Kohlemainen (11:06)
2010	Gordon Byrn & Jonas Colting (9:09)	Åsa Annerstedt & Annie Gustafsson (11:15)	Rebecca Nordholm & Johan Nyqvist (11:32)
2011	Antti Antonov & Björn Englund (9:07)	Annika Åström, Karin Edvinsson (12:28)	Åsa Annerstedt & Joakim Axelsson (11:10)
2012	Magnus Olander & Lelle Moberg (9:11)	Helena Lindahl, Linda Sernfalk (13:47)	Annika Åström & Fredrik Åström (11:16)
2013	Paul Krochak & Björn Englund (8:35)	Charlotta Nilsson & Bibben Nordblom (10:54)	Annika Eriksson & Fredrik Selmered (10:33)
2014	Daniel Hansson & Lelle Moberg (8:16)	Charlotta Nilsson & Bibben Nordblom (10:26)	Ulrika Eriksson & Jonas Udehn (9:52)
2015	Paul Krochak & Björn Englund (8:29)	Annika Eriksson & Maja Tesch (10:30)	Marika Wagner & Staffan Björklund (8:55)
2016	Daniel Hansson & Lelle Moberg (7:59)	Annika Eriksson & Kristin Larsson (9:32)	Eva Nyström & Adriel Young (8:49)
2017	Daniel Hansson & Jesper Svensson (7:58)	Annika Eriksson & Kristin Larsson (10:03)	Eva Nyström & Adriel Young (9:01)
2018	Fredrik Axegård & Alex Flores (7:39)	Annika Eriksson & Kristin Larsson (8:56)	Martin Flinta & Helena Grbanova Karaskova (8:16)

American Swim Coaches Association Coach of the Year Award

Year	Coach	Affiliated swimmers
1961	Doc Counsilman, Indiana University	Chet Jastremski, Mike Troy, Alan Somers, Frank McKinney
1962	Peter Daland, University of Southern California	Robert Bernnett, Sharon Finneran, Jon Hendricks, Hans Klein, John Konrads, Lance Larson, Per Ola Lindberg, Roy Saari, Tsyoshi Yamanaka
1963	Dick Smith, Dick Smith Gym	Bernie Wrightson, Leslie Bush (Smith is the only diving coach to receive the award.)
1964	George Haines, Santa Clara Swim Club	Donna de Varona, Steve Clark, Don Schollander
1965	Don Gambril, Arcadia High School	Sharon Stouder (Gambril later coached Mark Spitz, Gunnar Larsson, Jonty Skinner, and Matt Biondi.)
1966	George Haines, Santa Clara Swim Club	Don Schollander
1967	George Haines, Santa Clara Swim Club	Don Schollander
1968	Sherm Chavoor, Arden Hills Swimming	Mark Spitz, Debbie Meyer, Mike Burton
1969	Jim Montrella, Ohio State	Susie Atwood
1970	Don Watson, Hinsdale Central High School	John Kinsella
1971	Jim Montrella, Ohio State	Susie Atwood
1972	George Haines, Santa Clara Swim Club	Mark Spitz
1973	Bob Miller, Totem Lake Swim Team	Lynn Colella, Rick Colella
1974	Dick Jochums, Long Beach State	Tim Shaw, Bruce Furniss, Jack Babashoff
1975	Mark Schubert, Mission Viejo Nadadores	Shirley Babashoff, Maryanne Graham, Brian Goodell, Casey Converse, Jesse Vassallo
1976	Mark Schubert, Mission Viejo Nadadores	Shirley Babashoff, Maryanne Graham, Brian Goodell, Casey Converse, Jesse Vassallo
1977	Paul Bergen, Nashville Aquatic Club	Tracy Caulkins (Bergen later coached Dutch Inge de Bruin to 3 Olympic golds in 2000.)
1978	Paul Bergen, Nashville Aquatic Club	Tracy Caulkins
1979	Randy Reese, University of Florida/ Holmes Lumber	Tracy Caulkins, Craig Beardsley

American Swim Coaches Association Coach of the Year Award

Year	Coach	Affiliated swimmers
1980	Dennis Pursley, Cincinnati Pepsi Marlins	Mary T. Meagher, Glenn Mills, Greg Rhodenbaugh
1981	Mark Schubert, Mission Viejo Nadadores	Steve Barnicoat, Jesse Vassallo, Robin Leamy, Jerry Spencer
1982	Dick Shoulberg, Foxcatcher	Sue Heon, Karen LaBerge
1983	John Collins, Badger	Rick Carey (Collins swam for Counsilman at Indiana.)
1984	Randy Reese	Rowdy Gaines, Mike Heath, Mary Wayte, Tracy Caulkins, Matt Cetlinksi, Dara Torres
1985	North Thornton, California	Matt Biondi, Mary T. Meagher, Connie van Bentum
1986	Richard Quick, Stanford University	Jenna Johnson, Susan Rapp
1987	Bud McCallister, Fullerton Aquatics	Janet Evans
1988	Bud McCallister, Fullerton Aquatics	Janet Evans
1989	Dick Shoulberg, Foxcatcher	Dave Wharton, Erika Hansen
1990	Jon Urbancheck, University of Michigan	Mike Barrowman, Eric Namesnik, Eric Wunderlich
1991	Eddie Reese, University of Texas	Josh Davis, Shaun Jordan, Doug Gjertsen, Hans Dersch
1992	Richard Quick, Stanford University	Jenny Thompson, Lea Loveless, Janet Jorgensen, Lori Heisick
1993	Skip Kenney, Stanford University	Jeff Rouse, Brian Retterer, Joe Hudepohl, Kurt Grote, Trip Zeidlitz, Derek Weatherford
1994	honor removed	
1995	Jon Urbancheck, University of Michigan	Tom Dolan, Michigan's Men's NCAA title
1996	Murray Stephens, North Baltimore	Beth Botsford, Anita Nall
1997	Mark Schubert, University of Southern California	Lenny Krayzelburg, Lindsay Benko Mintenko

American Swim Coaches Association Coach of the Year Award

Year	Coach	Affiliated swimmers
1998	Richard Quick, Stanford University	Jenny Thompson, Misty Hyman
1999	Richard Quick, Stanford University	Jenny Thompson, Misty Hyman, Dara Torres
1999	Mark Schubert, University of Southern California	Lenny Krayzelburg, Lindsay Benko Mintenko
2000	Peter Banks, Blue Wave	Brooke Bennett
2001	Bob Bowman, North Baltimore	Michael Phelps
2002	Teri McKeever, California	Natalie Coughlin, Haley Cope, Jessica Hardy
2003	Bob Bowman, North Baltimore	Michael Phelps
2004	Eddie Reese, University of Texas	Aaron Peirsol, Brendan Hansen, Ian Crocker
2005	Eddie Reese, University of Texas	Aaron Peirsol, Brendan Hansen, Ian Crocker
2006	Eddie Reese, University of Texas	Aaron Peirsol, Brendan Hansen, Ian Crocker
2007	Bob Bowman, University of Michigan	Michael Phelps, Scott Spann
2008	Bob Bowman, University of Michigan/ North Baltimore	Michael Phelps, Tyler Clary, Scott Spann
2009	Eddie Reese, University of Texas	Dave Walters, Ricky Berens, Eric Shanteau
2010	Gregg Troy, University of Florida	Ryan Lochte, Gemma Spfforth, Teresa Crippen, Shaune Fraser
2011	Gregg Troy, University of Florida	Ryan Lochte, Conor Dwyer, Brett Fraser, Elizabeth Beisel
2012	Bob Bowman, North Baltimore	Michael Phelps, Allison Schmitt
2013	Bruce Gemmell, Nation's Capital	Katie Ledecky
2014	Bruce Gemmell, Nation's Capital	Katie Ledecky
2015	Bruce Gemmell, Nation's Capital	Katie Ledecky
2016	Dave Durden, California	Nathan Adrian, Anthony Ervin, Ryan Murphy, Josh Prenot
2017	Ray Looze, Indiana University	Lilly King, Cody Miller, Blake Pieroni, Ian Finnerty

THE MYSTIC SQUARE

Training to perform isn't easy. Our weeks are limited to 144 hours, and there are often plenty of distractions when it comes to our swim or triathlon training. Finding a safe and sound training program that works for your week may benefit from the following.

The Mystic Square or "The 15-puzzle" is a sliding puzzle that consists of numbered square tiles within a frame. The titles are in random order with one tile missing. The object of the puzzle is to place the 15 tiles in numerical order by sliding each tile, using the empty space.

Imagine your training as this 15-puzzle. The following workouts below become your tiles and the week (or whichever period you choose) becomes your board. The game is designed to make planning your training an easy and fun process. With limited time, it becomes even more important that the training you do have time to undertake makes a difference. That's why the focus is not on how far or how long, but to find a clear purpose for each session.

The "tiles" below explain the objective of the training session and describe its main set. A week is a common "magic square," but you may certainly pick whatever period of time works for you.

Around these main sets in the pool, add other warm-ups, drills, and cooldowns.

Example of Main Series

LETTER indicates whether it's swimming (S) or weight training (W).

(S) DISTANCE

Swim at a low speed with continuous muscle movements. Drink before and after if you don't intend to rest.

Stresses muscular endurance needed for endurance events.
Long sessions increase your fat burning.

60 min without rest (90–120 etc.)/Own interval for example 6 × 1000/Increase length after each time

COLOR indicates the toughness of the series. High on the stress thermometer means that your muscles and immune system require recovery time after a well-performed workout.

EXAMPLES of main sets make it easy for you to come up with your own variations.

STRESS THERMOMETER. Blue is recovery. Red is exhausting. The exact shade of red mainly depends on the amount of anaerobic work required. An unusually long workout might also call for prolonged recovery. The recovery, however, will be faster the more adapted you are to the content of the workout.

(S) DISTANCE

Swim at a low speed with continuous muscle movements. Drink before and after if you don't intend to rest.

Stresses muscular endurance needed for endurance events.
Long sessions increase your fat burning.

60 min without rest (90–120 etc.)/Own interval for example 6 × 1000/Increase length after each time.

(S) RECOVERY

When you feel worn out, a swim could still be your best choice. Whichever intervals you choose are okay, as long as the speed is slow and pleasant. Whether it is 15 or 75 minutes is less important.

Allows the body to build up muscles and strengthens the immune system.

(S) DRILL WORKOUT

Swim drills mean that you execute the stroke a little bit differently. This helps you to gain control over desired kinetics.

Improves your water position.
Improves your coordination.
Improves your flexibility.

(S) GENERAL AEROBIC

Basic training session for a triathlete, limited to three workouts a week with a little bit of each. Feel free to use every stroke for a well-rounded muscular workout. Reasonably continuous work on your heart rate.

Prepares your heart and muscles for tougher and more event-specific training.
Increases the stroke volume of your heart.
Increases muscular recovery in slow-twitch muscle fibers.

Medley/Fartlek (Speed Play)/Water Polo/Ladders/ Descending Sendoffs/Hypoxic work

(S) AEROBIC THRESHOLD

Persistently grinding at the speed that meets your aerobic limit. Duration above 30 min. Try to swim with the same stroke frequency and stroke length the whole set. 30–60 beats below your maximum heart rate.

Moves your aerobic threshold to a higher speed.
Increases your capillary density for optimum transportation of oxygen

40 × 25 rest 5–10 sec/2–40 × 100 rest 10–20 sec/8–20 × 200 rest 10–20 sec. Short rest! Effective form of training when maintaining your technique.

(S) DESCENDING SETS

Repetitions with the objective of a clear progression in terms of both intensity and speed.

Stresses a good relationship between invested intensity and scored speed.
Uses all energy systems.
Speeds up recovery following muscular fatigue.

10 × 50 descend 1–10 rest 30–45 sec/8 × 100 descend 1–8 rest 40–60 sec/6 × 150 descend 1–6 rest 40–75 sec
If distances are too long, the speed won't be fast enough if target is anaerobic.

(S) CRITICAL SPEED

Swimming at the highest possible even speed given the set. Short distances promote the best technique possible. Sets are not very long.

Gets your body accustomed to high intensity.
An alternative that doesn't wear out your body too much.
Promotes good technique in high speeds.

8–12 × 50 rest 10–15 sec/4 × 100 rest 10–20 sec/20–40 × 25 rest 15–20 sec/32 × 12.5 rest 6–10 sec
The longer the distances, the harder it is to maintain your technique.

(S) WATER STRENGTH

Most frequently used as a filler between other exercise sessions.

Muscular strength training in the water with a focus on increasing muscular endurance.

Treading water/strength-oriented technique exercises/vertical kick/sculling/swimming against hose/swimming followed by screen. If you only swim, you also need to carry out strength training on land to prevent injuries.

(S) STARTS OF TURN

Showing some flair in the set pieces that aren't swimming, including push-offs, breakouts, starts, and turns.

Improves coordination.
Provides muscle memory for the task.

Starts without push off/turns in pool/starts from starting block/relay exchanges/underwater boosts.
Times valid parts of your race.

(S) ANAEROBIC THRESHOLD

A somewhat higher speed than the aerobic threshold. Shorter duration, but still a pretty short rest. If you're fit, you may stay at 80–90 percent of your VO_2 maximum.

Improves toughness for high speeds.
Speeds up recovery following muscle fatigue.
Increases aerobic capacity even for fast-twitch muscle fibers.

3 × (6 × 100 rest 20–35 sec)/20–40 × 50 rest 20-25 sec

(S) VO_2-MAX

High speed on slightly longer distances so that both your heart and muscles get a good workout. Longer (sometimes active) rest, most often 1:1.

Exercises the maximum capacity of your heart.
Exercises your maximum muscular activity.

2–6 × (25 all out, rest 10, 150 AeT, rest 10, 3 × 50) easy/600 fast—active fast—300 fast—active rest—100 fast

(S) SPEED

Where your muscles get to move at speeds close to or above short race pace.

Gets your muscles and nervous system prepared for race speed or even faster.

10–14 m/yds all out (starting from the blocks, from a push or without)/running + dive + fast swimming/swimming assisted with elastic cord

(S) RACE

Imitating a race. Warm-up swim (or other form of warm-up) plus an all-out effort in a race event. Mimic the race as close as possible. Analyze.

Prepares the body for competition.

One distance in open water at target intensity/ 1–3 shorter races (>200m)/1 longer race
If more repeats, rest for as long as you need to recover.

(S) LACTATE PRODUCTION

Hard intervals above the lactic acid threshold. Long rest.

Improves toughness for high speeds. Prepares you for quick recovery following muscular fatigue.

4–6 × 100m max rest 5–8 min, some active/3×200m max rest 5–8 min/8–5 × 100
1:1 or 1:2 swimming/resting
Long repetitions may thrash technique, but may benefit whoever can keep good form.

(W) INJURY PREVENTION & CORE WORK

Often before or after workouts on the pool deck. 10–60 min. No heavy loads. Possible to execute at any coordinate—at the gym or in a hotel room without any equipment. Abs and lower back are important in every exercise.

Strength training with a focus on preventing injuries.
Strength training with a focus on improving muscular endurance.

Squats/lunges/triceps dips/the plank/back extensions/push-ups/shoulder exercises with or without band.

(W) INCREASING STRENGTH

Resistance work in the gym more or less to fatigue.

Weight training to enable the generation of power for a more explosive start dive or turn, or a more powerful stroke.

Lat pulldowns/pull-ups/bench press/power cleans/squats/bicep curls/tricep press

Find exercises at the gym that match your stroke.

THANK YOU!

A solo project is best completed with the help of others. An enormous thank you for contributing to the book and for discussing its contents.

Daniel Adams-Ray, pop genius and swimmer, Sweden.

Ahmed Firass Afeef, swim coach Male Lifeguards, Maldives.

Linus Ahlberg, photographer, diver and swimmer, Sweden.

Reem Ahmad Al-Boainain, club manager, Al-Saad Swimming, Qatar.

Mats Andersson, original swimrunner, Sweden.

Richard Andersson, swimrun partner, Sweden.

Johan Annerfelt, photographer and swimmer, Sweden.

Antti Antonov, triathlete and swimrunner, Sweden.

Marcus Åradsson, swim coach, Sweden.

Jane Asher, masters swimmer, Great Britain.

Petter Alexis Askergren, rapper and swimrun partner, Sweden.

Randall Bal, swimmer, Stanford University.

Bengt-Arne Bengtsson, swimmer, Sweden.

Hans Bergqvist, swim coach, Sweden.

Anders Berlin, masters swimmer, Sweden.

Lena Bragesjö, swim coach, Sweden.

Mats Briseneldt, swim coach, Sweden.

Dan Bullock, swim coach, Great Britain.

Daniel Carlsson, swimmer and swimrun partner, Sweden.

Martin Dahlberg, MD and PhD in organic chemistry; Sweden.

Sofia Demnert, swimmer and swimrunner, Sweden.

Bernie Dietzig, British Swimming Association.

Djordje Djordjevic, triathlete, Serbia/Sweden.

Tyler Fenwick, swim coach, University of Virginia.

Chris Flodén, HEAD Swimming.

Gunnar Fornander, swim coach, Sweden.

Henrik Forsberg, Swedish Swimming Federation.

Anne Forsell, swim coach, Sweden.

Lars Frölander, swimmer, Sweden.

Nikos Gemelos, swim coach, Greece.

Spyridon Gianniotis, swimmer, Greece.

Daniel Giray, Apollo Sports, Sweden.

Gary Hall, Sr. swim coach, The Race Club.

Åke Hansson, swim coach, Sweden.

Marty Hendrick, swim coach, Swim Fort Lauderdale.

The Henning Library and Archive.

Yasunari Hirai, swimmer, Japan.

Anders Holmertz, swimmer, Sweden.

Simon Huitenga, swimmer, Australia.

Ron Jacks, swim coach, Canada.

Margot Jacobs, swimmer, Dartmouth College, Sweden.

Mattias Janvald, swim coach, Sweden.

Carl Jenner, swim coach, Sweden.

Victor Johansson, swimmer, Sweden.

Peter Jonsson, journalist Swedish Television.

Ulf Jonsson, triathlete, Sweden.

Magnus Kjellberg, Head of Science, Japan Sports Science Center.

Wladimir Klitschko, swimmer and boxer, Ukraine.

Carl Lannerstad, MD, Sweden.

Kerri Lappi, swimmer, Michigan.

Filip Larsen, PhD in Physiology at the Karolinska Institute, Sweden.

Gunnar Larsson, swimmer, Sweden.

Terry Laughlin, swim coach, Total Immersion.

Michael Lemmel, Race Director ÖTILLÖ, Sweden.

James Lenger, modern pentathlete, Chicago.

Jason Lezak, swimmer, US National Team.

Daisy Lindros, swim teacher, Sweden.

Mike Litzinger, swim coach, Notre Dame.

Michael Lohberg, swim coach, Coral Springs.

Daniel Lönnberg, swimmer, Sweden.

Ray Looze, swim coach, Indiana University.

Petter Løvberg, swim coach, Norwegian National Team.

Jon Maccoll, swim coach, Rutgers University.

Filippo Magnini, swimmer, Italian National Team.

Kenneth Magnusson, Swedish Swimming Federation.

Anders Malm, original swimrunner, Sweden.

Tobias Marklund, swimmer and swimrun partner, Sweden.

Jesper Mars, original swimrunner.

Niko Martikainen, swim coach, Sweden/Finland.

Mikael Mattsson, PhD in Physiology at the Royal Karolinska Institute.

Oussama Mellouli, swimmer, Tunisia.

Carly Miller, swimmer, California.

Glenn Mills, swimmer and technique expert, USA Swimming.

Måns Möller, comedian and swimmer, Sweden.

Ed Moses, swimmer, University of Virginia.

Anthony Nesty, swimmer and swimming coach, University of Florida.

Hasse Nilsson, Swedish Swimming Federation.

Stefan Norman, triathlon statistician, Sweden.

Mattias Nykvist, publisher, Sweden.

Stefan Nystrand, swimmer, Sweden.

Nadja Odenhage, swimmer and photographer, Sweden.

Niclas Öhman, swimmer, New England Masters.

Ellen Olsson, swimmer, Saarbrücken/Sweden.

Erik Persson, breaststroker, Sweden.

Karin Pettersson, swimmer, Sweden.

Fernando Possenti, swim coach, Brazil.

Jim Reitz, swim coach, UNLV.

Nicolas Remires, swimrunner coach, France/ Sweden.

John Rodgers, swim coach, Australia.

Bill Rose, swim coach, Mission Viejo.

Lukas Ekenhill Rosén, son and swimmer, Sweden.

Evy and Glenn Rosén, parents.

Royne Rosén, swimmer and grandfather.

Björn Rosenthal, swimrunner, Sweden.

Michael Sage, swim coach, Australia.

Lovisa Sandberg, Pintxo.

Tommy Sarenbrant, Ironman, Sweden.

Erik Scalise, swim coach and swimmer, Northern Nevada Aquatics.

Ivan Sitic, swimmer, Croatia.

Slaven Sitic, professor in vessel technology and swim coach, Croatia.

Simon Sjödin, swimmer, Sweden.

Gert Sjöholm, swim coach, Sweden.

Sarah Sjöström, swimmer, Sweden.

Mats Skott, Race Director, ÖTILLÖ.

Michael Soria, police officer, California.

Ola Strömberg, swimmer, Sweden.

Niklas Svidén, Ironman, swimrunner and author.

Gustav Swedenborg, swimmer, La Salle, Philadelphia.

Sheila Taormina, swimmer etc., Sarasota.

Jon Urbanchek, swim coach, Los Angeles.

Vansbrosimningen, open water race, Sweden.

Hannes Vitenze, swim coach, Germany.

Andrei Vorontsov, swim coach, Russia.

Johan Wallberg, swim coach, Sweden.

Fredrik Wannerstedt, swimmer and photographer, Sweden.

Andreas Waschburger, swimmer, Germany.

Mattias Wernqvist, swim coach, Sweden.

Bosse Westergren, swim coach, Sweden.

Josh White, swim coach, University of Michigan.

Lee Williams, swim coach, Sweden/Australia. Anna Wretling, Power Woman swimsuits.

Nils Zetterström, director Ångaloppet swimrun, Sweden.

Fredrik Zillén, running coach, Sweden.

Plus everyone who's swum in Human Ambition, those keeping up with @human_ ambition on Instagram, as well as swimmers and coaches in the groups I have trained or trained with.

SOURCES

In addition to meetings with swimming personalities throughout the world, my sources consist of around 400 books about swimming that are in my own possession or located at the library of the International Swimming Hall of Fame, the PubMed medical database, and newspaper articles and email. The following is a selection of the literature used.

David A. Armbruster and Lawrence E. Moorehouse,
Swimming and Diving (1950).

Cecil Colwin, *Swimming into the Twenty-First Century* (1993).
Swimming Dynamics (1999). *Breakthrough Swimming* (2014).

David L. Costill and Ernest W. Maglischo,
Handbook of Sports Medicine and Science, Swimming (1992).

James E. Counsilman, *The Science of Swimming* (1968).
Competitive Swimming Manual for Coaches and Swimmers (1978). *The Complete Book of Swimming* (1979). *The New Science of Swimming* (1994).

Lynne Cox, *Open Water Swimming Manual* (2013).
Swimming to Antarctica (2005).

Rick Cross, *The ASA Guide to Better Swimming* (1987).

Emma Davis, *Open Water Swimming* (2013).

Penny Lee Dean, *Open Water Swimming* (1998).

Frank W. Dick, *Sports Training Principles* (2014).

Anthony D. Fredericks, *Surprising Swimmers* (2000).

Don Gambril, *Swimming* (1969).

David L. Hoof, *Demythologising Michael Phelps* (2014).

Tim Johnson, *History of Open Water Swimming* (2005).

Filip Larsen and Mikael Mattsson, *Kondition och Uthållighet* (2013).

Terry Laughlin and John Delves, *Total Immersion* (2004).

J. E. Lindsay Carter and Timothy R. Ackland, *Kinanthropometry in Aquatic Sports* (1994).

Alan Lynn, *Swimming: Technique, Training,
Competition Strategy* (2006). *Conditioning for Swimmers* (2007).
High Performance Swimming (2008).

Ernest W. Maglischo, *Swimming Faster* (1983).
Swimming Even Faster (1994). *Swimming Fastest* (2003).
*A Primer for Swimming Coaches. Volume 1: Physiological
Foundations.* (2015) *Volume 2: Biomechanics Foundations* (2016).

Ian McLeod, *Swimming Anatomy* (2009).

Paul McMullen, *Amazing Pace: The Story of Olympic
Champion Michael Phelps* (2006).

R. McNeil Alexander, *Principles of Animal Locomotion* (2006).

Steven Munatones, *Open Water Swimming* (2011).

Paul Newsome and Adam Young, *Swim Smooth* (2012).

Diana Nyad, *Other Shores* (1978).

Francois Oppenheim, *The History of Swimming* (1970).

Michael Phelps and Alan Abrahamson, *No Limits* (2008).

Michael Phelps and Brian Cazeneuve, *Beneath the Surface* (2004).

Rob Price, *The Ultimate Guide to Weight Training
for Swimming* (2005).

Scott Riewald and Scott Rodeo, *Science of Swimming Faster* (2015).

David Salo and Scott Riewald, *Complete Conditioning
for Swimming* (2008).

Ludovic Seifert and Didier Chollet, *World Book of Swimming:
From Science to Performance* (2011).

Bob Shalter, *Michael Phelps—The Untold Story
of a Champion* (2008).

Joel Stager and David A. Tanner,
Swimming—Second edition (2005).

Joel Stager and David A. Tanner, *Swim Speed Strokes* (2014).

Sheila Taormina, *Swim Speed Secrets* (2012).

Charles M. Tipton, *ACSM's Advanced Excercise Physiology* (2006).

Dara Torres, Age Is Just a Number (2010)

Chuck Warner, *And They Won Gold* (2012).

David Wilkie and Kevin Juba, *The Handbook of Swimming* (1996).

Jeff Wiltse, *Contested Waters* (2010).

Abbott, Taylor, 177

Abouheif, Abdellatief, 252–53

Abraham, Rich, 172

Adams, William, 198

Adrian, Nathan, 65, 114, 118, 153, 161, 283

aging, 167–73, 182–87, 197–203

Agnel, Yannick, 150

anchoring, 106

Andersson, Mats, 210–11

Andrew, Michael, 116–17, 124

Andrews, Theresa, 194

animal swimmers, 131–36, 142–49, 152, 161–62. *See also individual animals*

Antonov, Antti, 211

Armbruster, David, 293–94, 299

Armstrong, Duncan, 110, 141

Arnesen, Tim, 264–65

Asher, Jane, 166, 171, 202

asthma, 289–93

Atkinson, Alia, 63

awards, 335–46

Babashoff, Jack, 33

Babashoff, Shirley, 32

backstroke, 45, 141, 147–48, 306

Bainbridge, Richard, 44

Baranyi, Stefan, 15, 17

Barnea, Guy, 327

Bauer, Sybil, 55–57, 82

Bauerle, Jack, 216

Belmonte, Mirea, 127

Berkoff, David, 42, 44–45, 50

Berzelius, Jöns Jacob, 139

Biondi, Matt, 48, 137–38, 141, 154, 226

body rotation, 27, 28–30, 49

Borg, Arne, 91–93, 241

Bovell, George, 284

Bowman, Bob, 119, 135

breaststroke, 43

Breen, George, 29, 49, 299–300

Brigitha, Enith, 83, 286–87, 288

Burgess, Thomas, 50

Buric, Damir, 224

Burton, Mike, 228

butterfly, 44–45, 137–39, 141–42, 306

Caldwell, Nicholas, 91

Cameron, Kirsten, 222

Carlile, Forbes, 109–11, 124

Caulkins, Tracy, 183, 194

Cederqvist, Jane, 202

central fatigue, 99

Cielo, Cesar, 283

Clements, Kevin, 88

coaches, awards for, 344–46

Colting, Jonas, 260

Cooper, Brad, 228

core exercises, 26

Corse, John, 198

cortisol, 99

Costill, Dave, 123, 172–73

Counsilman, James "Doc," 104, 114, 234, 294–300

Coventry, Kirsty, 82, 86, 252

Cox, Lynne, 83, 254, 260

Crippen, Fran, 266, 268

Csik, Ferenc, 298

Cuba, swimming between Florida and, 80–82, 256–58

Cunha, Ana Marcela, 282, 339

Cureton, Thomas, 19–20, 28

Darnyi, Tamas, 320

Deissler, Ines, 38

DeLorme, Thomas, 93

DeMont, Rick, 316

DiCarlo, George, 98

Digby, Everard, 256

distance training, 101–2, 112

do Carmo, Allan, 266

Dolan, Tom, 127

dolphins, 137–38, 140, 141, 162

Dowling, Robert, 71

drafting, 222–24, 258

Dressel, Caeleb, 153, 162

drills, 315–27

drowning, 247–49, 256

ducks, 144–45, 146

Dunford, Jason, 252

Durack, Fanny, 63–65

du Toit, Natalie, 252, 339

Dzaburia, Oleksander, 300

East German athletes, 286–89

eating disorders, 195

Ederle, Gertrude, 55

Ekblom, Björn, 139

Elionsky, Ida, 71

Elwani, Rania, 250–51

Ender, Kornelia, 286, 287

English Channel, 50, 74, 83, 223, 245–46, 253, 256, 260, 266, 269, 291

equipment, rules concerning, 22–23

Eriksson, Jon, 260

etiquette, at swimming pools, 329–30

Evans, Janet, 83, 126–27

Fall, Malick, 252

female swimmers, 55–57, 63–69, 82–83, 186–87, 190. *See also individual women*

Fick, Peter, 298

FINA, 45, 266, 337, 339

fins, 46, 142, 310

Fischer, Helmut, 298

fish, 152, 162

flexibility, 46, 107–8, 115

flip turns, 49

Fokaidis, Antonis, 177–81

Ford, Alan, 20

Fraser, Dawn, 24, 83

Fratus, Bruno, 153

Fredriksson, Gert, 191

Freese, Hans, 299

Frodeno, Jan, 187, 342

Frölander, Lars, 289

Gaines, Rowdy, 48, 183

Gambril, Don, 321

Gay Games, 75, 76–77

Geehr, Carly, 187

Gemelis, Nikos, 177, 179, 180, 181

Gerschler, Woldemar, 103–4

Gianniotis, Spyridon, 124, 176–81

goggles, 22, 50

Goodell, Brian, 97

Goss, Sandy, 194

Gould, Shane, 110–11, 242

Graves, Edwin, 198

Groselle, Jack, 118

Gross, Michael, 75–76

Hackett, Grant, 110, 231

Haines, George, 225–27

Hall, Gary, 234–37

Halsall, Dano, 113

hand paddles, 213–15

Hargitay, Andreas, 234–37

Hasse, Dagmar, 218

Hayes, Bruce, 75–77

Heibel, Hermann, 299

height, 279–85

Hencken, John, 32, 34

Henricks, Jon, 21, 50

Heyns, Penelope, 251

Higgins, Herbert, 296

Hinds, Natalie, 63

Ho, Chad, 251, 281

Hogshead, Nancy, 291

Holland, Stephen, 110, 127

Holmertz, Anders, 34, 35, 141

Holmes, Tiger, 198

Hosszu, Katinka, 233, 242

Huitenga, Simon "Hoots," 229–33

Humphries, Kris, 202

Hundeby, Chad, 223

Hunger, Daniela, 287

Hurst, Ky, 231–32

International Swimming Hall of Fame, 20, 62

interval training, 102–3, 112

Ironman, 231, 268, 340–41

Iwasaki, Kyoko, 202

Jackson, Trina, 126, 218

Jager, Tom, 226

Jameson, Andy, 141

Jendrick, Megan, 43

Jenner, Carl, 135

Jochums, Dick, 96–98

Johannsson, Greta, 65

Jones, Cullen, 63

Kahanamoku, Duke, 65

Kawaishi, Takuro, 299

Kidder, Lew, 219

Klim, Michael, 110, 320, 323

Komisarz, Rachel, 241–42

Kromowidjojo, Ranomi, 65, 141

Kruger, Harold, 55, 82

Krumpholz, Kurt, 225–29

lactic acid (lactate), 139–41

Lane, Frederick, 110

Larsen, Filip, 211

Larsson, Gunnar, 227, 234–37

Laughlin, Terry, 49, 152

Leamy, Robin, 113

le Clos, Chad, 319

Ledecky, Katie, 34, 68

Lemmel, Michael, 210, 213

Lewillie, Léon, 213–14

Lindeberg, Jan, 211

Lindquist, Barb, 220

Lindsay, David, 299

Liukkonen, Ari-Pekka, 283

Ljungberg, Hasse, 235, 236

Lochte, Ryan, 23, 183, 242, 274

Looze, Ray, 297

Lopez-Zubero, Martin, 194

Lundquist, Steve, 183

Madison, Helene, 65

Magee, Matt, 232

Malm, Anders, 211

Manaudou, Florent, 141, 284

Manhattan, swimming around, 70–72, 74

Mann, Matthew, 295

Manuel, Simone, 63

Maroney, Susie, 256–58

Mars, Jesper, 211

Marsh, David, 321

masters swimming, 165–67

Matteoli, Marcus, 203

McBreen, Tom, 228

McEvoy, Cameron, 284

McKee, Tim, 235–37

Meagher, Mary T., 38, 40, 183

medley, 233–37

Meilutyt, Ruta, 43

Mellouli, Ousama, 251

Meyer, Alex, 266

Miller, Jim, 173

Mills, Glenn, 37–41

Miyazaki, Yasuji, 65

Moffet, John, 38, 40–41

Montgomery, Jim, 33, 34

Morozov, Vladimir, 284

Munatones, Steven, 259

muscles, diagram of, 308

muscular endurance, 302

muscular strength, 66–69, 170, 189–90, 301, 305–6

Myers, Henry, 137

Mystic Square training program, 348–52

Mythbusters (television show), 160–61

Naber, John, 32, 35

Nagy, Richard, 126

Navid, Nick, 39

Neal, Lia, 63

Neethling, Ryk, 242

Negris, Dimitrios, 177–81

Neilson, Sandy, 65

Nelker, Mikael, 151

Nesty, Anthony, 63, 141, 194

Newton's laws of motion, 25, 149, 154, 155–56

Nyad, Diana, 70–71, 72–74, 80–82, 254

obstacles, managing, 39

Olasz, Anna, 126

open water swimming
  awards for, 338–39
  body temperature and, 174–75
  competitive, 261–63, 270–71
  currents and, 264–65
  distance and, 263
  feat, 254–55, 260–61
  history of, 245–47, 268–70
  packing list for, 333
  pool swimming vs., 259, 281–82
  salt water vs. freshwater, 263–64
  types of, 259–61
  water temperature and, 265–68
  weather and, 265

ÖTILLÖ race, 210–11, 213, 237, 238, 268, 343

overload principle, 93–94

overtraining, 94, 98–101

pace list, 328

packing, 331–34

Paltrinieri, Gregorio, 34

Payne, Keri-anne, 282

Peaty, Adam, 43

penguins, 131–33, 144, 145–46, 161, 162, 326

pentathlon, modern, 221–22, 332–33

Peppe, Mike, 296, 299

Perkins, Kieren, 110, 257, 322

Phelps, Michael, 35, 61, 96, 99, 116, 117, 119–20, 134–36, 183–84, 186, 202, 233, 242, 252, 275, 277–78, 281, 335

Poenish, Walter, 80

Polianski, Igor, 45

Pollack, Andrea, 287

Popov, Alexander, 48, 65

Prefontaine, Steve, 175

Priemer, Petra, 286

"pruning" effect, 90–91

Pugh, Lewis, 254, 260

Pursley, Dennis, 37, 38, 39, 40, 41

Quick, Richard, 195, 196

racism, 57–63

repetition training, 103–4

Reymond, Axel, 124, 126

Rhodenbaugh, Greg, 38

Rieckehoff, German, 37

Ris, Wally, 299

Rocca, Peter, 32

Rongione, Isabella, 91

Rose, Murray, 21, 50, 110

Rosenthal, Björn, 238

Rushall, Brent, 114, 116

Ryan, Sean, 300

Scherer, Fernando, 318

Schneider, Josh, 300

Scholes, Clarke, 65

Schollander, Don, 49

Schumacher, Brad, 229, 241, 319

Seleznyov, Aleksandr, 250

Selye, Hans, 109–10

sharks, 256–57

shaving, 21, 23, 50

Shaw, Steven, 303, 305

Shaw, Tim, 96–98

Shioura, Shinri, 141

shoulder problems, 115, 309, 310–12

Sieg, Jack, 50

Silva, Chris, 62–63

Sitic, Ivan, 223

Sjödin, Simon, 184–86

Sjöström, Sarah, 24, 118, 134–36, 154

Skinner, Jonty, 33–34, 48

Smith, Clark, 69

Smulders, Tom, 90–91

Soni, Rebecca, 43, 310

Soria, Mike and Brian, 87–89, 125

Spitz, Mark, 33, 51, 65, 96, 141, 226, 233–34, 291

sprint training, 104

Steadman, Charles, 92

Steffen, Britta, 196

Stengård, Ingrid, 343

Stockwell, Mark, 194

Stovall, Gil, 281

Stoychev, Petar, 266

Streeter, Allison, 291

Strel, Martin, 260

strength training

  benefits of, 300–304

  exercise selection, 304, 307, 314

  frequency of, 304

  history of, 51, 293–96, 299–300

  overload principle and, 93–94

  timing of, 304–5

  young people and, 189–90

stress, 109–10

stroke frequency, 29–30, 108, 150–51, 214

stroke length, 27, 29–30, 108, 150–51

Summers, Byron, 71

Suzuki, Daichi, 45, 50

Svensson, Jonatan Torshall, 238

Swammerdam, Jan, 213

swimming. *See also* open water swimming; training; *individual swimmers and strokes*

  aging and, 182–87, 192, 197–203

  analyzing your, 105–8

  evolution of, 133–36

  gender differences and, 66–69, 186–87, 190

  history of, 249–50, 255–56

  human body and, 275–84, 313

  physics of, 153–59

  in syrup vs. water, 160–61

  underwater, 44–47, 50, 141

swimming bench, 305

swimming caps, 22

swimrun, 208–13, 237–40, 334, 343

swimsuits, 22, 23

Szöke, Katalin, 65

Takaishi, Katsuo, 16–19, 21, 26, 28–29, 30, 48, 49

Taormina, Sheila, 216–22, 241

tapering, 110

Teuscher, Cristina, 217, 218

Thompson, Jenny, 217, 218

Thorpe, Ian, 54, 77, 110, 275

Thulin, Vera, 65

Timmerman, Jaring, 202

Tonkonogi, Michail, 188, 189

Torres, Dara, 83, 164, 193–96, 203

track starts, 51

training. *See also* strength training

  aerobic vs. anaerobic, 95

  with asthma, 292–93

  drills, 315–27

  optimum program for, 190–92

  over-, 94, 98–101

  planning, 117–22, 348–52

  programs, suggested, 78–79

  research on, 89–95, 123–24

  types of, 101–4, 112–15

  upper body exercises, 312

  for youth, 187–90

Travello, Julio, 253

triathlon, 219–21, 222–24, 239, 332, 342

Ultra Short Race-Pace Training (USRPT), 114–16, 124

underwater swimming, 44–47, 50, 141

Val, Laura, 172

van Almsick, Franziska, 218

Vanderkaay, Peter, 291

van der Weijden, Maarten, 281

Vande Weghe, Al, 49

van Dyken, Amy, 291

Vassallo, Jesus, 33, 35–36, 41–42, 48, 50

velocity

  angular, 159

  average, 154

  definition of, 153–54

  factors influencing, 24–25, 28, 31

Vendt, Erik, 126

Vollmer, Dana, 194

Waddell, Tom, 75

Walker, Rick, 87

Waschburger, Andreas, 124

water polo, 224, 226

water resistance, 21, 23–24, 27

water temperature, 174, 265–68

Webb, Matthew, 70, 245–47, 253, 256, 269–70

Weertman, Ferry, 124

Weissmuller, Johnny, 14–17, 20, 29, 55, 83, 117, 294, 298

Westerblad, Håkan, 139, 170

wetsuits, 23

Whitney, Ashley, 217

Wylie, Mina, 64–65

Wynmann, Nikolaus, 256

Yong, Zhuang, 65

Zenhum, Tamer, 250